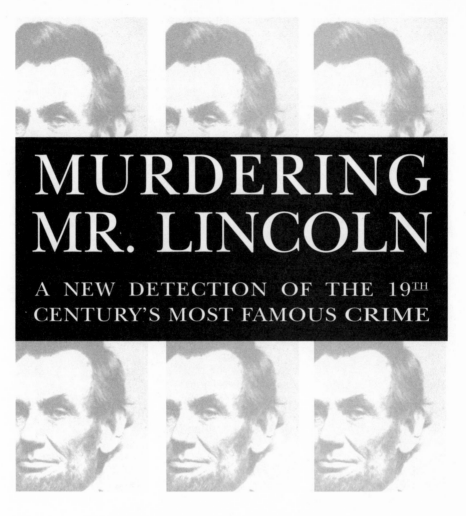

MURDERING MR. LINCOLN

A NEW DETECTION OF THE 19TH CENTURY'S MOST FAMOUS CRIME

CHARLES HIGHAM

New Millennium Press
Beverly Hills

Also by Charles Higham

Politics
THE DUCHESS OF WINDSOR
TRADING WITH THE ENEMY
AMERICAN SWASTIKA
ROSE: THE LIFE OF ROSE KENNEDY

Literature
THE ADVENTURES OF CONAN DOYLE
AUSTRALIAN WRITING TODAY
THEY CAME TO AUSTRALIA

Film
THE FILMS OF ORSON WELLES
ORSON WELLES: THE RISE AND FALL OF AN AMERICAN GENIUS
THE ART OF THE AMERICAN FILM
HOLLYWOOD IN THE FORTIES (with Joel Greenberg)
THE CELLULOID MUSE (with Joel Greenberg)

Poetry
A DISTANT STAR
SPRING AND DEATH
NOONDAY COUNTRY
THE EARTHBOUND
THE VOYAGE TO BRINDISI

Copyright © 2004 Charles Higham

First published in the United States of America in 2004
by New Millennium Entertainment, Inc.
301 N. Canon Drive #214
Beverly Hills, CA 90210

Library of Congress Cataloging-in-Publication Data available upon request.
ISBN: 1-932407-40-5

Interior design by Carolyn Wendt

Printed in the United States of America
www.NewmillenniumPress.com

10 9 8 7 6 5 4 3 2 1

For Richard V. Palafox
And
Dorris Halsey

PHOTO INSERT CREDITS

Crush the despots of the world in their very dens!

—George Nicholas Sanders

Yes! We're coming Abraham Lincoln
With curses loud and deep,
That will haunt you in your waking,
And disturb you in your sleep.

—BATTLE HYMN OF THE
SONS OF LIBERTY, 1864

I long ago made up my mind that if anybody wants to kill me, he will do it. If I wore a shirt of mail and kept myself surrounded by a body-guard, it would be all the same. There are a thousand ways to getting at a man if it is desired he should be killed.

—ABRAHAM LINCOLN TO THE
WRITER NOAH BROOKS,
N.D., (SPRING 1863)

I really believe, it would have been a happier day for *us* now, and my idolized husband would now have been living, if those, *en masse* holding office would have abhorred and sternly treated those Copperheads as I *would* have done.

—MARY TODD LINCOLN TO
ALEXANDER WILLIAMSON,
JUNE 15, 1865

CONTENTS

INTRODUCTION

Few Presidents have been as revered in memory as Abraham Lincoln; none, from his first inauguration, has been so continually threatened with death. Assassinations are usually committed when the killer feels behind him a strong swell of support, either real or imagined. When John Wilkes Booth shot the President at Ford's Theatre in Washington, D.C. on the night of April 14, 1865, he was not only fulfilling the imagined goal of millions of Southerners who supported slavery, and that of the terrorist groups to which he belonged. His act of murder was the culmination of anarchistic purposes, hatched in the assassination bureaus of London in the 1850s and inspired by the inflammatory policies of the Young America and Manifest Destiny movements, of which, ironically, Lincoln had once approved.

Lincoln's legion of prominent enemies was not impressed by the generous and noble qualities that made him so popular with much of the citizenry and were exemplified in the Gettysburg Address. His protectionism of American industry through a tariff destroyed his reputation with the power elite of England; his desire to remove the curse of slavery annoyed countless Americans; his love of the common people whom his influential and undemocratic critics saw as serfs, his joy in telling analogous stories and his brusque country humors irritated sophisticates raised amid city intrigues. The tall, gaunt figure in his stovepipe hat that so appealed to the masses was, to those bent upon his destruction, a vision both grotesque and monkeyish, the very image of the Missing Link.

The deepest reason for hatred of Lincoln was what Democrats, Southerners and radical Republicans saw as a presidential assumption of despotic powers, of the attitudes and exercises of a royal figure on European lines. This rancor drove the revolutionary diplomat George Nicholas Sanders, a principal architect of

Lincoln's destruction, with the same fervor Sanders directed against the French Emperor Napoleon III, whom he had sought to assassinate. His enemies saw Lincoln destroying daily the basis of the Constitution. He refused to admit the legality of secessionism, the right of the state governors, senators and congressmen to leave the Union if they so chose; they objected to his suspension of the fundamental human privilege of habeas corpus, so that he could collaterally authorize arrest, imprisonment and punishment without a warrant under wartime special provisions.

They objected to his ordering military searches of homes, driving men and women from their loved ones without hope of communication and, in some cases, even without legal counsel. They despised his rejection of free speech: newspapers suffered closure when they dared criticize his administration. Small wonder then that Sanders and his political colleagues Clement C. Clay and James P. Holcombe, as well as John Wilkes Booth, John Surratt and others of their stripe saw Lincoln in the same light as Emperor Napoleon III, Czar Nicholas I of Russia, Emperor Franz Joseph I of Austria, Queen Isabella II of Spain or King Pedro V of Portugal.

Lincoln's assassination was proposed again and again, starting with a fanatical group of supporters of George Sanders' idol, the Italian patriot Giuseppe Mazzini, in Baltimore in 1861. His death was planned at a meeting between Sanders, Clay and Holcombe at Niagara in August, 1864 but was defused when Dean Richmond, Chairman of the New York State Democratic Party, who hated the President but stopped short of the idea of murder, reported the matter, through a go-between, to Washington.

Assassination was again planned by the same group. It was to take place on the eve of the Presidential election, on November 7, 1864, but it was delayed by a number of factors, including increased security and the failure of the egregious organization known as the Sons of Liberty to act according to plan and bring about a *coup d'état.* Another factor was the unexpected and extraordinary value of Lincoln to the very people who threatened his life.

On July 2 and then on September 24, 1864, the most upright of American Presidents wrote into law Acts allowing for trading with the Confederacy. Robert E. Coxe and Beverley Tucker, both part of Sanders' murderous group, and Sanders himself, benefited considerably from this largesse. For the time being, as they earned a fortune from shipping pork south in return for cotton, turpentine and rosin, and more modest sums from medical supplies in the hands of Booth, Surratt and others, Lincoln was worth more to the conspirators alive than he would be if he were dead.

Confederate President Jefferson Davis and his Secretaries of State, Treasury, Army and Navy did nothing to stop such trade. Three States governors, of New York, Massachusetts and the Union-controlled area of Virginia, oiled the machine from which Lincoln's circle of friends corruptly benefited. Among these beneficiaries were such figures as Lincoln's bodyguard and Marshal of the District of Columbia Ward Hill Lamon, the Republican power broker Thurlow Weed, his intimate associates Orville H. Browning and James W. Singleton, and his Illinois admirer and supporter, the lawyer Leonard Swett.

Collusion between North and South while thousands died in the field also benefited Lincoln's two sisters-in-law, Mrs. Benjamin Helm and Mrs. Clement White. Familial connections eased the breaking of the blockade of shipments of goods and arms by sea. Rear Admiral Samuel P. Lee, chief of the North Atlantic Blockading Squadron until November, 1864, had as a father-in-law none other than the champion cotton speculator and trader with the enemy, the peace commissioner Francis Preston Blair, Senior. David Levy Yulee, Confederate Congressman and millionaire who owned the Fernandina plantation and railroad that made shipments north and south through north Florida an easy matter had, as his wife's sister's husband, Lincoln's advocate general, Joseph Holt.

Collusion continued untrammeled until January, 1865, when a moralistic congressman from Illinois, Elihu B. Washburne, completed months of investigation into the matter of treasonable trade, interviewed dozens of those involved at hearings of the Committee on Commerce, and so severely threatened to confiscate the appropriate privileges that Lincoln nervously began to shift the decisions on the trading to its chief opponent, Lieutenant General Ulysses S. Grant. Once that transfer was made, Lincoln's usefulness was thought to have expired. The road was clearly set for the night of Good Friday, April 14, 1865.

ONE

THE

MISSION

In Richmond, Virginia, in the early months of 1864, almost three years from the inception of the Civil War, Jefferson Davis, President of the Confederacy, raised the colossal sum of five million dollars (equivalent to $57 million today) from the Confederate Congress for a Secret Service fund that would unofficially be operated by Judah P. Benjamin, his accomplished and ingenious Secretary of State.

The talk of the spring season was that President Lincoln and his Secretary of War, Edwin M. Stanton, had ordered Brigadier General H. Judson Kilpatrick and the dashing Colonel Ulric Dahlgren to invade, conquer and burn Richmond in a surprise attack, release the Union prisoners at Bell Isle, and destroy the southern capital's mills, garrisons and the canal and river boats.

An order carried from the Headquarters of the Third Division, Cavalry Corps, Division of the Mississippi, was said to have been found on Dahlgren's body after his death in action on March 2, 1864, containing the words:

Once in the city, Jefferson Davis and his Cabinet (must be) killed.

It was the Dahlgren note that, even more than previous threats against his life, compelled Jefferson Davis, strongly supported by Judah P. Benjamin and Secretaries of Navy and War Stephen R. Mallory and James A. Seddon, to embark upon the conspiratorial policy of early 1864 that involved the support of large numbers of anti-Lincolnians in Britain and British North America (Canada) in arranging guerrilla raids on the northwest and northeastern United States, releasing and stirring up prisoners in Union military jails and, most importantly of all, provoking war between England and the Union. It was hoped that such a conflict would result in Davis's installation as head of a recognized independent government of the South, with states' rights in North and South at last fully recognized and Lincoln rendered useless.

Until 1864, such dreams had scant hope of fulfillment. Expeditions into British North America by poorly-briefed and untutored secret agents, unfamiliar with the craft of espionage, had proved no more than irritants in the North. It was clear that Davis would have to invest a considerable amount of his government's rapidly draining treasure to secure the results he needed.

To find suitable subversives was no easy task. Southern males above the servant class saw themselves as gentlemen and an expedition to British North America, no matter how generously financed, was a journey to which no gentleman could comfortably look forward. There were no slaves up there, as the British government had abolished slavery; instead, a Southern arrival would be sure to find, annoyingly, successful travelers by the Underground Railroad, enterprising African-Americans who had slipped across the border and were working at small businesses of their own or as paid workers in cities and on the land. A popular center of Black settlement was the very town which had been chosen, based upon a recommendation by a visiting Mrs. Robert E. Lee, wife of the general, as a Confederate headquarters: St. Catharines, Ontario, a pleasant leafy hamlet where Harriet Tubman had once made her home.

And who knew whether life was civilized in that remote Northern province? In the antebellum years, a grand tour of Europe was in the cards for the well-to-do; British North America most emphatically was not. Would the hotels of those little-known metropolitan centers offer mint juleps? Were brass spittoons supplied or, for that matter, Cuban cigars? Were there proper leathery clubs with African mahogany fixtures where a man could escape, in a pleasant fog of smoke and conversation, the immediate presence of women? Were there billiard rooms where gas chandeliers glowed over green baize tables and a man could wager his house on the success of a double carom?

And above all, how could gentlemen, raised in a world where quarrels were settled by fists or guns or swords, trained in the army or navy, serving as congressmen or senators at a time when paid leaves were long and states' service minimal, turn by reverse alchemy into intriguers and underground operatives, involved in spying, subversion and intrigue, making or breaking codes, smuggling messages in bottles, boots or baskets under the cover of night, slipping information in dispatches through the Union blockade when the moon was past her waning?

Service in the armed forces was one thing: proof of manhood to the women and children and old folks at home. Not to carry sword, pistol or rifle was always a cause of contempt. But in the American tradition, as in the British and Irish, the stool pigeon, the spy, the informer were degrees below the criminal as forms of lowlife. And now gentlemen of the South would have to engage such creatures by the wagonload.

For Jefferson Davis who, when he was President Franklin Pierce's Secretary of War, had played a crucial role in seeking the services of leading revolutionaries and anarchists as U. S. consuls in Europe in the mid-1850s, the idea of stirring up rebellious and dangerous activities in North America and its British neighbor was scarcely foreign.

Davis was sorely prompted by Benjamin, whose surreptitious nature leant naturally to intrigue. And there was his Secretary of the Treasury, Christopher Memminger, who, like Benjamin, was foreign-born. Memminger was German; as a European he was thought to be heir to a centuries-old tradition of skullduggery. He was not felt to be a specimen of that mythological species, the innocent American.

Judah P. Benjamin was marked down in the racially prejudiced South as something worse than a European immigrant: he was a Sephardic Jew and thus of Spanish ancestry. Disliked by Jewish figures of German, French or Russian origin and even by the Sephardics themselves, he failed to preach or practice his hereditary faith. Born in the then British Caribbean island of St. Croix one year before the War of 1812, he rose from humble origins to an impressive career in New Orleans, first as a successful attorney, then in Washington as the Democrat Senator from Louisiana, then, after Secession, as, in turn, Attorney General, Secretary of War and Secretary of State in the Jefferson Davis cabinet.

Round, short and rosy-cheeked, with a high-pitched but well-modulated voice, Benjamin offered so perpetual a Cheshire cat smile that one might have suspected a chronic rictus of the face muscles or an excessive degree of self-approval. His unruffled

demeanor partially concealed one of the South's most able and
nimble brains. Secretive, he burned his papers on a regular basis,
partly because of his subversive plans in Britain, France and
British North America and partly because of his compulsive habit
of gambling. In a lesser being that indulgence might have been
thought a sign of manliness, but in a Secretary of State who must
at all times sustain an image of blameless rectitude, it most
decidedly was not.

A lasting blemish on his record was that he had been accused
of stealing at Yale. His metal traveling trunk had been found
stuffed with money, watches, gold pencil cases and penknives
purloined from his fellow students (or planted there, perhaps, by
anti-Semitic freshmen). He left in his second year to avoid expul-
sion; later, much unnecessary gossip was expended when his
attractive Creole wife, Natalie St. Martin, departed his home with
their five-year-old daughter for Paris, never to return.

At Montgomery, the first and distinctly unsuitable Confederate capital, Benjamin became so conveniently if platonically intimate with Varina Howell Davis, the accomplished First Lady, that
he was able to compose much of her ailing husband's correspondence. With Jefferson Davis's collateral consent, he forged
the Presidential signature on official documents and in general
acted as both comptroller and glorified secretary—a workable, if
highly questionable, combination.

As Secretary of War from November 1861, Benjamin showed
a polished capacity for surviving not only criticism but actual disaster. An amateur irritant to the general staff, he began promis-
ingly with the Confederate victory at the first Battle of Bull Run
but foundered on the loss of Roanoke Island and his adoptive
city of New Orleans. When the wealthy and arrogant Robert M.T.
Hunter stepped down as Secretary of State on February 17, 1862,
Benjamin, Hunter's social inferior, was well-prepared to occupy a
post to which at last he was suited. Diplomacy, not militarism, was
always his delicate *forte*.

It can only have appealed to Benjamin's humor that he now
was the Secretary of a state that did not, in legalistic terms, actually
exist. Unrecognized internationally, self-invented, the Confederacy could send no ambassador to foreign parts, only ministers

without portfolio whose acceptance in official circles was reluctant at best.

Benjamin found from the first a willing if unpopular ally in Memminger, whose determined eyes and wide, thin mouth suggested a stern capability unaccompanied by charm. A penniless immigrant, as Benjamin had been, he had been abandoned by his mother to a Charleston orphanage; like Benjamin, he rose to become a successful attorney, fighting the local bureaucracy to create the local public school system and acting as a chairman of the committee that established the provisional Confederate constitution in Montgomery.

Though his marriage at age 29 and his eight children scarcely suggested austerity, Memminger had few of the qualities of appearance and character that were prized at the time. Men of position were supposed to be erect, military in bearing, glowing with masculine confidence and equipped with expensive cigars. Memminger was prematurely stooped, thin, pale, not a smoker, a gray little church mouse who spent hours in bookstores seeking out obscure religious texts.

Neither in Montgomery nor later in the more attractive capital of Richmond did this somber and dry-hearted pedant show a penchant for the serious comforts of the table and the hotel bar; asked by President Davis or Benjamin for money for military, naval or surreptitious activity, he had the whimsical habit of pulling fistfuls of banknotes from his pockets and announcing that they were all that the Treasury could offer.

Since greenbacks, the accepted Union dollar bills, were of little use in the South, he was compelled to print that doomed form of currency, the Confederate dollar. He obtained the paper from disloyal Unionist stationers in New York, a city so heavily operated by Copperheads that it amounted to a Confederate center.

The bill's design also was prepared in New York, the engraving performed by an old friend and German colleague who lived in Richmond, Virginia. Memminger from the first preferred to use the internationally viable form of bullion, much of it shipped in gold bars or coins from the Northern states or plucked from the vaults of the Confederate rich; more still was imported through the Union blockade from England via the Bahamas or Cuba, to Halifax, Nova Scotia and thence through the blockade to Wilmington.

Memminger's arrangements were often maladroit until, in 1863, he assisted Benjamin and the Confederates' Paris agent John Slidell in obtaining a substantial loan from the French Erlanger bank. Much of the money he squirreled away went to Secretary James A. Seddon's War Department for the purchase of armaments in Britain and France; he often handled these arrangements awkwardly. He bungled particularly in the matter of cotton; instead of exporting that product in quantity in the early part of the Civil War to England and France where it would soon be needed, he, with the approval of Benjamin and Davis, burned it in quantity to prevent it falling into Northern hands. The secondary purpose was to force Britain and France to recognize the Confederacy as a separate nation: if they did not, they would receive no cotton. But the two nations had stockpiled; their profiteers were making millions while the work force was being laid off to save money. It was not until 1862-63 that the cotton famine of Europe led Memminger to change his ill-advised policy, only to have it undermined when cotton supplies to the enemy in the North were found to be profitable.

In the early months of 1864, he had to support Davis's and Benjamin's establishment of a subversive operation in British North America. Since his treasury was depleted by the costs of fighting the war, he had to make arrangements through his associate and later successor, the polished and personable George Alfred Trenholm, who anomalously occupied the positions of unofficial Assistant Secretary of the Treasury and senior partner in Fraser, Trenholm, the British-Charlestonian piratical shipbuilding enterprise in Liverpool, with blockade-running branches in Nassau, Havana and Bermuda. Trenholm, assisted by Edward Lawrence, Mayor of Liverpool, who ran a marauder warship, *The Night Hawk,* and a furiously anti-Lincolnian British associate, James Prioleau, broke the Union blockade to bring to Richmond arms on a scale that helped prolong the war, as well as importing cotton, tobacco, turpentine and rosin in quantity to England until Lincoln's blockade clamped down.

On February 15, 1864, the aforementioned sum of five million Confederate dollars, or $57,000,000 in 21st century terms, was voted by Congress for Secret Service. That sum could not all be obtained locally. Instead, some four million of it was raised in England, where the rich and powerful, including almost the entire membership of the House of Lords and William Edward Gladstone, the Chancellor of the Exchequer, were pleased to encourage a policy that would bring Lincoln down. They saw Lincoln correctly as a protectionist, whose approval of the Morrill tariff, which restricted British imports, was sufficient on its own to make his removal desirable. The same attitude prevailed in France, where hatred of the tariff combined with contempt for the thrust and energy of the Union. Even when both England and France enjoyed the benefits of imported North American wheat, expressions of gratitude were seldom heard.

The first and most serious Confederate effort to provoke war between England and the United States occurred in the fall of 1861. In a plan hatched in Richmond—the progenitors were Navy Secretary Stephen R. Mallory and Judah P. Benjamin—two emissaries, the wealthy John Slidell of Louisiana and James M. Mason of Virginia, the latter an architect of the Fugitive Slave Law, were sent to France and England respectively as ministers without portfolio or diplomatic recognition to obtain still more support for the Confederate cause; but first, they would be involved in an episode that would, it was hoped, provoke Britain into a declaration of war.

The diplomats arrived in the tropical port of Havana on October 22, after riskily running the blockade from Charleston. The British ship *Trent* was to pick them up in the sewage-filled harbor for passage to Southampton, England. French documents show that they made financial arrangements with the Union adventurer Captain Charles F. Wilkes of the U.S.S. *San Jacinto* to stage a boarding and seizure of themselves, their secretaries and, in Slidell's case, next of kin; this was, in legal terms, an act of war since no British ship could be boarded in that manner, according to the peculiar maritime rules, unless the ship herself were declared a prize and sailed to a North American port.

Running to plan, and following much fine food and vintage champagne at the Havana home of the Confederate resident Mrs. Sarah E. Brewer, Captain Wilkes met his obligations and intercepted the *Trent* with two shots over her bow in the Bahama Straits, sailing carefully within territorial British waters to enhance the illegality of the attack. With well-staged protests amounting to hysteria, Slidell's daughter added false authenticity to the occasion as Mason and Slidell surrendered and were shipped off to Fort Warren in Boston Harbor, where they were accommodated in comfortable staff quarters and given the best of liquor and the finest of meals.

Unaware of the conspiracy, the British government and people talked of war with Lincoln; troops by the thousand were shipped to Canada to prepare for a full-scale invasion of North America to the tune of "Dixie," played by bands on the Liverpool wharves; only the intercession of a dying Prince Albert, Queen Victoria's typhoid-stricken consort, prevented a repetition of the conflict of 1812. But British anger against the North continued, as Benjamin (and presumably Davis with him) intended—even after the two captives were released.

To send a Confederate secret mission to British North America to disrupt the loyal American states and enlist support for possible invasion, arson and murder was to endanger the now seriously imperiled state of transatlantic neutrality. Yet this was the risky purpose entertained by Davis, Benjamin, Memminger and the Confederate Secretaries of War and Navy in 1864. Again, the underlying hope was that, believing the subversive activities were launched with the approval of British North America, Lincoln would declare war on England and that, in turn, England would give the Confederacy recognition and diplomatic and political status as the only official American state, launch an attack on Boston, Washington and Chicago, and bring Lincoln to his downfall.

To head up this Canadian expedition, Jefferson Davis, as its co-initiator, had to rely on trusted friends. From the first, Memminger and his associates made the unwise decision not to require their dubious emissaries to supply a regular accounting of their expenditures.

The North Carolinian, former Mississippi Congressman and Secretary of the Interior Jacob Thompson was Davis's first choice. About to turn 54, he had outlived the then current life expectancy of a male by 14 years; he felt, incorrectly, that he had also outlived his usefulness. He boasted a high, pale, intellectual forehead, conveniently enhanced by receding gray hair, large, reflective but sharply observant dark brown eyes and an expertly-clipped spade beard. Somehow, this combination of not unpleasant features failed to make him more than passably appealing; some even called him ugly.

The fact is he was too invulnerable, self-contained, shrewd and obviously calculating to gain a warm circle of friends. Although he showed a manly pleasure in the table and the wine bottle, he failed to display in his daily business more than an austere assertiveness and control of others. His avoidance of brothels, hard spirits, gaming and adultery made him less than popular among his peers. His chief acceptable weakness was his lack of caution and common sense in the matter of money. He was extravagant to a fault in dress, houses and furnishings; it was as if his masculine firmness in business affairs were contradicted by an almost feminine interest in décor.

From the beginning of his life in his native state he suffered from an inferiority complex, brought on by a stern and unyielding father, who compared him unfavorably with his dashing and athletic brother Young. The physically beautiful Young Thompson enjoyed hunting, steeplechasing, fast women and cards. If Young rode to college on a spanking thoroughbred, Jacob had to make do on a spavined workhorse. When, in 1837, the brothers found themselves in Pontotoc, Mississippi, where they made a living as fledgling attorneys, Young enjoyed the pleasures of bars and whorehouses while Jacob shut himself up in musty offices or rode to the circuit courts to fight corruption and political speculation with all the zeal of a militant Calvinist.

He married early in Oxford, Mississippi. A motive was money as well as love, because his 15-year-old future child bride, Catherine Anne Jones, was an heiress. With characteristic austerity, at a time when men often married women of that tender age, he made it clear he would require no bedtime pleasure of Catherine until she was 20. She left for a sojourn abroad.

After their marriage, they settled in the pleasant, leafy town of Oxford, where Thompson bought a plantation. He ran slaves with such oppressive harshness that difficult servants from other properties were sent to him for punishment. For more than a decade, from 1839 to 1851, he ably represented his adoptive state in Congress as a states' rights Democrat, becoming President James Buchanan's Secretary of the Interior in 1857. When he was certain Buchanan supported anti-secessionism, he resigned his post; always recessive and diffident, he had grown to dislike the cut-and-thrust of politics; devoted to his wife and family, he longed to retire to his plantation at an early age. But in 1860 he had perked up briefly when asked to become host for Edward, Prince of Wales, the eldest son of Queen Victoria, on a popular private visit; an Anglophile, he was pleased by the assignment. His wife, in consequence, was received by the Queen in England and given the practical if parsimonious gift of a solid gold thimble.

The Thompsons' warm acquaintance with Lincoln surmounted the President's Republicanism and the presence of his annoying first lady, until Secession tore them apart.

With the outbreak of war, Thompson showed his duplicity by protesting Buchanan's Navy relief expedition to Fort Sumter by the vessel *Star of the West* and advising the Confederacy of the ship's imminent arrival. Firmly in the Southern camp, he became in his middle age an improbable Lieutenant Colonel, acting as aide-de-camp successively to Brigadier General Pierre G. T. Beauregard, the hero of Fort Sumter, and to Brigadier General John C. Pemberton.

Wearied of warfare and furious at the ill-treatment by Union forces of his elderly mother-in-law at Vicksburg, he resigned his commission and again retreated to his Oxford home, whence Jefferson Davis summoned him from work in the Mississippi legislature to Richmond for Secret Service duty that spring of 1864.

Those whom Davis and Benjamin chose to accompany Thompson were no more suitable for the assignment. The Alabaman Clement Claiborne Clay was, like Benjamin, Memminger and Thompson, a lawyer by profession and, like Thompson, a plantation owner. He was a frail asthmatic, whose sparse hair, pallid, weakly-bearded face, unconvincing stare and narrow, sloping shoulders inspired little confidence. Pampered by an early life of ease led in the political shallows, he was frequently on the brink of destitution because of an addiction to gambling he shared with Judah P. Benjamin. He was bailed out by his State Governor father, who awarded him the post of assistant editor of the family-owned *Huntsville* (Alabama) *Democrat,* a job to which he was conspicuously unsuited.

Like Thompson, he was an admirer of the legendary states' rights Democrat John C. Calhoun, and shared with that firebrand orator a need for expansion of American power. But as Congressman and then Senator from Alabama, he lacked the dash and sparkle of his populist idol.

Clay's most sensible act was to marry, in 1843, the appealing Virginia Caroline Tunstall. A Southern belle of great charm, she was a feather in his cap until there followed the disappointing news that, at a time when fathering a brood was considered a necessary sign of manhood, Clay was apparently incapable of siring an heir.

Clay's claim to fame was that he had once averted a duel between Benjamin and Jefferson Davis that led to a lifelong friendship among the three. His refusal of the Secretaryship of War in 1861 did not enhance his image of manliness and led to the unsatisfactory successive appointments of Leroy P. Walker and Benjamin himself. When Davis summoned Clay to discuss the British North American expedition, he had, in February, concluded his two years in the Confederate Senate and was looking forward to a recuperative trip to Florida, where one of that state's first two Senators, David L. Yulee, was his reliable friend.

The third of the Davis-Benjamin appointees was already in the North. James P. Holcombe was also a skilled lawyer. A Virginian doctor's son, tall, spare and bewigged, his bony good looks were undermined when he smiled or laughed by a conspicuous set of store-bought teeth. Like his *confrères,* he was a Calhounian, concerned with foreign expansionism and States' Rights—the ravenous antithesis of Lincoln. Of the group Davis sent to the North, he was easily the most ardent secessionist.

He had early produced valuable law books on commercial and maritime issues and had, ironically, become Professor of Law at the same University of Virginia he had quit before graduation. He was a supporter of slavery and had backed James M. Mason, unofficial Confederate emissary to London, in the Fugitive Slave Act, which allowed African-Americans to be arrested in flight without warrant and punished without trial. Holcombe made fiery addresses in lecture halls, preaching to the converted about the dangers of abolition, of which he saw Lincoln as the prime political supporter.

Holcombe was the eloquent dark star of the Virginia Convention in March 1861, addressing the subject of slavery with his customary fire and brimstone. From February 1862 he was among the angriest and most vociferous members of the Richmond Congress, representing the interests of the Virginia slaveholders with racist declamations. He fought daily for increased taxation, taking on Christopher Memminger in the process, and pushed Memminger to his later action of stripping assets of gold and jewelry from the coffers of the Southern rich.

He demanded a draft for able-bodied men, as well as an increase of rank-and-file eligibility to the advanced age of 40. At the end of 1863, Davis sent him to Halifax to settle, with his skill at naval law, the problem of the Union-authorized vessel *Chesapeake,* which had been seized by privateers posing as Confederates. He soon discovered their true identity and, skating expertly on the thin ice of British North American adjudication, avoided the most difficult issues to settle the matter. At that moment he was approached by Davis and proceeded to become, unlike his colleagues, unequivocally committed to the British North American enterprise.

Thompson appointed a private secretary, a miserable young Kentuckian named William C. Cleary, whose diary of the time complains of his state of despair, occasioned by the Richmond spring rains, his separation from a young and pretty wife in Lexington, his uneven health and the dismal prospects of the trip North.

After their meeting with Jefferson Davis at the Confederate White House in Richmond at the end of April, Thompson, Clay and Cleary set out from various points to Wilmington, the favored port for blockade runners at the time. On the 29th, Clay wrote in transit to his friend, the cantankerous Congressman Louis T. Wigfall, who detested Davis and refused to stand in his presence:

> It is a very responsible, difficult and delicate duty for which I am not suited by my talents, tastes or habits. I cannot enjoy secret service . . . I must incur the perils of the sea and capture by the enemy.

His notes of the time indicate that he would like to have backed out at the last moment—his health would have been a proper excuse, his reason, among others, that his wife was about to appear in a play in Richmond following her amateur triumph as Mrs. Malaprop in Sheridan's *The Rivals*—but he could not, because of a sudden and shocking incident.

On the day of Clay's note to Wigfall, the President's beloved five-year-old son Joseph had fallen from the piazza of the Presidential home and had been killed. How could Clay relinquish his assignment after that?

It was appropriate that the vessel chosen to take the Commissioners—for that was their egregious title—to British North America should be a product of the Liverpool blockade runners Fraser, Trenholm, whose most active partner was Christopher Memminger's associate George. For Jefferson Davis and Navy Secretary Mallory to authorize a Fraser, Trenholm blockade runner to take Thompson and Clay to British North America was the equivalent of making an arrangement with Blackbeard the Pirate.

Sailing under the Union Jack, the 500-ton side-wheeler *Thistle* carried cotton, turpentine and rosin as well as the Commissioners. Moored at the entrance to Cape Fear River, the vessel was delayed from sailing for a week, partly by unfavorable tides and weather, partly by the burning of cotton on the wharves by opponents of export to England and the North.

When at last the Commissioners were told it was time to sail, there was a further delay for the waning of the spring moon. Only in the deepest darkness could the *Thistle,* a minnow trying to slip past a pack of sharks, manage to evade the Union's thirteen massive wooden ships and ironclads.

Yet the side-wheeler was a nimble craft, unusually fast in the water, as even the nervous trio of Confederates boarding her with $25,000 in gold pieces had to admit. She could manage, with sufficient current and anthracite in her bunkers, a spanking 14 knots of speed. Painted a dull camouflage gray, her side wheels so assiduously oiled that she made no more than faint slaps on the water, she had an iron-hooded furnace that would show the enemy no betraying flicker of fire.

As the *Thistle*'s master eased her into the swell and dropped the pilot off shore, the Union blockaders rocked lightly in the waves. Lookouts were notoriously lazy in those days, but one observant seaman perched high up in the U.S.S. *Connecticut*'s crow's nest spotted the *Thistle* sneaking past. He climbed down and informed the skipper. The *Connecticut* set off in pursuit.

Thompson, Clay and Cleary woke at dawn, Thompson in the Captain's cabin, to see through the portholes the *Connecticut* chasing them, her funnel pouring smoke. They conferred anxiously, deciding, if they were boarded, to jettison the cotton and divide the $25,000 gold pieces and hide them—an impossible task. And they would burn their papers of instruction in the *Thistle*'s furnace. Pessimistic by nature, they—even the abstemious Thompson—began drinking the available liquor to give them Dutch courage, since they had very little of the other kind.

In sunshine and storm, the chase went on all day and into the night, until at last the lumbering *Connecticut*'s hard-pressed boilers overheated and her Captain ordered a return to the waters off Cape Fear. The *Thistle* sailed on unmolested, for refueling to the port of St. Georges, Bermuda; an African-British pilot guided the little ship through tricky offshore shoals. Four skiffs sailed up, brilliantly colored, with cheering citizens in welcome.

Accommodated by Clay's fellow Alabaman, the island trader and blockade runner Norman S. Walker, the Commissioners met at his welcome dinner party the grave and accomplished Thomas Connolly, Roman Catholic Archbishop of Halifax, a strong opponent of Lincoln, who worked constantly to encourage subversive Confederate activities in British North America.

Connolly joined the Commissioners aboard the British ferry *Alpha,* bound for Halifax. On a day of brilliant sunshine, the visitors had on arrival at that Nova Scotia port only to walk one block to check into the red-brick Halifax Hotel, a converted army barracks run by the expansive Southern sympathizer Henry Hesslein. They were joined by James P. Holcombe, who was housed in uncomfortably cramped quarters over a confectionery store he could now afford to quit.

Entertained by Archbishop Connolly, who provided instructions to every pro-Confederate in the province, the arrivals met at his house two pirates and blockade runners, the British Benjamin Wier, who worked with Norman Walker of Bermuda to ship arms illegally to Richmond, and Alexander Keith, freebooting Scots nephew of a local brewer, who was starting to grow wealthy from making trading arrangements with the South.

Thompson and Cleary decided to move to Montreal as soon as possible with the $25,000 in gold, to deposit it at the Ontario Bank in that city. Clay, suffering from asthma and general debility, briefly stayed behind. There he met with a young rebel First Lieutenant, the handsome if baby-faced Bennett H. Young, who, on June 16 of that year had, with authorization from Confederate Secretary of War James A. Seddon, formed a force of 20 Kentuckians, feisty escapees from Union prisons whom he called the Confederate States' Retributors. Uses would be found for Young, who left shortly after meeting Clay to run the blockade to Richmond for War Secretary Seddon's military advice.

Unable to take ship on the St. Lawrence River because of lingering pack ice, Thompson and Holcombe traveled to Montreal by wagon and stagecoach, a bumpy miserable journey that lasted several days, through wild scenery under threatening or sundrenched skies, way stations offering food not much more appetizing than fried jackrabbit, the exhausted and ill-watered horses replaced at regular intervals. It was May 29 before the weary travelers arrived.

Montreal was a surprise: a civilized haven in the Canadian wilderness. It was a thriving metropolis of some 75,000 souls that could, by the look of it, have been transported, stone by stone, from Europe. Compared to stinking, filthy, ill-paved New York City, or the muddy mess that was Washington, it had all the qualities of an unlikely urban paradise.

Mount Royal, the limestone mansions of the very rich, the Parisian sidewalk cafes, the twin-towered neo-Gothic Roman Catholic cathedral, a modest echo of Nôtre Dame, the Corinthian marbled splendor of the Banks of Montreal and Ontario, and the Doric Bonsecours Market building dominated a proliferation of well-appointed churches, schools and office buildings.

Headquarters for Thompson and Cleary, and for all Confederates in the city, was the luxurious St. Lawrence Hall hotel. Run by the popular and ruddy-cheeked Henry Hogan, a British Southern sympathizer who combined virtual illiteracy with a passion for billiards, the hostelry offered the only mint juleps to be found north of the Secessionist states. With its rotunda dining room, lounge filled with ferns and flowers, bootblacks and flocks of maids and waiters, it offered a Southern gentleman almost everything he could want except for slaves.

The hotel was the headquarters of the British redcoat regiments, bristling with mustachioed generals and majors and colonels, alive with songs like "The Royal Fusiliers" and, more significantly, "Dixie" and "Maryland, Oh, Maryland." Here any agent of Davis and Benjamin could find unstinting support both financial and military; here, plans could be hatched to stab the Union in the back; here soon, Lincoln's kidnap and death would be energetically plotted.

Thompson wasted no time in opening his account at the Ontario Bank, a riot of marble and gilt, whose manager lived in a sumptuous apartment on the second floor, with the sum in gold, bills of exchange or coin of some $130,000 or, in Canadian terms, 22,679 pounds sterling received from London. The rest he retained for distribution in banks at Toronto and St. Catharines, Ontario.

While at St. Lawrence Hall, Thompson formed an association with the wealthy and fierce-tempered James D. Westcott, whose wholehearted commitment to the South would prove invaluable in the months to come.

With David L. Yulee one of the first two Senators representing Florida in 1845, after that former Spanish province obtained statehood, and later acting Governor, Westcott hated Lincoln with all his heart, both on states' rights and slavery issues. He had once infuriated the former President James Polk when he stated that the only way to treat an unruly black was to "give him a damn drubbing at the start." Elected a Democrat, he angrily turned Whig when Polk refused to appoint his incompetent brother Attorney General. When he moved to New York City and became a successful lawyer, he became a member of the dominant Copperhead faction headed by Governor Horatio Seymour, Mayor Fernando Wood, and the millionaire Rothschild agent August Belmont. In 1862, he moved to Montreal to work underground with British interests against Lincoln.

Two days before Clay arrived belatedly from Halifax, Thompson and Cleary moved on to Toronto, too impatient to await his arrival and anxious to set up a separate headquarters at that city's handsome Queens Hotel. Soon the most furious and dangerous anti-Lincolnian of all would join them—a man who, almost single-handedly, converted their ill-defined and generalized plans for subversion, annoyance and infiltration into a plot aimed at Lincoln's personal destruction. That man was George Nicholas Sanders.

TWO THE KILLER

It is only appropriate that George Sanders should, while not related, be the namesake of the famous villain of 1930s and 1940s motion pictures, since he himself was a villain in the traditional mold.

With a shock of gray hair, incisive blue eyes, a bushy beard and a muscular middleweight's physique running rapidly to fat, Sanders in the 1860s resembled nothing so much as somebody's eccentric grumpy uncle rather than the destructive force of nature he really was. He defied the gentlemen's code—and not only in his violent utterances, bad language and betrayal of friends. He seldom combed his hair or bathed; he had about him the rank odor of a bear in a badly-kept zoo.

He paced and growled constantly, his metaphoric claws unsheathed if anyone should cross him. His clothes were old, baggy and shiny; his coarse manner was matched by his handwriting; his impatience and fondness for hyperbole made everything he said or wrote distinctly overwrought. And he scribbled inordinately—journals crammed from top to bottom of the pages, letters fired off with all the dangerous velocity of rifle bullets, newspaper editorials and articles like badly-bottled whirlwinds.

Yet he was a loving husband and father to his brilliant multilingual wife Anna, his three strapping sons, and his flirtatious, pretty daughter. He was so generous a host, so unabashedly extravagant in the supply of champagne and fine cuisine, so ready with overripe anecdote and witty insult that he attracted not a few. Sanders rejoiced in his murderous intrigues, and pirates have seldom been unpopular.

When he contacted Jacob Thompson in Toronto in June, 1864, he was already infamous as the power behind President Franklin Pierce in the ante-bellum era. Pierce, marked down with Sanders as a member of the terrorist Knights of the Golden Circle and a strongly anti-Lincolnian supporter of Jefferson Davis, remained one of his closest Copperhead allies.

Sanders, who called his fellow Kentuckian Lincoln a baboon and a What-Is-It?—showman Phineas T. Barnum's name for the Missing Link exhibited at his New York City museum—single-mindedly wanted Lincoln destroyed. He was the chief contact in Europe and British North America for the powerful New York secessionist group led by his close friend August Belmont, and by the Wood brothers, Fernando and Benjamin. As the intended assassin, 10 years earlier, of French Emperor Napoleon III, he carried considerable dubious prestige in revolutionary circles.

His arrival at Toronto in June 1864 was not comfortable for Jacob Thompson or for Clement C. Clay, who met him shortly afterward. These men saw him as too overt, crude and dangerous; he might say too much, he might betray their subversive operation before it had begun. Thompson never accepted him but Clay and Holcombe soon succumbed to his malevolent spell. None thought of him as one of their breed and class.

In truth, his lineage was at least as impressive as theirs. His family was prominent in Kentucky political affairs. Born on February 21, 1811, he was raised from puberty in the sprawling family-built log house named Grass Hills, near Ghent in Carroll County, surrounded by 750 property acres of rolling blue grass. There the Sanders clan raised sheep, cattle and thoroughbreds for breeding and racing. From his teenage years, Sanders was a wheeler and dealer in the brutal little world of horse-trading. He and his people laid the groundwork for the state's later fame as the location of the Kentucky Derby.

He grew up rough-handed, stocky, vigorous and thick in the shoulder, the very picture of corn-fed American country youth. He was loud, boastful, flashy, and ready with his fists; he could talk any man into the ground in an argument as readily as he would shoot off an expensive hat. Yet he was no illiterate; he quickly commanded at least a smattering of literature and foreign languages, and began reading, at an early age, the New York weekly literary magazine *The Passion-Flower,* whose attractive editor, Anna Reid, he decided to write to and win in marriage in order to obtain foothold in the influential salons of Manhattan.

Within a week of their first correspondence and a quick trip from Grass Hills to New York, Sanders' power of persuasion and healthy open good looks, soon to be lost to the joys of the table, conquered Anna's resistance. He even managed to persuade this hothouse intellectual with a command of many languages to abandon, for part of each year, the overcrowded pleasures of her city for the rustic isolation of his family estate. There they raised two sturdy older boys, Reid and Lewis, and their very pretty daughter, Virginia.

In 1844, Sanders, who had just turned 33, moved with Anna to Manhattan, where a third son, George, was born; he embarked at once upon his sulfurous political career, captivating or infuriating everyone with whom he came in touch. With no capacity to brook criticism, his ego was all-consuming. His brimstone presence was everywhere, noisy, aggressive, all-conquering, from Tammany Hall to Town Hall, from Mayor's mansion to Governor's ball, from club to club and street corner to street corner. He wasted little time in sleep; he could eat or drink almost anyone under the table, chain-smoked cigars with the best, and accumulated a flock of fair-weather friends.

Sanders was a founder member and camp follower of the Young America movement, the diplomat Edwin De Leon's dangerous reinvention of the Jeffersonian front line. It was an army of attack on old fogies and tyrannical European dictatorships. The movement was symbolized by its creators as a virile and powerful youth, a young Hercules who was America itself, stripped for action and swelling with muscle, ready to crush all those who stood against principles of United States supremacy at home or abroad.

Young America resembled nothing so much as Hitler Youth, some eighty years before the invention of that movement; today we would call it fascist, with its refusal to tolerate the old, the weak, the sick; its hatred of blacks, Jews, and native Americans; its emphasis on physique, pure racial strains and gladiatorial battle against the retrograde.

Young America cloaked its colonialist ambitions in a pretense of missionary idealism. Sanders and his associates took as their inspiration the Sanders family friend Aaron Burr, who had tried to swallow up Venezuela in 1805, and Alexander Hamilton, who had shared in that ill-fated adventure. A catch-phrase frequently on Sanders' lips was Manifest Destiny, a term coined by Massachusetts Congressman Robert C. Winthrop and promulgated by Sanders' friend and polemicist John L. O'Sullivan in the mid-1840s. Followers of Manifest Destiny believed, with Young Americans, that their nation was granted by God the right to filibuster and conquer any nation that stood in its way. They were certain that the Latin American countries, from Mexico to Chile and Argentina, and across the ocean to Cuba and Spain itself, were destined to become part of a vast slave empire, run from Washington by uniformed and strapping young men, like British India.

Sanders formed a close and lifelong association with August Belmont. Belmont was, like Benjamin and Memminger, of foreign origin, the son of a German-Jewish farmer; well-educated, softly handsome, cultivated, he was multi-lingual and early had a profound knowledge of painting and sculpture—a marked contrast with the rough-hewn Sanders. Arriving in New York City at 23, he soon grasped the opportunities in the world of finance; he had stumbled into a bank and business crash after which buying was possible from the bottom. He boldly took a room at 78 Wall Street and set up as agent for the Rothschilds, the greatest power brokers and bankers in Europe; he had worked for them earlier but they knew nothing of his plan. The move paid off; he became their American agent. Three years later, thanks to much skillful cotton and tobacco speculation, snapping up the Alabama state bonds and Arkansas and Missouri securities and notes, he was one of the richest men in the city. He was so attractive, with his dreamy liquid brown eyes, carefully disheveled black hair and almost feminine full-lipped mouth that it was said any woman would succumb to him at first sight and New York business leaders were advised to lock up their daughters. His banquets and balls were the rage of the city—despite his rare extravagance, he daily became richer than ever.

Sanders found another pugnacious supporter in the Illinois political figure known as the Little Giant: Stephen A. Douglas. Though at a little over five feet, Douglas scarcely filled the required picture of tall, athletic magnificence called for by Young Americans, he packed enough energy into his stubby, muscular frame to be dubbed a steam engine in britches; he had become a Supreme Court judge before he was 30.

Douglas fascinated Sanders from the outset; Sanders backed him as potential President. So red-faced and sore-throated was he from stumping in pursuit of a nomination in the 1852 campaign, so plagued by headaches in pursuit of his ambition, the pint-sized contestant sometimes appeared to be on the verge of spontaneous combustion, his eyes about to pop out of his head.

Yet another of Sanders' revolutionary idols was Lajos (Louis) Kossuth, the Hungarian national hero whose cowardly exile in Turkey had been transmuted by publicity into a fund-raising venture with the Sultan in Constantinople. Snatched from arrest and execution in his native land by American gunboat, he was brought to New York, and to Sanders' front door, in December, 1851. So short that his ceremonial sword clanked on the sidewalks behind him, he scarcely presented an heroic figure despite his darkly romantic good looks, but he captivated women, and men hailed him in triumph down the stinking stretch of Broadway. So popular was he that he even got away with criticizing George Washington and with grumbling petulantly when military brass bands drowned out his speeches. For years, Abraham Lincoln often wore a Kossuth hat.

Sanders fastened on Kossuth, became his friend, and supported his seldom-stated but consuming cause: the assassination of the Emperor Franz Joseph of Austria, the egregious monarch of Hungary.

In January 1852, Sanders showed his hand openly as a would-be terrorist and assassin. He became editor of *The United States Magazine and Democratic Review* in place of his fellow scholarly and devious Young American, John L. O'Sullivan. The transportation tycoon George Law acquired a financial interest in the publication along with August Belmont, the Woods and others of their stripe and handed Sanders co-ownership.

Sanders converted the magazine from a mildly inflammatory organ of opinion, laced through with contributions from Poe, Hawthorne and sundry other literary figures, into the revolutionary platform of Young America and Manifest Destiny. In his ominous first editorial of January, 1852, he announced:

> What the Ides of March were to the Roman despot and the threat-
> ened republic of antiquity, the year "1852" upon whose first day we
> at last enter, is to the modern system of republican peoples and
> antagonistic governments throughout the world . . . a gigantic Bru-
> tus, armed . . . to bring death to tyrants . . . it beats the drumbeat
> of insurrection.

On page after page, he called for American invasion of Europe, a destruction of crowned heads, and glorious bloodshed in the name of freedom.

Sanders targeted Napoleon III, Emperor of France, by reprinting Victor Hugo's murderous manifesto *Napoleon the Little,* a document circulated in France from Hugo's Channel Island exile in baskets of game birds. He trumpeted the glories of the assassination-minded Italian revolutionary Giuseppe Mazzini and gave support to a terrorist group, a precursor of the Knights of the Golden Circle and The Sons of Liberty, The Knights of the Silver Star.

He approved George Law's vessel *The Crescent City*'s voyage to Havana, a ship loaded to the gunwales with cannon and musket to launch a filibuster backed by Young Americans against the local Spanish authorities to plunder sugar, tobacco and slaves. From New Orleans, where he practiced law, Judah P. Benjamin endeared himself to Sanders and Pierce by stating that the local government's overnight act of seizure of the vessel was cause for the invocation of Mars, god of battle, against Spain and that America would be entitled to annex Cuba in retaliation; any excuse, it seemed, was better than none.

While not exemplifying it physically, Jefferson Davis was yet another adherent of the Young American movement. In his forties, the Mississippi delta politician seemed prematurely aged, tall, erect in his military posture but gaunt and hollow-cheeked and as cadaverous in body as Lincoln himself. He suffered from recurrent bouts of malaria and an excruciating condition known as facial neuralgia or *tic dolorosa,* a nervous ailment that had been known to drive some sufferers to suicide. But Davis was made of sterner stuff; he had an unbending stubbornness of will and enterprise and he was intent, vigorous and mentally strong. His far-flung interests, stemming from his service as colonel-hero in the Regiment of First Mississippi rifles volunteers in the Mexican war, included an interest in Mexican silver mines. Soon he would be Secretary of War in the Franklin Pierce cabinet and very much behind Sanders' expansionist adventures. James M. Mason and John Slidell, manipulators of the *Trent* incident, were also on the presidential team; Mason became Pierce's Chairman of the Department of Foreign Relations, adding yet another threat to Latin American and European sovereign interests.

According to William Need, a printer and military officer who spent years researching the subject, in a report made to Union War Secretary Simon Cameron on September 27, 1861, Davis was involved in extensive expansionism in the Americas. He swayed Franklin Pierce into obtaining Arizona and to protecting his silver mines in Chihuahua. "With an eye that never winked and a wing that never tired has Jeff Davis turned his thoughts and desires to the Mexican line for infinite expansion," Need wrote.

Of the Young American group, none was more dangerous than Pierre Soulé, Benjamin's associate as New Orleans lawyer and later Senator from Louisiana. He was the very image of a heroic Apollo, glowingly described in Sanders' editorials in *The Democratic Review*. Tall and square-shouldered, with streaming crow-black hair, dramatically pale skin and Byronic flashing eyes, he had lived a life as colorful as that of a Victor Hugo hero, his idol and fellow revolutionary. At fifteen he had emerged as a would-be assassin of the French King Charles X. Escaping from prison when condemned to the guillotine, he had fled to England, where he found approval for his plans for regicide; then, like Benjamin, he had founded his brilliant career in the same Creole-dominated city.

When Pierce swept the polls in 1852, Sanders greeted the President as if he were a new star in the heavens. In an exhortatory editorial in *The Democratic Review* he predicted that Pierce would "crush the despots of Europe in their very dens"—an open call to invasion, massacre and assassination. Strongly supported by Jefferson Davis as War Secretary, and bucking the influence of William L. Marcy, the cautious Secretary of State, Sanders had no difficulty in influencing Pierce, who was distracted by the tragic death of his infant son in a train wreck, to create what, in effect, was an anarchistic network abroad.

Pierce, reduced to a puppet President, appointed Sanders' and Davis's diplomatic choices, not on the basis of any capacity for negotiation and accord, nor of experience in consular and ambassadorial affairs, but upon the ability to stir up revolution, destroy monarchies by gun, poison, bomb, or sword, and clear the way for American control of the Western world as far afield as Russia. Only England was excused, as she gave safe harbor to revolutionaries, famous or obscure, not so much because of reasonable influence but because she hoped to increase British power by seeing the European monarchies destabilized and wrecked.

Sanders, knowing that the local Consulate would be the focus of terrorism, secret intelligence from spies across the Channel, and a contact for anti-royalist intrigue, made sure he secured the post. He managed to wangle the astonishing salary of $10,000 a year, or the equivalent of $231,000 in money today, out of Pierce; it isn't surprising that Pierce, defying Marcy, made this a recess appointment—that is to say, made without benefit of Congress.

Sanders and Jefferson Davis needed a man they could manipulate as Minister to the Court of St. James. The perfect choice was the austere and gentlemanly white-haired bachelor James Buchanan of Pennsylvania, who had twice been defeated as Democratic nominee for President and who could be relied upon firmly not to say boo to a goose. Abashed and semi-retired as a political washout, he was a manipulatable Old Fogey, sure to be molded by Sanders once they were both in London.

To bolster Sanders' cause still further, the unscrupulous firebrand Young American Daniel E. Sickles from New York was made London consular attaché and first secretary; later he would murder the son of the composer of "The Star Spangled Banner" and get away with it.

Sanders and Davis turned to other crucial appointments. Grateful for August Belmont's continuing financial support and Fifth Avenue hospitality, Sanders fixed him up with the job of Minister to the Netherlands, which gave Belmont (and the Rothschild Bank) access to the rich treasure of the Dutch empire in the East Indies. It also gave Belmont, and the other Young Americans, much to offer in terms of opposition to the Dutch monarchy, and the chance to interfere, not to say meddle, in local and colonial politics.

Pierre Soulé, with the conquest of Spanish Cuba uppermost in his mind, was awarded outrageously the post of Minister to Spain, where he plotted to bribe, suborn or cajole Queen Isabella II and her dominant mother Queen Maria Cristina into selling that island colony for a bargain price or risk surrendering it to American-backed military forces. John L. O'Sullivan, as a reward for handing over the editorship of *The United States Magazine and Democratic Review* to Sanders, and continuing to supply anonymous revolutionary articles, was given the enviable post of Minister to Portugal, where he schemed against the already embattled King Pedro V and harbored, in short order, Victor Frond, a French assassin Sanders had hired. In Paris, the vigorous Young American John Y. Mason could be relied upon to sustain the anarchist cause.

Even the smaller diplomatic posts were laced with revolutionaries. As an example, Sanders fixed up his friend, the radical novelist Nathaniel Hawthorne, with the position of consul in Liverpool, a crucially important post because from that Northern port spies, treasure and armaments could be shipped on forged permits to foreign parts. From Moscow to Cairo, the undergrowth of subversion spread and flourished.

Arrived in London in November, 1853, Sanders, his wife Anna and four children moved, after a brief stopover, into a handsome, three-story Victorian house at 45 Weymouth Street, off Portland Place, and at once Sanders joined the Central Democratic Committee, a polite name for an all-out assassination bureau under constant surveillance from its formation in 1851 by Sanders' hard-working namesake, Inspector John N. Sanders of Scotland Yard.

Situated at various locations, most notably at rooms in Windmill Street, and financed by American and French supporters to the tune of five million dollars, the Committee ran a death-to-tyrants society of some 600 members, operated an illicit telegraph service to Paris and Marseilles, and numbered among its members Victor Hugo, Giuseppe Mazzini and Lajos Kossuth. The Committee's manifestos were drawn word for word from the terrorist utterances of Maximilien Robespierre, bloodstained leader of the French Revolution, and called for, among other things, the assassination of Napoleon III.

When Sanders became a figure of the Central Democratic Committee, his messages were smuggled (as they would be during the American Civil War), written in tiny, inked words on scraps of silk, sewn into knees, elbows and armpits of travelers' clothing. The Committee manufactured hand grenades, bombs and infernal machines at a headquarters hidden away in a cellar in Rotherhithe. Sanders used the diplomatic pouches, with Daniel Sickles' collusion and without James Buchanan's knowledge, to send insurrectionist manifestos abroad. Oblivious, the Old Fogey Buchanan was concerned chiefly with whether or not to wear breeches at official court receptions.

Sanders befriended the leading revolutionaries of the world, all of whom found safe haven in xenophobic England, a country which had no liking of the French after the Napoleonic wars, had not forgotten the Spanish armada and soon would be spoiling for the Crimean War against Russia.

Giuseppe Mazzini, with his slender, tense body and brimstone eyes, surrounded by twittering greenfinches in wooden cages at his rooms in the Fulham Road, and the equally handsome would-be assassin Felice Orsini, brooding in his headquarters at the Café Etoile in Windmill Street, were very close to Sanders.

The talk of London was the recent (July, 1853) attempt on the life of Napoleon III with pistol and dagger at a performance of Auber's *Haydée* at the Opera Comique in Paris, an attempt backed by the political hothead Hippolyte Magen, to whom Sanders gave shelter and succor. This attempt, including the location of a theatre and the choice of weapons, foreshadowed John Wilkes Booth's murder of Lincoln eleven years and nine months later.

The Central Democratic Committee was investigated by the Black Chamber, Napoleon's secret service, whose members had to write their names on kettle-steamed glass doors before they could be admitted. The Chamber was particularly on the alert after an extraordinary dinner party Sanders held on his own birthday, and the eve of George Washington's, on February 21, 1854, for the revolutionary figures of Europe.

At Weymouth Street, with James Buchanan as co-host, the guests included Giuseppe Garibaldi, who had just arrived, at the height of his fame, in England; Mazzini; Kossuth; Orsini; the French revolutionary Alexandre-August Ledru-Rollin; the French socialist Louis Blanc; Aleksander Herzen, the leading Russian insurrectionist and protégé of the Rothschilds; Ferenc Pulsky from Hungary and Stanislas Worcel from Poland. James Buchanan, the only weak man at the feast, was heard to ask Anna Sanders whether she wasn't afraid that, given so combustible a guest-list, the house might not explode, with everybody in it.

After dinner, Anna struck up the revolutionary strains of "La Marseillaise" on her guitar, with its theme of the destruction of tyrants; although it was the militant hymn of both Garibaldi and Mazzini in their Italian campaigns, some of the guests were too drunk to join her in remembering the words. Then Sanders provided all those who hadn't left early with samplings of his lethal Kentucky punch.

In April, while Anna was in Paris, and the Crimean War, which Sanders hoped would bring the downfall of Czar Nicholas I, was beginning, Sanders was often closeted with Kossuth, his old friend from New York, who kept in a locket a strand of George Washington's hair; and, all summer long, with the huge, grizzled Ledru-Rollin, who was constantly plotting against Napoleon III. These anarchists differed with Sanders only on the slavery issue; he protested repeatedly that the enslavement of blacks was nothing compared with the enslavement by monarchies of millions of white people in Europe.

Disturbed by word of Sanders' plots with terrorist leaders stemming from the February revolutionary dinner, Pierce's Secretary of State, William L. Marcy, called for his dismissal in the spring, a dismissal that both Sanders and Buchanan chose to ignore. At word of his removal, Sanders' admirers deluged him with letters of support. Victor Hugo wrote from the Channel Islands in anger and shock ("When you write it is your soul, elevated and free"), Garibaldi wrote in sorrow ("Of my unhappy land, you are the model") and Nathaniel Hawthorne joined the chorus with an equally sympathetic note from Liverpool. Sanders was retained by Buchanan who, despite disapproval in Washington, trusted him to issue passports, in those days single-page documents, under the ambassadorial seal. They were signed by Buchanan in every case, to be endorsed only with the names of those on official business in view of the current Crimean War and the revolution in Spain led by General Leopoldo O'Donnell.

Quite illegally, Sanders had his British clerk attaché, William Henry Walsh, knowingly enter the former Paris fire chief and present terrorist Victor Frond (also called Frondé), on one of these passports as a diplomatic courier and silk merchant, to enable him to leave the Central Democratic Committee assassination bureau in London for Lisbon, Madrid and Paris. In those cities he would contact successively John L. O'Sullivan, Pierre Soulé and John Y. Mason and then proceed, with their personal blessing and financial support, to Biarritz, where he would waylay and murder Napoleon III at a theatre or at his vacation home at the Villa Eugenie, named for his wife, the Empress. He would stir an uprising in Marseilles, former headquarters of Mazzini and Ledru-Rollin, as the beginning of a full-scale new French revolution.

The plan backfired. U.S. Paris envoy John Y. Mason, who had established a degree of friendship, quite against revolutionary principles, with Napoleon III's foreign minister, Drouyn de L'hys, leaked the plan to a horrified James Buchanan, who at once advised Marcy in Washington; Marcy told Franklin Pierce, who, in turn panicked and advised Napoleon. The Emperor changed his holiday residence to a safehouse outside Biarritz. Forced to abandon his plan but never brought to justice, Frond, sheltered by John L. O'Sullivan, settled permanently in Lisbon, where he became, paradoxically, a society photographer.

Sanders was not prosecuted for being a party to a murder plot. Buchanan, though annoyed with him, suggesting he should leave England, was too weak to call for his arrest. Instead, Buchanan encouraged Sanders and others of Pierce's revolutionary diplomats to frame the so-called Ostend Manifesto of October 18, 1854, in which Buchanan, Belmont, Mason and Pierre Soulé met in that city to issue a statement that, if the revolutionary government of Spain should refuse to sell Cuba, the United States would be justified in invading and conquering the island colony. Nothing came of this reckless proposal.

On December 27, 1854, Sanders and his family left England for New York. Word that Spain planned to release the Cuban slaves in defiance of Young American interests, resulted in Sanders, George Law and Belmont, among others, again planning a Cuban invasion; Law offered thousands of muskets for such an adventure, but the order was cancelled by an increasingly nervous Franklin Pierce, who did not want to risk a war with Spain.

Weak as ever, Buchanan forgave Sanders everything; he sent him encouraging notes from London to Manhattan in the early months of 1855. Treacherously, Sanders planned to bring about Franklin Pierce's defeat for the Democratic party nomination; he energetically backed Buchanan.

Old fogey though Buchanan was, Young Americans rallied behind the candidate. Judah P. Benjamin and August Belmont were in the forefront of his supporters; Belmont's uncle by marriage, John Slidell, was another. A certainty if Buchanan were elected would be the convenient redemption of these intriguers' Texas state bonds; Sanders' close friend, the heavy-drinking and devious Beverley Tucker, often misdescribed as his cousin, was another bondholder.

Thirty-five years old at the time, Tucker was born in Winchester, Virginia, in 1820. The son, grandson and brother of distinguished figures of that state's legislature, a graduate of the University of Virginia, he helped the engineer Charles Ellet build the James River and Kanawha Canals. Married in 1841, he became the owner of a plantation, Hazelfield, in Jefferson County and raised eight children.

He began his career as a munitions manufacturer during the Mexican war of the 1840s; from 1853 to 1856 he was editor of the Washington *Sentinel.*

He was tall, fleshy, with the shambling uncertain gait of a drunken bear; he was also duplicitous, smart and of plausible and boisterous manners. In his own way, he would turn out to be as dangerous as Sanders himself.

On February 15, 1856, Sanders wrote to Buchanan, promising that Tucker and his six brothers would do everything possible in Richmond to secure the Virginia delegates; the promise was kept. In April, Sanders was busy addressing a Canal Street, New York assembly to launch the Tennessee adventurer William Walker in a planned filibustering conquest of Nicaragua; Pierre Soulé gave a similar speech at a St. Louis meeting. Judah P. Benjamin, to whom Buchanan promised support in developing the trans-Mexico Tihuantepec railroad, also rallied to the cause, as did Jefferson Davis, who was promised the job of War Secretary and favors in Mexico as well.

At the Democratic National Convention in Cincinnati in June, with Sanders as aggressive spokesman, Soulé headed the Louisiana delegation calling for a resolution that sought support for William Walker and the defeat of Latin American sovereign interests in the interests of North America. Supporting such colonialist ambitions, Buchanan was nominated, with the pro-slavery John C. Breckinridge of Kentucky as Vice-President. He would one day become Confederate Secretary of War.

On September 22, 1855, at a meeting of anarchist sympathizers at Washington Hall in New York, to celebrate the 63rd anniversary of the formation of the French revolutionary republic, Sanders delivered an inflammatory speech calling for death for tyrants and stating that he would be happy to work the guillotine himself (he meant, to execute Napoleon III) "by steam, by God." The promise provoked a chorus of grateful cheers.

After Buchanan's election, the grateful new President seriously—and incredibly—considered reappointing Sanders to the London consulate, there, no doubt, to recommence his terrorist activities. This time Sanders would only accept if the appointment was confirmed in Congress. But there were too many opponents in both Houses and instead Buchanan handed his errant former Consul the useful sinecure of Navy Agent in New York, as approved by the Secretary of the Interior, Jacob Thompson.

With his customary shrewdness, Sanders managed to obtain for Beverley Tucker, despite that man's enhanced habit of drinking heavily, the post of Consul in Liverpool in replacement of Nathaniel Hawthorne. If Civil War should come, and it was already in the cards, it would be crucial for the South to have access to the wealth and maritime connections of that British port, with its vigorous firm of Fraser, Trenholm, half-owned in Charleston, half in Lancashire, and its adherents who could supply ships to maraud the United States Navy with Sanders acting as cooperative agent. Tucker could, and did on arrival in England, secure the support of all of those who would soon oppose Buchanan's increasing restrictions on British trade.

In March 1858, Sanders was attacked in an inflammatory pamphlet, issued by Napoleon III himself, and published in the London *Times* on the 11th of the month, following Felice Orsini's attempt on the lives of the Emperor and Empress outside the Paris Opera on January 14, and Orsini's subsequent summary execution. Napoleon named Sanders directly:

> (Hippolyte) Magen invented bombs which were to explode through a single shock. Convicted in Belgium by default, he fled and took refuge in London, where Sanders . . . in the midst of conspirators and assassins . . . received him as a brother.

As a fellow Kentuckian, Sanders had for years been aware of the rising power and influence of Abraham Lincoln, the epitome of everything he disliked, from his appearance to his country manners and cheerful homilies, to his high-handed desire to reduce states' rights and his need to cause emancipation of slaves. Lincoln's down-home humors, simplicity of expression and deep-seated populism were equally infuriating to Sanders, for whom duplicity and wickedness were second nature. And now, in the late 1850s, Lincoln offered the possibility that he might be President.

Sanders found many who shared his views, particularly in New York City, including August Belmont and the former (and future) Mayor Fernando Wood, co-owner with his brother Benjamin of the New York *Daily News* from 1860. And, of course, the inescapable George Law.

The Woods were of Scots-Quaker origin, their father a failed Philadelphia dry goods merchant. The young men grew up strong and broad-shouldered extroverts in New York City, and rapidly emerged as hard-working, feverishly intense figures of the city's life. Fernando was careful, polished, a smooth operator of the political machine; Benjamin was impudent, rascally, blunt and obvious.

Both were ardent slavers and despised Lincoln from the outset. At a mass meeting in New Rochelle, Westchester County, on October 19, 1859 Fernando denounced Lincoln's party as "a fiend which stalks within the narrow barrier of its Northern cage." He mentioned that—a theme which would recur after the Civil War broke out—"hundreds of millions of Northern capital are invested in the South and . . . the wealth of New Yorkers depend on Southern use of slavery . . . the profits, luxuries, even necessities, nay even the physical existence, depend upon the products only to be obtained by continuance of slave labor and the prosperity of the slave master."

Such sentiments helped to carry him to the mayoralty and he was not handicapped when he called for his city to secede from the Union. On January 7, 1861 he urged the Common Council to follow that purpose. With war pending and sporadic conflicts already occurring between North and South he had the effrontery to state that "as a free city, New York could have the united support of the Southern states." Since the Union had been disrupted, New York City and state, he averred, must become a Southern independency.

His brother Benjamin rallied to the cause and for the rest of the war, despite a brief hiatus when Lincoln had his *Daily News* banned from circulation, maintained a policy of outright sedition and treason that never changed.

Nor did James Buchanan fail to undermine the Lincoln presidency even before it officially began. On April 4, 1861, the London *Times* correspondent William Howard Russell published the result of an interview with the newly-appointed Union Secretary of State, William H. Seward:

> (Buchanan's) cabinet had [Seward said] tampered [sic] with trea-
> son and contained traitors . . . one Minister had personally sent
> away the navy of the United States to distant and scattered stations;
> another had purposefully placed the arms, ordnance and other

munitions of war in undue proportions in the Southern states, and had weakened the Federal Government so that they might easily fall into the hands of the traitors and enable them to secure the war *materiel* of the Union; a Minister had stolen the public funds for traitorous purposes—in every port, in every department of the State, at home and abroad, on sea and by land, men were placed who were engaged in the deep conspiracy.

Despite such useful intrigue, Sanders abandoned Buchanan when there seemed no likelihood of his succeeding in the nomination. As before, Sanders turned his slippery attentions to Stephen A. Douglas, who forgave him for the disastrous *Democratic Review* editorials of 1854 and accepted his support at the successive and famous debates with Lincoln of 1858 which Douglas won.

Sanders' approval was enhanced by Douglas's introduction of the Kansas-Nebraska Act, which nullified the Missouri Compromise prohibiting slavery in the Louisiana Purchase territories.

However, on another matter Sanders was opposed. Douglas was angered by the Lecompton pro-slavery constitution for Kansas, stating that it was an abrogation of states' rights and that the majority of citizens must have the ability to decide on the matter. This placed Sanders in a difficult position and infuriated Southern leaders on Capitol Hill, but Sanders was sufficiently filled with hatred for Lincoln and so, certain only Douglas had a chance of electoral victory, he continued in dangerous support.

When Lincoln won the election in November, despite furious stumping by Douglas, who lost much support on the Lecompton issue, Sanders was devastated. Civil war was now a certainty. While Belmont, the Wood Brothers and Seymour stayed in the North to betray the new President, Sanders went South, but retained these men's allegiance to the last.

From January 1861, Sanders was in Montgomery, Alabama, the short-lived Confederate capital, commuting several times to Washington to set up contacts that could be sustained treasonably during the coming conflict.

Montgomery was an unappetizing excuse for a city. It was negotiated by shabby, insecure omnibuses and carriages that often foundered in ill-paved, uneven streets, flanked by largely undistinguished buildings. The one hotel for the well-to-do to stop at was the Exchange. So overcrowded was this wartime hostelry that married couples had to separate and three men or three women had to share; sometimes an uncomfortable trio was forced to occupy the same bed.

Flies and fleas made noisy competition. The dining room was closed at all times and food had to be obtained down the street where, at a fly-blown restaurant, toads, possums and raccoons were on the menu and the tablecloths had been in need of washing for weeks.

The habit of tobacco chewing and spitting seemed as much a mark of manhood as donning a uniform and strapping on a sword. The firing distance of the spit, and the refusal to acknowledge the existence of a spittoon, also indicated virility and a proud disdain of manners. Every man who called himself a man carried on him a gun or a knife. The most persistent topic at the Exchange was the Knights of the Golden Circle, described by William Howard Russell of the London *Times* as

> A Protestant association for securing the Gulf provinces and states, including . . . those in the Southern Confederacy, and creating them into an independent government.

Jefferson Davis was, as President, forced to conduct much of his affairs at the Exchange.

It was there that William Howard Russell met Sanders, amid much talk of the newly-fledged Knights, and described him as "a pig, but a learned pig withal, and weatherwise—catching straws and whisking them upward to detect the currents (of the wind)."

In February 1861, Sanders was briefly in Cincinnati for no apparent reason of business or politics, except to contact members of the Knights of the Golden Circle, which had made its headquarters there. On the 12th of the month, Lincoln was in town on his inaugural national tour, greeted by Mayor Richard M. Bishop at City Hall. He stayed that night at the Burnet House, where Sanders and the Knights' leader Clement L. Vallandigham were also stopping. That evening, Lincoln gave a speech from the balcony of his suite to a large and enthusiastic crowd.

At some stage during the celebrations, somebody placed a carpet bag on board the Presidential private railroad car at the Cincinnati depot. A suspicious attendant heard a mysterious ticking sound emerging from inside it and at first thought it might be a clock. But on second thought, he decided to call in a bomb defusing expert.

A bomb was, in fact, inside the bag, timed to be set off when the President boarded the car next morning. It is known that Sanders and his friend Beverley Tucker were, at the time, inventing and developing infernal machines of this kind; Vallandigham was, as they were, thinking constantly of ways to eliminate Lincoln. And the use of a bomb exactly mirrors the attempts made against Napoleon III under Sanders' specific instruction.

The matter was rapidly buried; it has surfaced in no published work in the 140 years after that. It was referred to only once, in the Syracuse N.Y. *Journal* for February 18, 1861 and that was the end of the matter. For fear of unsettling his supporters and adding strength to his enemies, Lincoln made a policy of suppressing stories of attempts on his life. He sought no investigation from the leading government detectives Lafayette Baker, Allan Pinkerton or Ward Hill Lamon.

Another scheme was afoot. According to an entry in the diary of Orville H. Browning, senator, cabinet member and friend of Lincoln, on August 2, 1864, Douglas had plans, in the spring of 1861, to bring about a *coup d'état*. He promised Lincoln, his former rival, that he would give speeches in favor of war against the South on the understanding he would be given command of the army. Browning wrote: "It was Douglas's intention after achieving some military successes to turn against the Administration— depose Lincoln and set up a provisional government for his own benefit." The story, based upon comments by the political insider, Isaac N. Morris, indicates the fine hand of Sanders at work; but Douglas's death soon afterward, on June 3, cancelled any such destructive plans.

On March 4, and Sanders must have suggested it, "La Marseillaise" was played and sung in Montgomery at the unveiling of the Stars and Bars as the revolutionary flag of the Confederacy and the symbol of insurrection. Sanders could have asked for no more, but his daughter Virginia was far from satisfied. She complained to society leader Mary Chesnut that the crowd wasn't sufficiently frenzied in its response. "Our crowds are gentlemen," Mrs. Chesnut snapped, thus shutting her up for a moment or two.

Sanders was so often in Washington that there were those in Montgomery who thought him a Union agent whereas, in fact, he was acting on pro-Southern business. At the noisy and overcrowded Willard's Hotel, he was seen on the porch talking of Lincoln's assassination so overtly that Charles Sumner, the loyalist Massachusetts senator, advised Lincoln not to go out at night unattended. But Lincoln, then and later, again took the view that if he was going to be assassinated, he would be, and nothing was done about Sanders.

Unfazed, Sanders had to deal with another matter. How could he manage to travel to England on anti-Lincolnian Confederate business? The answer was Robert Bunch.

Bunch was British Consul in Charleston, where George Trenholm, of Fraser, Trenholm, in Liverpool, had his American headquarters. Bunch was a Confederate spy who issued passports to anyone in the South who wished to travel North as "Englishmen" in disguise, thus committing acts of outright forgery. On August 17, 1861, he was arrested in New York City; on him were found sealed and unsealed bags containing letters signed by him with secret military and diplomatic intelligence he was about to hand over in Richmond. Secretary of State Seward in a report to Charles Francis Adams, Union minister to the Court of St. James in London, stated that Bunch was "a British conspirator against the United States." A complaint was filed with British Foreign Secretary Earl Russell and Bunch, after a term at Fort Lafayette prison in New York harbor, was returned to London and dismissed from the diplomatic service. In the wake of the Consul's disgrace, Sanders still retained the British passport that later allowed him to enter British North America, England and France.

On April 1, 1861, in a letter reproduced in the *New York Times* on the 16th, Sanders, in a spirit of customary recklessness, addressed his New York associates August Belmont, Fernando Wood, and the Democratic New York State Chairman Dean Richmond with a fiery attack on Lincoln:

The entire South is under arms. The Negroes are strengthening the military. Peace will be quickly conquered. Northern Democrats are standing by the Southern states. People will not be held responsible for Lincoln's acts unless endorsing them. . . . Protect your social and commercial ties by resisting Black Republican Federal aggression. . . . Hoist your flag.

Sanders' old friend Belmont, appalled that his Copperhead commitments were so clearly shown at the outset of the new presidency, rushed off a denial to editors, lying that he had not received any such letter, nor had he had any dealings with Sanders since the previous Fall. Sanders was condemned by the *Times* itself, which compared his performance at the time of national crisis to that of "a chattering idiot at a funeral."

At the same time, Sanders became an arms dealer to the South, shipping as many as 140,000 muskets to Montgomery from the traitorous New York City arms dealer A. A. Belknap, using a crude box code later adopted in a different form by John Wilkes Booth and others aiding the Confederacy. Davis was Dot, the Confederacy Sam, peace was Pit Toes and so forth: a code more suitable for children in party games. Sanders was again involved with Beverley Tucker, who returned to Montgomery from his consular post in Liverpool in March, to build a cannon that could fire a ball through a tree from a distance of two and a quarter miles. Through Sanders' and Tucker's contacts in Charleston and Liverpool, plans were advanced for Fraser, Trenholm to build battleships and cruisers to sink Union merchant and militant vessels in the North Atlantic.

Lincoln infuriated high-powered British interests from the outset of the war. His support for the restrictive Morrill tariff, that levied up to 45 percent on imported goods, had been bad enough. Now he started a blockade to prevent cotton, turpentine and rosin reaching England from Southern ports, and arms, pistols, cannon, and rifles from being sent there from London. True, in 1861 British merchants had stockpiled their cotton, so essential to the textile industry that was the heartbeat of the nation, whether for clothing, sails, sheets or a score of other essentials. But that stockpile would only last a year; afterward, without cotton, the British economy could easily founder, and the same was true of the French.

At first, the blockade itself was little more than a threat. The Union fleet under Secretary of the Navy Gideon Welles was a mere phantom flotilla of ramshackle vessels, mostly survivors of the War of 1812. The Southern coastline provided a formidable obstacle course for all save the most skilled of skippers. Its 3,500-odd miles consisted of tricky and threatening inlets, complicated twisting creeks, uncharted shoals, quicksands, rocky escarpments and promontories battered by unpredictable storms. On the other hand, the British captains of blockade-running vessels were veteran seadogs and masters of navigation, and nothing could match the Liverpool and Glasgow shipbuilders, peerless merchants of the seven seas.

By the summer of 1861, the situation had changed. From a bedraggled fleet of rotten wooden hulks and some 60 shaky steam-driven vessels, Gideon Welles had managed to whip up supplementary ships that gave chase to and sank Confederate vessels. Sanders and Beverley Tucker, with Stephen R. Mallory's blessing, increased their shipbuilding arrangements with Fraser, Trenholm; their purpose all along was to provoke, by sinking Union ships, the United States to declare war on England, which, they were certain, would win.

The Confederate agent Captain James D. Bulloch arrived in Liverpool on June 4, 1861, to start arrangements with Fraser, Trenholm's James Prioleau and Liverpool's piratical Mayor Edward Lawrence. Under Bulloch's efficient control, Fraser, Trenholm built the formidable screw steamer *Oweto,* her keel laid on June 30, her design cheekily copied from Queen Victoria's royal gunboat and her registration forged as coming from Palermo, Italy; her guns were mounted only when she left British shores. Bulloch supervised the engine-driven barque rig the *Alabama,* armed offshore to escape any breach of neutrality, and soon to be a powerful enemy of the United States on the high seas.

By July, 1861, with the aid of Tucker, who commuted frequently in secret missions direct to Liverpool from Havana, where he stayed with Mrs. Sarah M. Brewer, soon to be the hostess of James M. Mason and John Slidell, Sanders had Fraser,

Trenholm ship through the blockade to Wilmington 6,500 British Enfield rifles, 20,000 cartridges, 50,000 army boots and 20,000 blankets, all packed in crates labeled *Earthenware.* One of Sanders' purposes was to build fast-running small vessels that could make 14 knots and slip unobserved in or out of ports under cover of moonless nights, carrying not only supplies but secret messages to and from Halifax and Liverpool, via St. Georges Bermuda, Nassau, and Havana, which was no longer a target for expansionism since the Spanish proved cooperative in illegal shipments to and from their popular refueling ports. In Nassau especially, which became a boom town, the British rejoiced in helping the Confederacy; the downfall of Lincoln was on many tongues in the waterfront bars. Soon, Matamoros, Mexico, across the Rio Grande from Brownsville, Texas was added to the favored ports, and used by Sanders himself.

Matamoros swelled, in two short years, from a sleepy tropical fishing port to a thriving jerry-built boom town, a vibrant entrepot of men, women, cotton, tobacco, arms and treasure, with busy brothels, bars and slave markets, its streets alive with the sound of guitars and drunken ditties, its pervasive odor an unholy blend of magnolia, urine and horse manure.

Sanders spent much of that first summer of the war trying to wrest the divided state of his native Kentucky from alliance with the Union. In June he sent his son, the handsome and capable 18-year-old Reid, to Lexington; Reid wrote his father that the Blue Grass state preferred to remain neutral, but if "the Lincoln administration forces us, we will go with the South immediately." On July 4, Reid reported that the State had 50,000 of the best riflemen in the nation and that women were trained in the use of revolvers and "many are excellent shots." Sanders and Beverley Tucker supplied many of the arms that were used.

In late April, the Davis government moved to Richmond, that gracious city's artery the easy-flowing James River, its broad and handsome thoroughfares green with elm and live oak, the houses of the rich set beyond well-tended lawns with banks of spring flowers, its social leaders extravagantly disrespectful of the state of war.

The Sanders offspring, Virginia and Lewis, cut handsome figures at cotillions and dinner parties; two young bucks fought a duel for the beautiful Virginia's hand; but Sanders, unable to obtain a cabinet post because of his brash unpopular manners and unkempt appearance, had to move to Nashville, Tennessee, where he and Tucker increased their armaments supplies, as well as offering rash advice on field maneuvers to Brigadier General Felix K. Zollicoffer, who was killed in action on January 18, 1862.

Tucker was soon back in Liverpool. He was tireless in his efforts to build six mail steamers that could sail to and from Halifax and Liverpool with correspondences from Richmond, and from New York Copperhead supporters. A sympathetic Jefferson Davis, supported by Judah P. Benjamin and Stephen R. Mallory, signed the plan into law on April 19, 1862. Sanders would pay for the supply of vessels by selling cotton certificates to the wealthy of England—certificates that would guarantee the purchaser supplies of cotton as Britain faced famine in that commodity.

He found opposition in George Trenholm, Christopher Memminger's unofficial associate Treasury Secretary, whose objections were based less on fear of loss of neutrality than on Sanders' notorious unreliability. Trenholm was right; Sanders soon struck a treacherous and more profitable deal with the rival firm of William Schaw Lindsay, the richest shipbuilder in England, and an influential Member of Parliament who joined the British chorus of hatred of Lincoln in a loud, shrill voice.

On August 9, 1862, Sanders, after delays caused by his enemies in Richmond, at last left for England himself. Afraid of running the blockade, as he was known in the North for his threats of assassination, he made his way to British North America disguised as a Cornish tin miner, dressed in an anomalous outfit of straw hat, jacket, trousers of Kentucky denim and green goggles, the last in imitation of Jefferson Davis, who wore them at times for his serious eye problem.

Questioned before he crossed the border, at a stopover in Buffalo, NY, Sanders, using his Bunch-supplied British passport, lied to the Provost Marshal that he intended joining his brother, an imaginary wheat farmer, in British North America, to help out with the crop. Carpetbag in one hand and bag of miners' tools in the other, he made so convincing a picture that he was let through. When he arrived at the Suspension Bridge tollgate on his way to Niagara, he got away with paying one shilling instead of two. Once at the fashionable Clifton House, later the scene of some of his murderous intrigues against Lincoln, he was refused a room by a snooty desk clerk; whipping Confederate dollars out of the carpetbag brought an instant change of attitude.

At the Clifton House, Sanders formed one of his most powerful alliances, with the wealthy and influential Charles S. Morehead, former Governor of Kentucky, who had twice been imprisoned for commerce with the South.

He traveled on to Montreal to confer with leading British government officials there, assuring them that the Confederacy would increase free trade with British North America without such crippling restraints as the Morrill tariff, and promising insincerely that if slavery were to be a stumbling block to a transatlantic alliance, that stumbling block would be removed. He mentioned that Copperhead organizations—he clearly meant the Knights of the Golden Circle—were ready to bring about the overthrow of the Union forces in Kentucky, Maryland and Tennessee.

Although Sanders was stumbled in England by the cotton traders who demanded excessive discounts and price fixings on his certificates, he found a nation's upper class in irrepressible support of his masters in Richmond, and of plans for Lincoln's downfall. On a regular basis, the British Press still denounced Lincoln as a rail-splitter, a fool, a yokel, a dangerous and reckless tyrant. The furiously anti-Union polemicist James Spence, neighbor and brother-in-law of Fraser, Trenholm's Charles Prioleau; Arthur B. Forwood, leader of the Conservative party; Liverpool Mayor and pirate Edward Lawrence; the Earls Shaftesbury and Salisbury; Lord Robert Cecil and countless other leading figures supported Sanders and James M. Mason in London.

Few issues of *Punch* lacked scurrilous caricatures of Old Abe. He was portrayed as the devil incarnate, a raccoon up a tree, a greedy Jack Horner in the nursery rhyme, an evil chemist making poisonous potions, or a hunched accountants' clerk at a bench calculating vicious corrupt financial arrangements. It is only necessary to state that Sanders found in England an atmosphere of hatred that to him fully justified his dream of seeing Lincoln dead.

Back in Richmond in October, Sanders embarked on plans
for trading in flour across the North Atlantic and for his sons
Reid and Lewis to run a dispatch service between Halifax and
Liverpool. These proposals foundered when Reid was arrested
while trying to cross into British North America; exchanged for
a Union prisoner, he became an assistant to Judah P. Benjamin's
chief associate, L. Quentin Washington, in Richmond. Sanders
wrested him from that sinecure and dispatched him dangerously
from Charleston to England while he himself, after leaving the
Confederate capital, more safely embarked from Matamoros.

BEFORE HE LEFT MEXICO ON THE FIRST DAY OF JANUARY, 1863,
Sanders fired off an inflammatory letter to the chief Copperheads
of New York, this time leaving only Belmont, for safety reasons, off
the list. Among those to whom he wrote were Horatio Seymour,
newly-reelected Governor of New York, the Wood brothers, John
Van Buren, son of the former President and known as the Prince
of Manhattan, and James Brooks, secessionist co-owner of the
New York *Evening Express,* a hater of Lincoln who called him "a
thief in the night." Describing them as "Men of the Triumphant
Revolutionary Party of New York," Sanders urged them:

> Let heart and brain into the revolution, accelerate and direct the
> movement, get rid of the Baboon (what is it?) Lincoln . . . com-
> mercial relations (with us) are attainable, and every hour of alien-
> ation is your loss.

On January 3, Sanders suffered a setback. His son Reid had
unwisely trusted Arnold Harris, nephew of a friend of the family,
to sail him to England; instead, Harris, cutting a deal with the
Union to secure his release from jail, deliberately sailed his vessel in sight of the Union ships *Quaker City* and *Powhatan* and
again Reid was arrested and imprisoned, this time for good.
Worse, the secret correspondence on the cotton certificates, mail
and flour ship deals Reid had tried to throw overboard in oilskin
bags was captured.

As Rear Admiral Samuel F. Du Pont, commander of the South
Atlantic Blockading Squadron, reported to Secretary of the Navy

Gideon Welles on January 8, 1863, among the letters from Sanders were those detailing the construction of ships in Liverpool to be disguised as merchant vessels and then armed in overseas British waters with British collusion. Also discovered was the secret box code devised under Davis' and Benjamin's control in Richmond and used for spies; among the emissaries who would soon employ it was, as we know, John Wilkes Booth. All of the damaging contents of Reid Sanders' trunk appeared, doubtless to the extreme discomfort of the Confederate cabinet, on the front page of the *New York Times* on January 18, 1863.

Soon afterward, Sanders again betrayed Fraser, Trenholm, which had resisted his plans in England, through the agency of Beverley Tucker. One of the strongest opponents of confederate shipbuilding was Frederick Hamel, chief solicitor-adviser to the London Board of Customs and a rigid adherent of neutrality. On April 17, 1863, Tucker brought a letter to Hamel from A. F. Squarey, of the Liverpool solicitors Duncan, Squarey and Blackmore, urging the government to confiscate Fraser, Trenholm's ironclads as soon as they came down the slipways. The government acted by seizing the new Trenholm ship *Alexandria.* At the same time, the Lindsay company proceeded unmolested, no doubt through much influence peddling by Sanders in Whitehall.

On March 14, 1863, supported by such major backers of the Confederate cause as the prominent lawyer Lord Wharncliffe, the London Confederate Bank was formed in that city with two million pounds in capital, and was floated as a public company on the stock market, with 22,000 shares at one hundred pounds each; the issue was subscribed almost overnight.

The Bank acted in connection with the Confederate States' Aid Association, set up also in London with a committed anti-Lincolnian agenda. James M. Mason supported the C.S.A.D. with moneys from the British aristocracy, including Alexander Beresford-Hope, M.P., who condemned Lincoln as "a despot . . a Robespierre."

By the end of 1863 Beverley Tucker, ever vigilant in his own and Sanders' interests, realized that the Union would soon complete its blockade of Southern ports and that he must find a solution to benefit them both. He succeeded in January 1864 with an act of characteristic boldness. He made a contract with Lieutenant Colonel Frank G. Ruffin, Commissary of Substance and Chief Quartermaster in Richmond, who was in charge of military and civilian supplies, to supply meat and arms from Canada and North America in return for cotton from the South. The arrangement was helped corruptly by the fact that Ruffin's Union counterpart trader was none other than Lincoln's brother-in-law, Ninian Wirt Edwards, former Governor of Illinois; the President and Mary Todd were married in his house. For discretionary reasons, Edwards conducted his quartermaster's affairs in Chicago, in collusion with the Washington authorities.

THREE

ALARMS

AND

EXCURSIONS

When, on June 1, 1864, Sanders arrived in British North America from Paris, he was full of plans for Lincoln's assassination. Jacob Thompson was not impressed with Sanders' sophisticated political schemes and, presumably to annoy him, assumed thenceforth the code name "Louis Napoleon," as well as his previous "Captain Carson." He wrote to Clement C. Clay from Toronto to Montreal on June 9:

> (Sanders) has come from abroad—Europe—to do what he says he did not know we were intended [sic] to do, and has gone on to do it. There is such a thing as spoiling the broth by having too many hands in it.

In turn, a nervous Clay wrote to Judah P. Benjamin on June 17:

> (I wish Sanders) were in Europe, Asia or Africa.

Although Thompson never crumbled, Sanders soon had Clay and James P. Holcombe under his maleficent influence.

At the same time, Sanders fastened on a visitor, the dashing anarchist Clement L. Vallandigham, former Ohio congressman, ardent supporter in his early youth of Young America and Manifest Destiny, and Supreme Commander of the Sons of Liberty. With black, wavy hair, a high intellectual forehead, large, liquid eyes underhung with dramatic pouches, and a wide, firm mouth, Vallandigham was a powerful orator whom Sanders had first encountered when they both supported Stephen A. Douglas at the 1860 National Democratic Convention.

On May 1, 1863, Vallandigham had given a speech at a political rally at Mount Vernon, Ohio, an outrageous occasion during which, as he stood addressing the crowd, 34 young women, dressed to represent all states of America, not excluding those in the South, passed by waving on a horse-drawn float, a Copperhead act of rejection of any consideration of rebellion as an illegal act. Vallandigham, referring contemptuously to Lincoln as a King, a wicked, cruel and unnecessary monarch, spat to loud cheers on the Presidential General Order 38, whose gist was that any habit of declaring sympathy for the enemy would not be allowed and would result in immediate arrest.

On May 5, charging Vallandigham with sedition and treason, Major General Ambrose E. Burnside, Commander of the Department of Ohio, originator of the sideburn and the true author of General Order 38, called for his seizure. Burnside dispatched troops to arrest him at his home at Dayton; officers banged on his front door, waking him in the early morning hours. Vallandigham's response was characteristic: dressed in his nightshirt, he fired at his assailants from his bedroom window. Bundled onto a train, he was rushed to Cincinnati for trial by a hastily assembled kangaroo court and found guilty. But on May 25, instead of having him shot as a traitor (Lincoln combined mercifulness with caution) lest Vallandigham be thought a martyr, he was shipped across the Confederate lines.

It is not surprising that Vallandigham was in British North America when he met Sanders in June, 1864, because he had been rapturously received there a year earlier. Arriving in Halifax on July 5, 1863, he had been cheered by the numerous supporters of the Sons of Liberty and haters of Lincoln who formed the majority of the country's British citizens. In Quebec, he had enjoyed a standing ovation at the pro-Confederate St. Anaconda Club, and the general manager of the Grand Trunk Railroad gave him a private car to take him to Toronto, Windsor and Niagara Falls.

Sanders could only warm to a man whose polemical journal, *The Old Guard,* denounced Lincoln as a besotted tyrant and the *padrone* of abolition and plunder, and as a coward who sheltered behind the army and thought only of devastation, bloodshed and burning. Vallandigham's battle cry was:

> We are coming, Abraham Lincoln
> From mountain, wood and glen,
> Yes! We're coming Abraham Lincoln

With the ghosts of murdered men,
Yes! We're coming Abraham Lincoln
With curses loud and deep,
That will haunt you in your waking
And disturb you in your sleep.

Although Sanders professed only to be interested in election influence buying and political intrigue, he was of course a vulture of the same feather, and the policies of Vallandigham and the Sons of Liberty exactly matched those of the London assassination bureau, dressed up as the Central Democratic Committee, to which Sanders had so conspicuously belonged in 1853-4.

The Sons of Liberty had begun as the Knights of the Golden Circle at the same time Sanders was Consul in London. Its founder was a self-important quack doctor named George W. L. Bickley, a Kentuckian supporter of Young America and Manifest Destiny; like Sanders, he approved of William Walker's filibustering Nicaragua, the Ostend Manifesto on Cuba, and the proposed death of Napoleon III; by 1860, he backed to the limit, with a few hundred followers instead of the thousands he bragged about, the actions of the revolutionary President of Mexico, Benito Juarez, against Napoleonic intervention, which would soon result in Napoleon's appointment of the puppet Hapsburg Emperor Maximilian in Mexico City.

Bickley sustained the ambitions of Young America in speeches and pamphlets promising, just as Sanders dreamed, a slave empire of Central and South American peons, the unpaid servants of American power. He dreamed of the Knights becoming a vast military police force, its membership achieved only by the applicant undergoing a series of complex rituals.

Initiates who revealed the secrets of the Knights would be caught and cut into four parts, the dismembered body hurled from the doors of the "castles" or quasi-Masonic lodges in blood-drenched disgrace. Letters were sent in code, elephants and stars carried hidden in clothing for identification purposes, meetings held in remote country locations at dead of night. In the Young America tradition, youth and fitness were required and those of superior physique given first place. No Jews,

African-Americans or women were admitted; the goals were assassination of Lincoln, murder, rape and pillage, and enforced peace between North and South with independence arranged for the Confederacy.

Vallandigham would brag, rightly or wrongly, of important members, including no less than Franklin Pierce, James Singleton (true), and Major General George B. McClellan, the Democrats' choice for President, who had been forced into retirement in New Jersey following a controversial military career in November, 1862; John Wilkes Booth and even (most improbably) Jefferson Davis. A major figure was Phineas C. Wright, Vallandigham's predecessor as Supreme Commander of the Knights and Benjamin Wood's editor of the New York *Daily News,* which used its personal column for secret messages to and from Richmond and British North America. Vallandigham had the unstinting support of August Belmont in New York (who was head of the National Democratic Committee, an extraordinary role for the representative of a foreign bank), as well as the Wood Brothers and Governor Seymour. And as if all this were not enough, Vallandigham used as his secret code NUOHLAC, the name of John C. Calhoun, Sanders' earliest idol, spelled backward.

If Sanders did not actually join the Sons of Liberty—and his membership is not recorded—that was merely a technicality; but Jacob Thompson, though not qualified for membership either in age or physique, joined the S.O.L. Third Degree that week in June, 1864 in a ritual that involved swearing never to betray the brotherhood on pain of death by quartering; and much crossing of feet and hands that must have seemed foreign to the tight-lipped former Secretary of State.

To the small group of Commissioners, Thompson added a recruit who, unlike Sanders, was decidedly unauthorized in Richmond. That man was the disgraced Brigadier General William H. Carroll from Tennessee, a man of incendiary disposition and profound hatred of Lincoln who, like Sanders, was on his mettle to prove himself valuable to Richmond.

At first, Carroll had attracted Jefferson Davis and Benjamin because of his activities in charge of his native state's first East

Tennessee Rifles; but when in April 1862 he was in command of Major General George B. Crittenden's 2nd division of the army of central Kentucky, he was, along with Crittenden himself, accused of inefficiency and drunkenness. Crittenden was allowed to resign more or less honorably that October, but Carroll was subjected to a court of inquiry that was little better than a court martial and was forced to quit the army the following year, moving in exile and disgrace to British North America. Now, in Toronto, Carroll could offer his military experience and "reformed" character in support of British-Confederate activities in the North.

After initiation by Vallandigham, who returned to Ohio to muster his forces on his home turf, Jacob Thompson set up a permanent headquarters at the stuffy, fern-and-gilt Queens Hotel in Toronto, with its potted palms, leather armchairs, atmosphere laden with cigar smoke, whispered conspiratorial conversations and heavy British food.

Clay, Holcombe and Sanders used as their own separate headquarters a comfortable redbrick house on Park Street in St. Catharines, a leafy, sparkling town of some 10,000 souls situated about 14 miles from the American border. The house's owner was the ebullient Robert E. Coxe, a trader on both sides of the war, whose carpet-bagging activities allowed him to maintain a residence in Poughkeepsie, New York. Beverley Tucker was often at Park Street, stirring up trade deals with Coxe and with the South.

Ironically, St. Catharines was the home of many refugee African-Americans, who had traveled there on the Underground Railroad and settled there, often as cooperatives, small business owners, as paid laborers, household help or indentured clerks; Harriet Tubman had at one time been a resident. For committed anti-emancipationists like Sanders, Thompson, Clay and Holcombe, the black population can only have caused discomfort. But the town's proximity to Niagara, used by so many colleagues crossing and re-crossing the famous Suspension Bridge, made it an ideal location for their operations.

In mid-June two visitors arrived, one at St. Catharines, the other at the Queens Hotel in Toronto, to see Thompson. The first visitor was Harrison H. Dodd, Grand Commander of the

Sons of Liberty in the State of Indiana, who wanted to play a major role in general insurrection and disposal of Lincoln; he was a fiercer figure even than Clement L. Vallandigham.

A new arrival in Toronto was Dr. Luke P. Blackburn. His purpose, he expressed to Thompson, was to kill Lincoln by sending him a present of dress shirts infected with yellow fever germs; he didn't know, for such was the state of tropical medicine at the time, that yellow fever can only be conveyed by mosquitoes.

Like Sanders (and like Lincoln), Blackburn was a Kentuckian; he was born in a small settlement in Woodford County on June 16, 1816. At 18, he graduated in medicine from Transylvania University and set up practice in New Orleans. His plan, first discussed with Confederate Canadian agent Alexander Keith in Halifax in May, was to ship the infected clothing from Bermuda, where an epidemic raged, not only to the White House, but to Washington, where he would distribute it.

In Halifax, a cross-eyed British shoemaker named Godfrey Hyams, a character out of a Grimm's fairy tale, who had been given funds by Holcombe, picked up the infected clothing in sealed trunks from the steamship *Alpha* that had carried Clay, Thompson and Holcombe from Bermuda the previous month. Dr. Blackburn explained that an extra valise was that intended for delivery to Lincoln; the rest of the suitcases were to be taken by Hyams to Norfolk, Virginia, as well as Washington, where "there are plenty of troops, who would catch the fever, weaken and die." He advised Hyams in handling the clothing to smoke strong cigars and sniff camphor as a protection. Hyams took the trunk and valise to Boston by train and checked into the Parker House Hotel under the name of James W. Harris; another guest that week was, by coincidence or not, John Wilkes Booth, who had plans against Lincoln of his own and discussed them there.

Once arrived in Washington, Hyams panicked and decided not to deliver the infected valise to the White House. Instead, he disposed of the trunks through a Washington auction house, W. L. Wall and Company. Infuriated by Blackburn's refusal to pay him his promised fee for this dangerous enterprise, he later turned states' evidence and informed on the doctor at a trial in 1865.

From their first arrival in British North America, Thompson

and his fellow Commissioners traveled constantly by canal and lake steamer, train and stagecoach, aided at every step by British supporters and agents. And at every step they were watched—by the Union's Canadian network of spies.

Vice-consuls in American offices were trained in ciphers; they were used to bribing hotel clerks, train conductors and coachmen to supply them with a constant flow of information on the commissioners' movements. In Washington, Lincoln enjoyed nothing so much as his nightly visits to the Telegraph Office, where the youthful and enthusiastic staff could hardly wait to turn over to him the intercepts of treacherous telegrams from British North America, or the latest reports from his agents there.

A typical report came from David Thurston, the young and capable U.S. Consul in Montreal, whose dispatches, even today, make entertaining reading. On June 25 he wrote that Beverley Tucker, lately arrived from Europe and staying at the Donegana Hotel in that city, was expecting the arrival of a tin box in which Confederate documents would surely be concealed; Thurston had the box intercepted and the contents seized. Such information can only have come from a hotel employee whom Tucker had asked to look out for the box's arrival. Thurston wrote in his report:

> There is no remission in the number of efforts these (Confederate agents) are making, scattered as they are across (our frontier) from Gaspe to Sarnia . . . They send money to each other.

One man on Thompson's team on whom the Union spies kept a particularly sharp eye was Captain Thomas H. Hines, of the Ninth Kentucky Cavalry, who had been in British North America since March. Restless, high-strung and driven, Hines had black, wavy hair, fanatical dark eyes, and a muscular, athletic physique. He had begun his career at the Masonic University of La Grange, and had risen rapidly through the ranks as a courageous and vigorous officer; Confederate Secretary of War James A. Seddon had arranged for him to coordinate Sons of Liberty activities.

On August 7, 1863, Hines and his commander, the famous raider, Brigadier General John Hunt Morgan, were arrested along with 66 officers at New Lisbon, Ohio and confined in the State Penitentiary at Columbus. From the first day of confinement, Hines made plans for escape; inspired by Sanders' idol Victor Hugo's novel *Les Miserables,* in which the convict Jean Valjean effected his flight from an even grimmer prison, he determined that his cell floor's lack of mold or even damp indicated an air chamber under the floor. Through this air chamber the prisoners could crawl out one by one.

With knives stolen from the hospital, Hines managed to cut through cement and bricks inch by inch until he reached the air chamber, hiding the chipped-off material inside his mattress. When the air chamber turned out to be blocked by coal heaps, several officers proceeded to make a tunnel at right angles, giving prearranged signals in taps as a warning if the guards should come nearby. While Hines sat on guard at the front of his cell, reading the pages of Gibbon's *Decline and Fall of the Roman Empire,* his cellmate covered the hole under the bunk with a leather satchel containing clothing.

Hines wrote to his sister in Kentucky, who sent money pasted into the back covers of selected books; this would finance the escapees once they were free. The night of escape was November 27; to make sure they heard the guard, the prisoners had managed unobserved to sprinkle coal dust along the front of the cells so that the slightest footfall would be audible.

In a drizzle of rain, in intense darkness, Hines, Morgan and the others crawled through the tunnel and broke through the thick stratum of earth at the end. They cut the alarm bell rope and climbed the wall with the aid of a grappling iron. They boarded the 1:15 a.m. train for Cincinnati, got off at Ludlow Ferry on the Ohio River, and found a warm welcome by Copperheads in Kentucky. While the wires hummed with telegraphic warnings of their escape and probable whereabouts, they assumed the disguise of cattle buyers. Arrested again near Bridges Ferry on the Tennessee River on December 13, Hines was dragged off to a prison camp, only to manage another escape. Hailed by gunshots, he fled into the mountains; posing as a Federal horse agent, he hired a canoe and crossed two rivers; on December 17, after many privations, he reached the Confederate lines near Dalton, Georgia.

In March, 1864, Hines, who was by now directly operating under Judah P. Benjamin's secret service operation, was sent to British North America to cause a full scale Order of American Knights outbreak, once the Commissioners headed by Thompson were appointed. In the meantime, he became a recruit to trading with the enemy, given, by Judah P. Benjamin's orders, numerous bales of cotton to be sold out of Memphis to northern buyers to finance his plans; he sold the cotton for $70,000 ($796,000) and received $5,000 ($57,000) from Benjamin as well. Hines reported to Thompson at the Queens Hotel in May, and thenceforth played a major part in his disruptive plans. On June 1, Hines advised Seddon from Toronto that he planned to assassinate the state Governors of Indiana, Ohio and Illinois; he intended to cut their heads off, a direct parallel to Sanders' threat to guillotine Napoleon III ("By steam, by God.")

That same month, Hines set up his headquarters at the Welland Hotel in St. Catharines, a short distance from Robert E. Coxe's rented house on Park Street. The popular hostelry had the advantage of standing next door to the hot mineral springs; in steamy wooden rooms of the baths, Thompson, Clay, Holcombe and other conspirators could sit in their towels, sweating and planning their future with little fear of being overheard.

Soon they acquired two helpers at the heart of the British North American government. The lean, broad-shouldered and bewhiskered Englishman Colonel George T. Denison was a formidable ally. Commander of Governor General Viscount Monck's personal bodyguard, known as the Active Force, Denison acted as a secret agent in Quebec, which was then the national capital, advising on any information that might leak via Monck to the British embassy in Washington, supported by anti-Lincolnian feelings in all British circles. Denison proved loyal, but another recruit did not.

The young New Yorker, Richard Montgomery, had powerful connections in the capital. He was slender, black-haired, with sulfurous dark gray eyes and pale, clear skin flushed with health; as romantically handsome as a Shelley or Keats, he was a spy in the grand tradition of seductive military intrigue. He assumed, with touching self-confidence, the pseudonym of Benjamin Courier, scarcely a sensible choice since he was acting for Judah P. Benjamin in precisely that role.

And in that capacity, no sooner did he receive messages for Richmond, sent by Thompson, Clay or Holcombe by his personal hand to avoid the vulnerable telegraph services, than he took them to Washington and the Telegraph Office for Lincoln's personal inspection. The envelopes were steamed open, then refastened; sometimes seals had to be broken and replaced with exact copies, not an easy procedure, and the envelopes duplicated on matching English-made paper, which had to be imported from London.

This prince among spies had started his career as a bookkeeper with green eye shade and leather sleeve protectors in Washington government offices; enlisted in Lincoln's personal lifeguard, he was let go for unreliability, only to apply to the Secret Service. At first denied admission, he obtained a position as the manager of a piano store, then became a clerk at the U.S. Treasury where he learned of that agency's dealings with the South; in an atmosphere of corruption and intrigue, he embarked on his career as federal agent in the summer of 1864.

In view of the fact that he was leaking every message sent to Richmond from British North America, it seems ironical that Clement C. Clay warned him not to say too much to Sanders, who, Clay said, could not be trusted to keep his mouth shut. Many of the intercepted messages concerned plans for running supplies of arms from England via Nassau or Havana and Halifax, with the aid of Alexander Keith and Benjamin Wier in Nova Scotia. Other reports concerned arrangements for uprisings of Copperheads, Sons of Liberty and associates in the Northwestern states.

Unaware of Montgomery's duplicity, Sanders was busy with a complex scheme to go to Washington on the excuse of bringing a peace offer to Lincoln in person. It takes no leap of the imagination to see that this unlikely encounter would, at the very least, allow him to obtain a clear picture of the President's movements, the location for the various offices he attended, and how best to assassinate him. And he, Sanders, had a clear-cut contingency plan: should Lincoln refuse to receive the so-called peace commission, he would be disgraced in the eyes of a war-weary public for having failed to act fairly to stop the slaughter of their fellow Americans.

Since neither Jefferson Davis nor Judah P. Benjamin could be approached to approve his scheme, as they might well dismiss it out of hand, Sanders had to come up with an approximation of the terms they would call for in any authorized approach. He would ask for the reparation to the Southern planters of some 400 million dollars for the loss of property and slaves following slavery's abolition; the Confederacy was to be a separate and self-governing nation within the restored Union; all states rights would be restored at a national convention called to settle disputes; and so forth in the same vainglorious mode.

Sanders figured that if Lincoln rejected these proposals, the way would be left open for a full-scale attack on the President by those industrialists in the North who found war an inconvenient interruption to trade; these included the cotton and tobacco brokers in New York and the textile mill owners in New England. But Sanders had overlooked the fact that many of these Capitalists were already trading with the South on presidential licenses and that in New York many were profiting in the arms shipments from Halifax to Richmond via Wilmington and Matamoros.

Even so, Sanders had much to rely on in his fraudulent peace plan, most notably the certainty of all save the general populace that Lincoln would lose the war if reelected. When the new Secretary of the Treasury, former Senator from Maine William P. Fessenden, took up office on June 30, he was forced to go hat in hand to the New York bankers for desperately needed war funds, only to be turned down by every one of them.

By now the general view among the rich and powerful was that, in the words of Professor Arthur C. Cole in the official history of Illinois, "Lincoln had assumed certain powers which made his role quite as significant as that of a dictator in the days of Rome's glory."

The President had continued to suspend the Writ of Habeas Corpus, the most valued of civil rights, without legislative warrant under wartime provisions and without precedent in American history. He had interfered with freedom of speech and had suspended newspapers. He had approved conscription, which was anathema to many immigrants and had resulted in the New York draft riots of July, 1863. He had, in short, as Cole summed up, "assumed more authority above the constitution than any President, or anyone such in history since Oliver Cromwell." Simultaneously, the radicals in Lincoln's own party resented his failure to put down the rebellion, using such terms as "squirting rosewater at the enemy," and "preferring the New Testament to the sword."

The Republican party was so severely divided that at a trumped-up convention on May 31 the Radicals called on Major General John C. Frémont for President, supported by the ever-treacherous, ever-changeable Horace Greeley of the New York *Tribune.*

Despite his intermittent shows of intellectual strength and considerable power as head of the most important newspaper in the nation, Greeley resembled nothing more significant than the White Rabbit in Lewis Carroll's *Alice in Wonderland.* Small, fussy, plump, with white hair and a white, twitchy face, he was a nervous shell of a human being, whose political affiliations depended on changes in the current climate and whose cowardice showed in his frequent switches of sides in the Civil War.

At the official National Convention in Baltimore, backed by the almost equally powerful Henry J. Raymond of the *New York Times,* chairman of the platform committee, Lincoln enjoyed a victorious sweep; but dissentients were heard noisily in the ranks.

Sanders, in addition to planning the peace proposal and backing peace candidate Major General McClellan, whose youth, looks and hatred of Lincoln made up a potent brew, had also to find a contact who could be relied on to carry out his scheme.

He again found hope in Benjamin Wood, who in July crossed the Niagara Suspension Bridge to confer with Clay and Holcombe at the elegant but gloomy Clifton House on the British

North American side of the Falls. Even as he arrived, the Lincoln-hating Wood was using his editor, the Sons of Liberty's Phineas C. Wright, to publish Union troop movements in the *Daily News* for immediate reading in Richmond.

On July 2, when Wood was in transit by train, a leading article in that newspaper gave the course of a march of a Union cavalry division, provided details of reinforcements arriving from Major General George G. Meade, commander of the army of the Potomac, and announced a secret meeting between Grant, Meade and Major General Benjamin F. Burnside, commanding the army of the James River at Burnside's headquarters. Just 10 days later, when Wood was at Niagara, the *News* published an account of troop movements from City Point, complete with details of military supplies.

Former Governor of New York Washington Hunt was also at Niagara and warned that the New York profiteers wanted no peace; with him came Lincoln's supporter from Illinois, James W. Singleton, who was about to amass his fortune in treasonable trade with the South.

Of all the visitors to Niagara and St. Catharines, the most significant was Singleton. Handsome, polished and slippery, with a nimble tongue, an old friend of Lincoln's, he was at the heart of North-South trading in what Union Secretary of War Edwin M. Stanton would one day call "the blood of our soldiers," namely carpet-bagging vital supplies with Lincoln's and Davis' approval on both sides of the war. The heir to a substantial fortune, he began life as an itinerant doctor, then as a circuit-riding lawyer; he rose rapidly in politics, lording it over a battalion of servants at Boscobel, his magnificent mansion and estate at Quincy, Illinois. He early became a prominent figure in the Knights of the Golden Circle, later in the Sons of Liberty; in 1862 he, it offers grim amusement to note, became a leading figure in an international commission to investigate water communications between British North America and the Union. The detailed marine and coastal charts and points of lake transit proved invaluable to him in laying out the routes whereby he could profit from treasonable trade and forge powerful links to future Southern/Canadian conspirators.

As a slick Illinois operator, "Peace" became his catchword, allowing him to journey across the frontiers of war from Washington to Richmond and back to make proposals which were at best fraudulent but which provided an umbrella for his neutralist's profiteering. In such matters, he was hand in glove with another glib and personable opportunist, Orville Hickman Browning, a high-powered Washington lobbyist who also claimed connections to Abraham Lincoln from earlier days when the President was an Illinois lawyer. Like Sanders a Kentuckian by birth, the polished and imposing attorney and political machinist settled in Quincy in 1831 and formed there his first association with Singleton. In 1843, he ran against Stephen A. Douglas for a seat in Congress and was defeated. He was less than enthused over Lincoln's rise to fame, their long and warm friendship imperiled by ambition and jealousy, as Lincoln easily outstripped him in the political arena. Deeply conservative, he was also duplicitous, since while he supported the first Non-Intercourse Act which called for suppression of treasonable trade, he carried on such treason without hesitancy. Another contradiction of his contradictory and immoral, not to say dangerous career, was that he, while opposing Lincoln at the 1864 election, continued to hold his forgiving ear, using his persistent and pernicious influence to secure favors for traders with the enemy and representing as an attorney virtually every significant figure in the Lincoln assassination plot whose activities as conspirators were covered by the treasonable commerce from which he benefited.

Sanders turned also to Horace Greeley, unaware that Lincoln was too shrewd not to have known that Greeley had been conspiring against him by backing the Frémont ticket and from the beginning of the presidency had never been a trustworthy supporter.

Sanders now made a very serious mistake. Instead of choosing a suitable contact of Greeley's—Judge Jeremiah Black, for example, who was distinguished and well-respected and was staying at Niagara—to initiate the "peace" proposal, he settled on a squalid adventurer of his own stripe, William Cornell Jewett, whose numerous boasts included an imaginary warm acquaintance with Mrs. Lincoln.

Shock-haired, craggily-built, Jewett was a worthless if plausible opportunist, an international adventurer from Manhattan who had kicked off his career as a swindler by claiming he had struck gold in Colorado and selling worthless claims. The scam earned him not a deserved stretch behind bars, but the contemptuous nickname of Colorado Jewett.

Without authorization from Davis and Benjamin, or for that matter from Lincoln and Seward, Jewett had, in January, 1863, embarked, with support from Horace Greeley, upon a plan to have the British and French governments negotiate an end to the Civil War, which would result in a relief of the two countries' critical cotton shortage. Seeing through the scheme as no more than an act of self-aggrandizement, the Union's able Attorney General, Edward Bates, who had played a critical role in averting war with England after the *Trent* incident, quashed Jewett's efforts, and Henry Raymond of the *New York Times* attacked Bates with derision.

The irrepressible Jewett again turned to Greeley for support in engineering this new phony peace plan. Lincoln could not have forgotten that in 1848 when Greeley served in Congress for a brief three months to fill a temporary vacancy, he had used the *Tribune* to charge Lincoln, as Illinois Congressman, with padding the accounts for travel expenses, or that when, in 1857, Stephen A. Douglas broke with the Buchanan administration, Greeley backed the Little Giant so strongly that Lincoln feared many Republican supporters would bolt the convention. "Greeley isn't treating me right," Lincoln told his law partner William H. Herndon at the time, as the latter reported in his multi-volume biography of the President.

It was only when Lincoln rose to the summit of mass popular esteem—he seemed to *be* America, with his home-spun country philosophy, his generosity, his open-heartedness and sense of justice—that Greeley characteristically crumbled and cravenly changed sides to support the winning team. On February 25, 1860, he chaired Lincoln's inspirational speech at the Cooper Institute, New York City, invited the candidate to his office to check proofs of the printed address, and in an editorial called the speech "[o]ne of the happiest and most convincing . . . ever made in this city . . . Mr. Lincoln is one of nature's orators."

At the Republican National Convention in Chicago in May, 1860, Greeley worked hard for Lincoln's nomination against William H. Seward, the front-runner, after years of posing as Seward's supporter, an act of betrayal occasioned because Seward withdrew an earlier promise to add him to his cabinet if elected.

Yet once Lincoln was elected, Greeley acted against his interests by calling for the secession of the cotton states, using the peculiar analogy of America's war of independence from England. "Let the Union slide," he wrote to Lincoln on December 22, adding ominously, "let Presidents be assassinated—we can elect more."

On February 23, 1861, in an editorial, Greeley addressed the matter of Lincoln's arrival in Washington prior to taking up office with the words, "If the slave states, the cotton states or the Gulf States only choose to form an independent nation, they have a clear moral right to do so."

His motive was scarcely love of Jefferson Davis but annoyance that Lincoln had failed to make him Postmaster General, a sinecure to which he had looked forward and which Lincoln had shrewdly if dishonestly dangled to ensure his support the year before. With the outbreak of war, the White Rabbit panicked: he saw victory for the North and dared not be on the losing side, calling, on June 26, 1861, for the wholesale destruction of Richmond and the seizure of the Confederate Congress. And he let that editorial run for an unprecedented seven days.

He panicked again on July 29 when the Union suffered defeat at the first battle of Bull Run: "If the Union is irrevocably gone, an armistice for 30, 60, 90, 120 days—better still for a year—ought at once to be proposed." This cowardly editorial was sealed up by Lincoln in a secret file until April 4, 1864, when he knew Greeley was working against his nomination and in favor of Fremont; Lincoln's secretary Major John M. Hay read it aloud at the White House and Lincoln laughed in contempt.

Greeley knew this, and was thus an ideal aide to Sanders, Colorado Jewett, and their associates to bring about the fake Niagara peace proposal of July, 1864. He in the meantime had exposed in the *Tribune,* as treasonably as Benjamin Wood in the New York

Daily News, Union troop movements to the South when he saw that the Confederacy was on a winning streak. Brigadier General Edward S. Canby saw his troop movements exposed repeatedly in the *Tribune,* and when Major General Winfield S. Hancock's Potomac River activity was similarly divulged, Lieutenant General Grant had the reporter arrested.

On July 7, 1864, Jewett sent Sanders, Clay and Holcombe's joint peace proposal to Greeley's townhouse in New York City, not stating that it was unauthorized in Richmond. Lincoln, who had been reading, courtesy of Richard Montgomery, the conspirators' rebellious missives in the Telegraph Office on a regular basis and knew what a rabbit Greeley was, saw through the proposal of which Greeley advised him from the outset. Yet with the war going badly for him—Atlanta and Richmond showed no signs of falling—he could scarcely infuriate the large numbers of his supporters who would welcome a negotiated peace, and he had at least to try to pull the carpet from under the peace arm of the Democrats by playing their own game. So he did not at once reject the offer that Greeley conveyed.

Lincoln, with his native shrewdness, at the same time as the way was left open for discussion with the commissioners in British North America, had planned his own peace mission to Richmond. This would serve the double purpose of finding out whether Greeley, Jewett and Sanders had approval from Richmond and of giving the public the impression he had peace plans of his own.

His own commissioners were mere pawns in his political chess game. Colonel James F. Jaquess of the 73rd Illinois Infantry, the former President of Quincy College, and a Methodist minister, the Reverend James R. Gilmore, learned very quickly from Davis and Benjamin that the Canadian proposals were not authorized, as Lincoln surely suspected, and that the conditions of peace expressed by Davis and Benjamin were unacceptable. The giving of sovereign independent rights to the South, the retention of slavery, or, if slavery were to be abolished, lavish compensation, was nonsense, of course.

Meanwhile, even as Clay and Holcombe were in support of the Sanders-Greeley-Jewett mission and of subversive warfare against

the Union, they were entertaining the Sons of Liberty's leaders at
the Welland House hotel in St. Catharines. Clay wrote to Thompson in Toronto telling him he must come at once to aid in the general revolution ("They only fear you will not be prepared for it.
You need not fear as they are of the sworn Brotherhood.")

At the same time, Lincoln wrote cunningly to Greeley that if
anybody had authorization from Jefferson Davis he would be
happy to receive them to discuss peace. Dodging the issue,
Sanders wrote to Greeley on July 12, stating that he and his colleagues were ready to go to Washington, provided—the require-
ment was typically cheeky—they would be given "complete and
unqualified protection"; in other words, a bodyguard and white
flag of truce in order to embark on an assassination plan of their
expectedly protective host.

It was at this stage that Lincoln engineered the Jaquess-
Gilmore mission, on July 17-18; he simultaneously sent his secretary, the young and keenly observant Major John M. Hay, to
Niagara, accompanied by a very nervous Horace Greeley himself,
in a mischievous effort to see what these so-called negotiators
were up to. On July 18, with Hay in transit, Greeley, jittery as ever,
wrote to Lincoln that he was by now "not convinced" of the Commissioners' authorization from Davis. In fact, he had doubted it
from the first.

Afraid that Greeley might slip out of his grasp, Sanders fired
off a letter on the 19th to James Gordon Bennett, the editor of
the *New York Herald,* whose London correspondent he had been
while American Consul in the 1850s. He asked Bennett to come
to Niagara and help with the negotiations.

Bennett disliked Lincoln more overtly and single-mindedly
than Greeley; at the first threat against Fort Sumter he had written (on April 10, 1861) an editorial stating that the only hope of
averting civil war was to overthrow "the demoralizing, disorgan-
izing and destructive sectional party of which 'honest Abe Lincoln' is the pliant instrument." Though somewhat less venomous
in his attacks by 1862, Bennett resumed them at full volume the
following year with onslaughts against Lincoln's "imbecile cabinet" at the same time that he called for Grant as President. When
Sanders approached him, Lincoln and Seward had let a rumor

float that Bennett might be offered the job of minister to France, at the same time as there was talk of joining forces with Juarez in a war in Mexico against Napoleon III. Sensibly, Bennett showed no interest in being a tool in a Lincolnian game. It wasn't much of a bribe anyway and it didn't work. Bennett ignored Sanders' letter; he had no desire to go to Washington on a peace mission and he knew Sanders too well as a former employee to believe the peace mission was genuine.

On July 20, with Jaquess and Gilmore on their way back defeated from Richmond, Major John M. Hay and Horace Greeley arrived by train at Niagara and checked into the Clifton House Hotel, where Sanders, Clay and Holcombe were now firmly installed. Clay, as it turned out, was temporarily absent at St. Catharines, conferring with Thompson and the Sons of Liberty on proposed acts of terrorism even while his colleagues were explaining to the two emissaries that all they wanted was peace.

Hay was unimpressed. He noted down his impression of Sanders: "A seedy-looking rebel with grizzled whiskers and a flavor of old clo[thes]," while Holcombe was "tall, spare, with false teeth, false eyes and false hair."

The visitors delivered a note from Lincoln that was addressed not to Sanders, Clay and Holcombe by name, but with a discreet touch of contempt, TO WHOM IT MAY CONCERN. Evidently, Lincoln couldn't bring himself to address those scorpions directly.

The note read:

> Any proposition which embraces the restoration of peace, the integrity of the whole Union, and the abandonment of slavery, and which comes by and with an authority that can control the armies at war with the United States, will be met by liberal terms on substantial and collateral points, and the bearers thereof shall be given safe conduct both ways.

Since Lincoln knew by now that not one of these to whom he wrote had any such authority, the note can be seen as a shrewdly humorous leg-pull, and Greeley's state of nerves on delivering it can only be imagined. Yet, paradoxically, the note was exactly what Sanders was looking for; if he had penned it himself, he could not have asked for more—short of being allowed to go to Washington and map out the ground for assassination.

He had the basis now for an assassination of Lincoln's character, for he could and did present the note to every secessionist or otherwise anti-Lincolnian newspaper in North America, as an example of Lincoln's refusal to relieve the Union, which Greeley in a letter to the President called "bleeding and bankrupt," of any chance of securing an armistice and rescue from financial disaster.

Although the letter circulated to the Press was not signed by Sanders, but rather by Clay and Holcombe, it was marked in every sentence with the fire and brimstone style of Sanders' *Democratic Review* editorials and was added to by Beverley Tucker at his most inflammatory. A passage read:

> If there is any citizen of the United States who has clung to a hope that peace was possible with this administration of the Federal government, (this Lincoln note) will strip from his eyes the last film of such a delusion . . .

And in addition:

> The stupid tyrant who now disgraces the chair of Washington and Jackson could, any day, have peace and restoration of the Union; and would have them, only that he persists in the war to free the slaves.

The diatribe, run in newspapers, had considerable effect; it not only preached to the converted, but swayed not a few against Lincoln.

On July 22, the President held a cabinet meeting on the matter, attended by Secretary of the Navy Gideon Welles, Secretary of the Interior John P. Usher, Postmaster General Montgomery Blair, and Attorney General Edward Bates. He gave a detailed account of the Niagara affair, and read out Greeley's devious and slippery letters one by one. Most of those present were hesitant to denounce Greeley; they were uneasy about his possible capacity for damage to them in the *Tribune*. But Bates feared nobody; he wrote in his diary that he saw Sanders' danger: "I can't see the color of the cat, but there is certainly a cat in that mealtub."

Lincoln was disgusted with Greeley; he told his cabinet on August 14, referring to his role as a shoe mender in Illinois:

> Sometimes, when far gone, we found the leather so rotten the stitches would not hold. Greeley is so rotten that nothing can be done with him. He is not truthful; the stitches all wear out.

On June 22, Greeley added fuel to the anti-Lincolnian fire, while corresponding with the President on a seemingly amicable basis. He published on July 22 on the *Tribune*'s front page only those portions of the correspondence between Lincoln and himself that would show the President in the worst possible light.

James Gordon Bennett in the *New York Herald* attacked Greeley unmercifully for embarking on so harebrained a mission in the first place. The New York *Post* screamed that Greeley shouldn't have disgraced himself by dealing with "rebels and slaveholders." The *New York Times* poured fuel on the fire, rejoicing in Greeley's public humiliation.

Also on July 22, the date of the Lincoln cabinet meeting, leaders of the Sons of Liberty held a conference with Jacob Thompson at Robert E. Coxe's house in St. Catharines. It was chaired by Idaho S.O.L. leader Harrison H. Dodd. Kentucky, Indiana, Illinois and Missouri had especially strong representation. The proposal agreed to by all was that on August 16, later postponed to August 29, thousands of their members would rise up in the North-West while Confederate troops would, by prearrangement with Jefferson Davis, Benjamin and Secretary of War Seddon, march into Missouri and Kentucky to distract the Union army away from attempts on Southern cities, and then begin an assault on Washington and eliminate Lincoln and his cabinet. Simultaneously, the army of the Sons, glorying in their youth and strength, would break into and unleash the prisoners at the military jails of Chicago's Camp Douglas, Rock Island,

Illinois, Johnson's Island on Lake Erie, Ohio, and Fort Lafayette, New York.

Delighted with these plans, which involved mass murder of civilians as the Sons would sweep burning and pillaging through the cities, Thompson agreed to everything and supplied $200,000 in gold or $2,270,000 in today's money to finance the revolution. What he had overlooked was that the Sons of Liberty had not the ability to bring off such an insurrection; their numbers were grossly exaggerated, their membership seldom trained in the use of arms or capable of killing civilians when it came down to it; their ability to release prisoners was minimal now that the Washington authorities had tripled security following various daring escapes. In truth, Thompson had been conned; the $200,000 sank into a well from which it had no possible chance of surfacing.

WITH SANDERS, CLAY AND HOLCOMBE AT THE CLIFTON HOUSE AND Sanders' son Lewis gone to Richmond in hope of finding support from Davis and Benjamin, the celebrated English author George Augustus Sala, a friend of Dickens and Thackeray, arrived at Niagara on August 2 for a one week stay. He found, as he wrote in *America in the Midst of Civil War,* a series for the London *Daily Telegraph,* later turned into a book, the Confederate commissioners and their friends wandering about the corridors, gaunt and sallow as a convention of ghosts, or brooding in wooden chairs on the veranda, spray from the Falls in the air, feet propped up against the railing:

> They come and go, these Confederate persons and foregather in corners where they hold stealthy counsel . . . they have generally newspapers in their hands . . . they pass them one to another, nodding and winking in an occult manner . . . it is as much as these exiles' lives are worth to cross (on) the ferry or the Suspension Bridge . . . they are marked and proscribed men . . . How the Yankees would rejoice to get hold of them! How the telegraph would flash news of their arrest from one end of the North to the other!

Sala reported a contrast with the International House on the American side of the Falls; that hotel was no phantom resort "but full, brilliant and gay," alive with music and revelry, champagne flowing and ice cream consumed by the bucket; the holiday crowd seemed to care "not a fig" whether there was a Civil War raging or not.

It was in the gloomy, furtive atmosphere of the Clifton House that, sometime in the week of August 2nd through the 9th, 1864, Sala spoke to George Nicholas Sanders.

FOUR

THE
NAME
IS
MURDER

Sala did not reveal the gist of the conversation until after Lincoln was dead, in the pages of the *New York Times* in an interview dated May 6, 1865. Inexplicably, he wasn't called as a witness in the trials of the conspirators, nor in the later trial of their associate John H. Surratt. The unsigned article reads in part:

> It would be interesting to have an explanation from Sanders of his conference with George Augustus Sala on the subject of these assassinations [the reference was to the attempted killing of Seward on the same night as the assassination of Lincoln] . . . Sala says distinctly that Sanders told him [of his plans].

The question is, why did Sanders choose a British writer of note and a correspondent of the London *Daily Telegraph,* to divulge anything so dangerous? The reason is that Sala was widely suspected—as he wrote later in his autobiography—of being an agent of the Confederacy. The Washington authorities refused him permission to travel to the South, where he might leak vital information—a futile gesture since so many of the Northern newspapers were leaking it anyway.

It is more probable, though not admitted, that Sala was a spy for the Union, and that his meeting with Sanders—whose name he is unlikely to have remembered from underground activities in London in the 1850s, in which Sala had no interest—was arranged by Washington, with Lincoln's and Seward's approval to determine the full extent of Sanders' murderous plans. Whether that was or was not the case, it is certain that Colonel Ambrose Stevens, another visitor to the Clifton House that week, was a Union spy, authorized by Major General John A. Dix, Commander of the Department of the East, whose headquarters was at the Astor House Hotel in New York City.

Dix knew Sanders well; he had been Postmaster of New York City in 1859 when Sanders was Navy Agent and was accused of padding accounts and stealing funds while complaining of inadequate office quarters and money; Dix was acutely aware of the man when he became Secretary of the Treasury for James Buchanan. His loyalty to Lincoln is exemplified by his celebrated warning, echoed by the notorious Major General Benjamin Franklin Butler in New Orleans, "If anyone attempts to haul down the American flag, shoot him on the spot." He had unmercifully suppressed the New York City draft riots in July 1863, and he would tolerate no further activity of that sort.

Sanders had no more formidable an enemy. Dix wasted no time after the farce of the Niagara peace mission in sending Stevens, his most trusted aide and the skilled head of his secret service operation, in civilian clothing to the Clifton House, to determine Sanders' plans.

Sanders recognized Stevens at once. But he knew nothing of the man's official position. He clearly remembered him for his vigorous noisy presence at the 1860 Charleston National Democratic Convention; Stevens had been an impassioned Democrat (before he turned Republican, a change Sanders knew nothing about), and had supported Stephen A. Douglas on the anti-tariff and other campaign issues, including pro-slavery.

Sanders said to him when they ran into each other:

> "You used to be a Democrat before the war."
> "Yes, and I am one now," Stevens replied.
> "That's right." Sanders said, rubbing his hands. "Come with me, I have something to tell you. We are not telling everybody, only a few to begin with whom we can trust."

Stevens reported to Dix:

> We walked apart and he deliberately gave me the main features of the infamous conspiracy that he was assisting to organize. Its object was no less than the assassination of President Lincoln! Its details were to be arranged with an eye to results which he thought certain to insure the recognition of the Confederacy and the end of the war. The plot was to be communicated to the leading Democrats of the North and they were to assist in making the

organization (of it) perfect. The plans were to be secretly and quietly matured, and the fatal blow was to be struck the night before
the [November] election.

The threat exactly matched Stephen A. Douglas's plan for a
military *coup d'état*. Sanders went on to tell Stevens that the assassination would cause the "utmost consternation" and that "thousands of Republicans would refuse to vote," not knowing who the
next President might be. The Republican party would be "utterly
demoralized"—a typical Sanders phrase—and, bewildered by
their "novel and distressing position," voters in "borderline
states" would at once vote for McClellan. The result would be a
negotiated peace with McClellan as President which would result
in "full sovereignty" for the South.

Sanders asked Stevens what he thought of the plot. Suppressing his indignation, Stevens could only reply that he
thought the assassination "impracticable as an idea"; that the
leading Democrats would not be drawn into it and that secrecy
in the matter would be "virtually impossible."

Sanders disagreed. He said that the conspiracy had met with
the approval of many leading Democrats—clearly he was referring to August Belmont, ex-Governor of New York Washington
Hunt, the Wood brothers and Horatio Seymour.

Finding no response from Stevens, Sanders hurried off to
meet with Dean Richmond, Chairman of the New York Democratic Committee, a wealthy newspaper and railroad owner whose
trains often carried Confederates into British North America.

Sanders was joined by Clay and Holcombe. They had reason
to believe in Richmond's reliability as a fellow assassination plan-
ner. They based their conviction of his potential support on the
fact that, like Ambrose Stevens, but on a much higher level, Richmond had been a belligerent anti-Lincolnian, a strongly pro-
Douglas figure at the same Conventions in which Stevens had
similarly figured. In his co-owned Albany, New York *Atlas and
Argus* newspaper, he had ceaselessly trumpeted sedition, calling
Lincoln a "slanging, whanging stump speaker of whom all are
ashamed." Dean Richmond had thundered against Lincoln's
Emancipation Proclamation and his continuing invasion of civil

liberties and his policy of the suspension of habeas corpus. This fire-breathing publisher had successfully pushed Horatio Seymour into the New York governorship with verbal cannon fire and much mendacious puffery.

What Sanders, Clay and Holcombe overlooked, in their state of manic tunnel-vision, was that Richmond was not a killer by instinct or intention, and knew that if Lincoln were to be shot in a *coup d'état,* it would ruin the Democratic party.

Richmond, who had come from his home in Buffalo to the Clifton House in answer to the conspirators' pleas, erupted in anger when he heard the plot. He was infuriated when Sanders, Clay and Holcombe told him that "the only way in which we can insure the election of McClellan is to kill Lincoln."

Richmond told the malignant trio that he would have nothing to do with such a scheme; that if they didn't abandon it at once he would publish it in all the papers in the morning; then he stormed out.

The Lincoln-hating editor Manton M. Marble got wind of the matter. Marble's newspaper, *The New York World,* was controlled by August Belmont and Fernando Wood and had changed at the outset of the war from a Republican to a radical Democratic newspaper. A passionate supporter of Clement L. Vallandigham, Marble had denounced the Sons of Liberty leader's arrest in a furious attack in the form of an open letter and narrowly escaped arrest himself when he published a fake proclamation by Lincoln calling for a draft; he claimed to be an innocent victim, but saw *The World* temporarily closed down.

He wrote to his friend George P. McClellan on August 22, stating that Richmond had told him of the assassination plan and that Richmond had told him he had said to the conspirators:

> Stop where you are. That is to say, do nothing and write nothing
> to anybody. You have Lincoln in a bad place. Leave him there.

With Richmond's expressed approval, Stevens went to New York to report the plot to Major General Dix, who in turn took the train for Washington and secured an audience with Lincoln. The President, who seldom took such assassination threats seriously found this one sufficiently menacing to call a special cabinet meeting.

The majority at the meeting urged Lincoln to have the scheme published in the press, as Richmond had suggested, but Lincoln followed his customary policy of suppressing the facts when they involved plans against his life. The members argued that to reveal the matter would provide a powerful stimulus to war feelings; that it would strengthen the national cause.

Lincoln's decision would finally cost him his life. If Sanders, Clay and Holcombe had been exposed at the time, they would have been extradited under British North American law, tried in Washington and imprisoned. But Lincoln was afraid that with Richmond and Atlanta still resisting invasion and destruction by Grant and Sherman, with Confederates raging through Maryland and Southern Pennsylvania and Sheridan acting only sporadically in the Eastern Theatre Valley Campaign, publicizing so "audacious and tremendous a conspiracy," he said, would "strike terror and despondency" into the hearts of "thousands of discouraged Unionists," and "do more harm than good, put off the support of him among the 'weak kneed and shaky'," and make "Copperheads correspondingly plucky."

THE SAME DAY, AUGUST 10, THAT DEAN RICHMOND LEFT NIAGARA with word for Major General Dix of the assassination plan, Jacob Thompson advanced, in the form of a bill of exchange on his British operation(Fraser, Trenholm and their Scots-London banker Isaac Campbell) the very large sum of $25,000 ($284,000) to Benjamin Wood, lately returned to New York City, to supply arms and treasonable rioters to assist in anti-Lincolnian terrorism in that city.

One day later, Holcombe wrote to Judah P. Benjamin that he had scoured British North America for any and all Confederate soldiers in exile, promising them safe conduct to the South (to assist in the general uprising, followed by the *coup d'état*) if they would promise to take up arms again. He promised Benjamin he would arrange for contacts in Windsor, Ontario, Niagara, Toronto and Montreal for these men to travel *en masse* to Halifax, where the indispensable Benjamin Wier and Alexander Keith would be ready to assist their journey south, by blockade running vessels.

Also on August 11, Clay wrote to Judah P. Benjamin with self-promotional zeal, in a letter supposedly dictated to him by Beverley Tucker but actually (as always) marked by George Sanders' hyperbolic style, boasting, falsely, that the so-called Niagara peace conference had been "promotive of our wishes," and that all but the most fanatical abolitionists were convinced there could be "no peace with Lincoln as head of government." The letter went on, promising "seas of blood," "utter demoralization," and "destruction of the Republican government" . . . many (in the North) would "gladly lock arms with our soldiers in crushing the common enemy, the abolitionists." The letter ended with a pat on the back for Sanders and Tucker, for their "earnest and active aid in promoting the object of Mr. Thompson's and my mission," this despite the fact that Tucker was considerably displeased with both of them and opposed to such violence which was against his commercial interests.

Another Clay letter on August 24 went overboard in its Sandersian tone. Addressed to James M. Mason in London, it asserted that the Yankees had "changed attitude" and were "yearning for peace"; that the "worshippers of Moloch" seemed sated now with "the blood Lincoln has shed," that (absurdly) "Lincoln sees the writing on the wall and trembles" and that (a direct reference to the assassination plot) "he will try to save himself from the ignominious fate which is justly due for his crimes against his country."

By separate mail on the same day, Clay wrote to Confederate agent John Slidell in Paris that the Commissioners were sending Holcombe to Europe, assuring Slidell that the American people were tired of "the iron heel of despotism" and "of bankruptcy, slavery, corruption and impotence," that the people no longer cheered the return from battle of the Union troops; that "apathy, fear and despair ruled everything." Referring to the To Whom It May Concern letter, Clay, again taking dictation from Sanders, added, "That letter is unconstitutional, infamous and intolerable" . . . Lincoln has inflicted "a mortal wound upon himself," with the "fatal indiscretion of the imperial rescript." The note was almost identical in content and style to Sanders' diatribes calling for the death of Napoleon III in 1853-4.

But nothing could equal in villainy a later paragraph that called for the murder of all slaves over the age of sixteen, a good million of them to be destroyed in a holocaust, because they might be incited by the North to murder, burn and rape.

Holcombe sailed for Europe at the end of August, carrying the two letters with him for safety's sake; on arrival, he found that, despite the fall of Atlanta on September 2, he had as much support as ever from the English aristocracy and banking fraternity. And especially from Lord Wharncliffe, James Spence and the Salisbury and Shaftesbury families. When mass meetings were held at the time in support of the Union, they were invaded by pro-Confederate mobs; later, when Lincoln was re-elected, a Bristol gathering was disrupted and wrecked, the invading mob screaming, in a grotesque distortion of "John Brown's Body," that Lincoln must be hanged "from a sour apple tree."

Holcombe found a continuing hatred of the cotton blockade expressed in the British construction of the marauding warships that wrecked the North American merchant fleet in an undeclared war in the Atlantic. He had no difficulty in raising large sums for Lincoln's elimination.

Meanwhile, Davis and Benjamin were far from pleased with the unauthorized fraudulent arrangements proposed by the Commissioners at Niagara, as well as threats of death and destruction of Lincoln. Sanders' son Lewis, after a perilous journey South, had arrived in Richmond on August 11, telling Davis that the Union wanted peace with the Confederacy and asking that for the time being the Confederacy should "remain quiescent." Davis listened with patience to the ill-advised young man but Benjamin exploded, asking Lewis why he had not brought an encoded message to that effect instead of generalized statements conveyed verbally.

Lewis replied that such an encoded message could have been intercepted and deciphered and he could have been arrested as a spy. Furious, Benjamin snapped that "any further discussion is useless," and walked out of the meeting.

Jacob Thompson thought the Niagara affair a disgrace; he was increasingly unhappy with Sanders and Clay during Holcombe's absence abroad; it is unlikely that he knew anything of the assassination plot. He must and would devote his attention to getting McClellan elected and Lincoln defeated, and to stirring up the Sons of Liberty and the escaped Confederate prisoners to support McClellan at the August 29-30 Chicago convention.

He saw an advantage in the schism within the Republican party between the peace and war factions; any weakening of the party from within would give strength to his peace democrats. Greeley was conveniently back on the anti-Lincolnian bandwagon; at a meeting at the New York City home of prominent attorney David Dudley Field, he called for a Radical Republican convention to correct the mistake in nominating Lincoln at Baltimore, and again called for the nomination of the former major general and Californian gold millionaire John C. Frémont, who had been put forward as a candidate as early as June. Greeley, in September, once more proved to be a paper tiger as the plans dissolved in acrimony and Greeley was seen yet again as vacillating, deceitful and unreliable.

Thompson could use the advantage of the Wade-Davis bill, passed on July 2. Introduced by Judge Benjamin F. Wade, Senator from Ohio and Chairman of the Joint Committee on the Conduct of War, and by Henry W. Davis, Chairman of the Committee on Foreign Relations, it called, in the event of victory, for stripping prominent Confederates of their citizenship, deprivation of slaveholders' properties and removal of the ability to vote.

As Republican hawk fought dove, Thompson was sure he could obtain unstinting support for McClellan, but he overlooked McClellan's inconvenient shift from a peace to a war platform; Atlanta had not yet fallen, and McClellan clearly believed that only a full-scale onslaught would bring the war to an end. Many pointed out that this attitude was a contradiction of the shilly-shallying that had cost him his uniform; that Lincoln's dismissal had come because he had been slow and diffident in much of his campaigning. The theory was that McClellan was still smarting from this disgrace and planned, as President, to regain the image of a man of action and a grand master of armies.

He was, in fact, not a bad candidate. Despite his downfall, he still cut a glamorous figure and at 38 would be an appealingly young occupant of the White House. Though shortish, he was comely, with a well-knit athletic figure and an expansive masculinity of bearing and in discourse. His dark wavy hair, broad pale forehead, and thick eyebrows arching over reflective, kindly eyes were irresistible to women. As for the military rank and file, they loved him. There was scarcely a man who didn't know he had protected his young forces, putting their safety ahead of easy victory at the risk of his military reputation. No commander in the field was kinder to the humblest rookie or more respectful to graduates from his alma mater of West Point. When Grant defeated McClellan at the April, 1864 ballot at the New York World's Fair, McClellan's young supporters tore the place apart. Thompson was sure he had a winner in him, even if McClellan's change to a warrior approach exacerbated the divisions in the Democratic party.

Yet Thompson, no more capable of raising a revolution than stirring up a thunderstorm in a thimble, was hopelessly adrift. McClellan didn't approve of the term McClellan Minute Guard cooked up by Vallandigham as a branch of the Sons of Liberty. Any uprising in Chicago during the Convention could result in citizens that might be supportive turning against the Confederacy, once they had their homes burned and their transportation upset. The idea of destabilizing the Northwest was not only reckless, but politically insane and would, if it succeeded, make it impossible for McClellan to accept the nomination, in view of the McClellan Minute Guard appellation which would give the false impression he had authorized the revolt.

At the Queens Hotel in Toronto on August 25, Thompson met with his young revolutionaries, Captain Thomas Hines and Captain John B. Castleman. He was aided by another firebrand, the same Lieutenant Bennett H. Young who had conferred with Clay at Halifax in May, to head up the enterprise in Chicago. He handed them $25,000 in gold ($284,000) and he also forwarded $12,000 ($136,000) to the Sons of Liberty's leader Amos Green in Illinois. Two days later, Hines, Castleman and Young left for Chicago posing as Britishers, with 70 Confederate soldiers, all equipped with forged passports, and checked into the expensive and appropriately-named Richmond House in that city, a remarkable fact in itself since the hotel had been fully booked for weeks for the National Convention. Only August Belmont as National

Chairman, Clement L. Vallandigham, or someone equally highly placed, could have arranged the reservations.

Meantime, leaks of the conspirators' plans had occurred through the Union spy Felix Grundy Stidger, at the heart of the Sons of Liberty, and very probably Richard Montgomery as well; and reinforcement troops were rushed to Chicago. Another problem was that Bennett H. Young had given Thompson wrong information at Toronto about the prison defenses. In late 1863, he had been a prisoner of Camp Douglas, the notorious Chicago military prison whose relief was at the top of Thompson's agenda, the prisoners to be freed to maraud the Federal forces during the Convention.

At the time Young was incarcerated there, the barracks buildings had no protective high picket fences, there were only two soldiers guarding a 300-foot stretch of cell blocks, and such Federal troops as were stationed represented the riffraff of skeleton volunteer regiments and artillery companies while most of the able-bodied and well-trained men in Illinois service were deployed in the field.

In January, 1864, and again that spring, the camp was ravaged by smallpox; those who were not stricken were weakened by inadequate rations. On February 24, Chicago's Mayor Julian S. Rumsey advised Major General Henry W. Halleck, United States Commander-in-Chief until succeeded the next month by Grant, that some of the contagious and desperate prisoners might escape and infect and burn down his city, with the result that soldiers were brought in to augment the security guard. Halleck ordered one third of all the inmates shifted to the Ohio State Penitentiary in Columbus. Many of the 5000-odd remaining were dead from smallpox by March and the few caught tunneling were shot on sight. As general punishment, men were forced to stand stiff-legged with hands flat on the ground until they dropped. They had no lighting at night and could barely find their way by stars or moon to the outside troughs that did service as toilets. Not a few got dysentery, which, in some cases, was fatal.

In May and June, after a long drawn out struggle with the authorities, the prison commander Colonel Benjamin J. Sweet pulled down the 33 barracks buildings brick by brick and raised them on four foot concrete blocks, so that any digging or crawling could be detected. For every Union soldier on guard, there was at least one Chicago policeman. By August 1864, Camp Douglas was a far different place from that which Young described to Thompson, and the latter's characteristically lamentable failure to seek up-to-date intelligence on its layout imperiled the release-of-prisoners plan.

Blindly, Young, Hines and Castleman continued with their plottings at the Richmond House. Even when word came of wholesale invasions, seizures and closures of Sons of Liberty headquarters in various cities they were not deterred. And now there was another stumbling block: the crowd of conventioneers and their families and the Chicagoans themselves, in honor of the late Stephen A. Douglas, whom they loved, not only swarmed around his grave in the local cemetery but around Camp Douglas itself, making a mass rescue impossible.

THE NATIONAL DEMOCRATIC CONVENTION OPENED IN OPPRESSIVE heat on August 29, 1864, at the wooden jerry-built structure used at the Republican National Convention in 1860. Designed to accommodate 15,000 people, it was known rudely as The Wigwam. The city was in a festive mood, some 25,000 out-of-town visitors stretching its facilities to the limit. To the tune of three brass bands and the waving of hundreds of Stars and Stripes flags and celebratory banners, the delegates and their horde of admirers and camp followers poured into the looming firetrap of a lobby, shouting at the tops of their voices, spitting tobacco juice where there was no cuspidor, filling the air with cigar smoke, greeting friends and swearing at timeworn enemies.

The anti-Lincolnian traitors were there in plenty. Horatio Seymour, talking loudly of his "friends in the south," was president of the convention and August Belmont, Fernando and Benjamin Wood were at their most vociferous. Belmont showed his hand with an opening speech that can only have been music to his old friend George Sanders' ears:

> Four years of misrule by a sectional, fanatical and corrupt party have brought our country to the very verge of ruin. The past and

present are sufficient warnings of the disastrous consequences if
Mr. Lincoln's re-election should be made possible by want of patriotism and unity. The inevitable results of such a calamity must be
the utter disintegration of our whole political position, among
bloodshed and anarchy.

The tone of the speech so closely resembles Sanders' manifesto in response to Lincoln's To Whom It May Concern letter as
to be a virtual copy of it; "utter disintegration" is pure Sanders,
the surrounding rhetoric untypical of the polished Belmont, who
went on to urge the cheering, sweating delegates, in the great
hall of the Wigwam, to forget about "Peace" and "War" platforms
and unite against the President. He added a threatening note:
Lincoln, he said, must "at all costs be removed to save the
nation." This was more than a call for Lincoln to be voted out of
office; it was a call for his annihilation.

Even more dangerously, the Ohio delegate Ben Allen
announced:

The people will rise soon, and if they cannot put Lincoln out of
power by the ballot, they will by the bullet.

Other speeches, led by ex-Governor William Bigler of Pennsylvania, had much the same tone; Bigler not only called for the
defeat of the Republicans but for the overthrow of the government, words more suitable for Sanders' idols Robespierre and
Danton in the French Revolution than for a contestant at a political rally; Bigler's friends supplied their full measure of rage and
seditious defiance.

Clement L. Vallandigham emerged as the dashing star of the
Convention, dazzling all save a few with his looks, his figure, his
superb tailoring, and his old-fashioned party rhetoric as he trumpeted peace while secretly planning insurrection and assassination.

The crowd was excited by his addresses, hands fluttering, his
voice rising from quiet assertions to a shrieking attack on Lincoln. Hundreds of supporters burst into the Richmond House
lobby to get a closer look at him, invaded his suite and stood for
hours in the heat outside to catch a glimpse of him.

So overcrowded and hysterical in mood was the Convention that at one stage a swarm of spectators climbing over the barricade fence inside the Wigwam to try to mingle with the delegates fell in a heap as the fence gave way under their collective weight. More than one delegate engaged in fisticuffs and one man was flung bodily into the street. The railroad trains kept grinding and puffing by, shaking the building and filling it with burning cinders and smoke.

McClellan, his war-to-the-bitter-end platform shakily in place, was under attack from the beginning. Many opposed him for his arrest of the Maryland state legislature in the early part of the war, even though, ironically, he had acted on Lincoln's instructions. Others accused him of supporting Lincoln against habeas corpus and states' rights; many called for Seymour as a better nominee or trumpeted Vallandigham's cause. Dean Richmond was present, no doubt tortured with the knowledge that he could not reveal the Sanders-Clay-Holcombe assassination plan, and barely able to tolerate his friend Peter Cagger's comical imitation of his large stomach, high white hat and blue-tailed coat, played at a window of the Richmond House before a loudly laughing crowd.

Again and again at the Convention, there were indications that a *coup d'état* against Lincoln was in the wind. Charles A. Wickliffe, the aging Congressman for Kentucky, actually stated Thompson's Sons of Liberty's purpose by promising that if McClellan were elected he should release all Confederate prisoners. He struck an ominous note:

> My colleagues and I in the West are of the opinion that circumstances may occur between now and March fourth [Inauguration Day] . . . which will make it proper for the Democracy of the country to meet in Convention again.

Lincoln's friend Noah Brooks wrote in his book *Washington in Lincoln's Time*:

> [Wickliffe's statement] was taken as a warning that the managers of the party expected something extraordinary to happen, and were determined to be ready for any emergency that might arise;

so the convention accordingly adopted a resolution to remain as organized, subject to be called at any time and place, that the Executive Committee (should) designate.

At the time Noah Brooks published his book, several of the people concerned were still alive and he had to be cautious. Nevertheless, it is clear that the contingency plan would be called for by August Belmont as D.N.C. Chairman in the event of the assassination, should he be re-elected, of President Lincoln.

McClellan was nominated over many protests; Vallandigham managed to insert a peace plank in McClellan's platform, thus sharing the victory with him. But McClellan made clear in his official acceptance on September that he would not allow defeatism:

I could not look in the face of my gallant comrades of the army and navy, who have survived so many bloody battles and tell them that their labor and sacrifice had been in vain.

The "labor and sacrifice" of the British North American conspirators might also have been seen as in vain, since the relief of Camp Douglas and the Sons of Liberty assault on Chicago had failed so singularly. But in fact, apart from Thompson, they had not countenanced any such plans, and they had achieved much because they could now (except for Tucker) enjoy the sight of Belmont, the Wood Brothers, Seymour, Wickliffe and others firmly bent on Lincoln's destruction. Political influence towards a *coup d'état* was Sanders' and his creature Clay's purpose, not random efforts by unreliable terrorists in the Northwest.

And indeed Clay put this into words in a letter dated September 14 to Holcombe in London:

I think he (Thompson) will ascribe his failure at Chicago to the negotiation for peace at the Falls, as creating the delusive idea of rescue from thraldom by the ballot box . . . thus his failures may be charged to our counter efforts: Look out for a coup d'état.

FIVE

RAIDS
AND
REBELS

That week, Sanders and Clay received adverse news. On September 2, troops stormed into Atlanta and the triumphant and newly-promoted Major General William T. Sherman was able to telegraph an equally exultant President with the words, ATLANTA IS OURS AND FAIRLY WON.

No sooner had Sanders received this shock than he suffered an even greater one. He was advised that his son Reid, stricken with dysentery and general debility, had died on September 3 in the prison hospital at Fort Johnson, Boston Harbor. For months, Anna Sanders had appealed to the highest authorities in Washington, sending letter after letter by white flag of truce; but in view of the plot by his father against Lincoln's life, and his own previous role as courier to Europe, Reid could not be released.

Jacob Thompson was still bent that same week upon his plan to embroil the United States in war with Britain, thus weakening the Lincoln administration to the point of ruin; he embarked on a scheme that would involve British North America in an attack on Union property and people. It would, he hoped, be taken by the uninitiated as authorized by the British North American Governor General Lord Monck who, in truth, was strongly opposed to any infringement of neutrality and had a guarded sympathy, not widely shared in Whitehall, for Lincoln.

The irrepressible Lieutenant Bennett H. Young, still smarting from his failure at Chicago, outlined a scheme, authorized by Thompson, to use the so-called Fifth Company, Confederate States Retributors, his own detachment of some 20 Kentucky cavalrymen in exile, augmented by British North American Confederate sympathizers, to maraud the Northern borders of Vermont and New Hampshire for 150 miles, thus drawing protective Union forces away from New York and Washington, and enabling Lincoln's destruction. In a note to Thompson dated September 20, 1864, he announced that he had bought a repeating air gun in Toronto that could shoot 30 times without reloading and kill a man at 80 yards' distance; given $600 ($6,830) to begin with, he would snap up more weapons in New York City; he warned Thompson to be careful not to tell "Nicol" (Sanders) about this, as "he is a very imprudent man and told all in Toronto what you said to him (about Chicago)."

After picking up arms in New York, no doubt with the assistance of Benjamin Wood and the $25,000 already advanced to that egregious newspaper publisher, Young was to relieve the military officers' prison at Johnson's Island, Ohio on Lake Erie, on the Canadian border, a plan as reckless and dangerous as the proposed release of Camp Douglas, and certain to set off a border war.

The plan had originally been hatched in February, 1863, not only by Young, but by two naval officers who had approached Jefferson Davis to bring it off. Once the prisoners were let go, the marauders would burn and scuttle the Union merchant vessels at Buffalo, blow up the Erie Canal and shatter the Ohio River locks before an all-out attack on Chicago.

Navy Secretary Stephen R. Mallory approved the idea and with him Admiral Franklin Buchanan, but Davis, who had been interested, got cold feet at the last minute. His cancellation of the plan shows that he would never have approved this new one—he was clearly concerned that England would see through the plot as one designed to drag her into war when her convenient neutrality allowed her to play both sides against each other, trading in wheat with the North while sneaking through cotton, tobacco, turpentine and rosin from the South, and supplying arms to both sides.

Conditions at Johnson's Island were worse than those at Camp Douglas. By late July, the prison was severely overcrowded; there were 2406 inmates, well over the prescribed limit, and 47 already had smallpox and the disease was spreading. The summer heat devastated the prisoners; the inmates had to eat rats; drains and sinks were dirty and blocked up; toilet-troughs overflowed with excrement. When the pumps that brought in fresh water from the lake broke down, the men had to form a duty detail to carry it in by bucket in their half-starved and weakened condition, and many fell unconscious on the ground.

On July 8, when Montgomery and others revealed that a relief of the camp was on Thompson's agenda, security was doubled. According to an agreement following the British-American war of 1812, only one foreign navy vessel was allowed the use of the Canadian Great Lakes; by 1864, this was the one-gun U.S.S. *Michigan,* skippered by the enterprising seadog Captain Jack Carter, and she was rushed to defend the island against marauders.

Showing more shrewdness than was customary, Thompson settled upon a device: he arranged for a member of his entourage, a certain Dr. Montrose A. Pallen, a former military doctor attached to the Vicksburg defense force, who allegedly had plans to poison the New York City water supply, to pose as a Britisher and go to Johnson's Island to make a report on conditions there. Pallen was able to give a clear picture on his return to Toronto.

Fort Johnson had been thrown up hastily at the outset of the war, the Lake Erie location chosen because lumber was cheap and available in quantity. The pinewood prison houses were jerrybuilt, erected in haste and surrounded by a picket fence that piggybacking men could vault over easily, and built flush with the much-rained soil so that digging and tunneling were easy.

High wooden watch platforms were set up, rickety and subject to collapse in bad weather. They were not properly patrolled because the scratch military guard detachment was seldom vigilant and the howitzers in the ramshackle barracks house were not often brought out for target practice.

There had been an attempted breakout early in September, in the midst of an electrical storm. The thunder and lightning and crashing of the waves distracted the guards, but the prisoners were caught trying to float a small ducking skiff from the shore and were clapped in irons. Again, security was increased and Captain Jack Carter was ordered by Navy Secretary Gideon Welles to remain indefinitely off-shore.

Instead of Bennett H. Young, who had so disappointed him at Chicago, Thompson changed his mind and settled on another young man to head up the Johnson's Island raid. The 29-year-old John Yates Beall's baby face and feeble beard suggested an overage choirboy rather than the fanatic he was. In some photographs, his heavy-lidded eyes in deep sockets, broken nose and wide slit of a mouth would make him look like the pirate he also was.

He was a virile, passionate and committed rebel against authority, who had jointly planned the raid at the same time as the naval officers in Richmond proposed it to Jefferson Davis. A wealthy Virginian of British high class origin, he had been a stout-hearted private in the Stonewall brigade and had the manly distinction of being wounded in the chest while serving under the controversial cavalry commander Colonel Turner Ashby.

With Thompson's permission, this picture of vigor and strength engaged as a sidekick a fiery Scot named Bennett H. Burley, aged 22, a round-shouldered bull of a youth whose reddish hair sprouted straight up from his head as if his scalp were seeded with carrots. Burley was a specialist in deadly weapons like his Glasgow inventor father; he had invented a bomb complete with time clock and a depth charge that a swimmer could carry underwater and attach by magnet to a vessel's hull. Beall, with another Scot, the hirsute giant John Maxwell, had already boarded, seized, rifled and burned a Union ship and had been briefly imprisoned for the deed. He was eager to start again.

A third man Thompson hired—his motive was enhanced by news that his Oxford, Mississippi plantation had been sacked and burned earlier in September—was the piratical Captain Charles Cole of the Fifth Tennessee Regiment, a hard-working spy who since July had supplied him with a stream of intelligence on Union troop movements, gun emplacements, arsenals and harbor soundings on the Great Lakes, and whose glamour was enhanced by the fact that his mistress, the beautiful Anna Brown, obtained much of the information by flirting with United States officers.

Beall, after researching the region with Cole's and Miss Brown's aid, decided that the only way he could achieve Thompson's purpose (still unauthorized in Richmond) was to hijack a Union passenger steamer and sail her against the U.S.S. *Michigan* and Johnson's Island.

He settled on the *Philo Parsons*. Built in 1861, she was a modest 222-ton side-wheeler used as a tourist vessel for visitors to and from British North America and Ohio ports, and for carrying a cargo of official and personal mail, food, pig iron, dry goods and timber. Owned by the half-American, half-British Fox family, she plied a regular route between Detroit and Sandusky, leaving on Mondays, Wednesdays and Fridays and returning the following day. She often made a stop at Malden, and less frequently at Sandwich, both on the British side of Lake Erie.

Cole made several visits to Johnson's Island, posing as a Union Oil businessman, to augment Dr. Pallen's reports. He boarded the *Michigan* on a nightly basis to entertain Captain Carter and his officers with fine food and champagne. His plan was to await the *Parsons'* arrival and then hold Carter and his cannoneers at gunpoint, ordering them to fire a volley across the officers' quarters at Fort Johnson to signal a general outbreak.

Beall went to Sandwich to await the *Parsons'* arrival; he would board there with his men. At 8 P.M. on September 18, 1864, Bennett Burley, beaming with all the charm that Scottish redhead could muster, stepped aboard the *Parsons* at Detroit pier and spoke to the equally youthful ship's chief clerk and co-owner Walter Ashley. He said he would be sailing in the morning with a group of friends and wanted to take a trip to Kelly's Island, a popular wooded picnic spot; others would join him at Sandwich. Then he bought the tickets.

The moment he left, Ashley, who was suspicious, walked over to the captain's cabin and spoke to skipper Sylvester F. Atwood. Atwood, in turn, advised Lieutenant-Colonel Bernard R. Hill, who was in charge of Detroit security as Federal special agent. At six A.M. the following morning, two hours before sailing, and before Burley and his team came aboard, Hill arrived to confer with Atwood.

The decision was that the *Parsons,* which had no guns, would be of little or no use against the *Michigan,* but at all events Captain Carter must be alerted, and so he was, by Navy Secretary Gideon Welles in a series of urgent telegrams from Washington. Setting a trap for Cole, Carter would let the supposed oilman go on supplying him and his officers with wine and food while all the time knowing his intention. Once the *Parsons* appeared off Johnson's Island, he knew what he had to do.

Atwood, while showing no suspicion of Burley, asked him, when he came aboard with his companions at 8 A.M., why he wanted to pick up more friends at Sandwich; why had they all not gone aboard with him? Burley replied that one of the men was lame and could not come to Detroit.

At the same time as the *Parsons* took aboard her regular passengers, border reinforcements were rushed to Lake Erie. Oblivious in their youthful optimism, Burley and his team enjoyed the clear weather to Malden, where British North Americans he had recruited brought aboard a large iron-bound pinewood box tied with thick ropes. It was filled with firearms and grenades.

Beall came aboard with his men, one faking a limp, at Sandwich. The vessel berthed briefly at Middle Bass Island, where Captain Atwood disembarked to visit with his family, who were vacationing there. Four more of Beall's team embarked, one posing as a sewing machine salesman.

Some 20 minutes off Middle Bass, in choppy waters under a threatening sky, Beall fired a signal shot off the taffrail to alert his men that this was the time to seize the *Parsons*. Burley and four of his men strode into the purser's office and confronted Walter Ashley, who was standing in front of his desk. They waved their guns at him and told him that if he resisted he was a dead man. He didn't resist.

The safe door was open and the men rifled it; others opened the pinewood box. They pulled out of it Colt revolvers, hatchets and knives and as 35 more pirates crammed into the small cabin, they handed out the weapons.

They rounded up the 28 passengers, ushering them at gunpoint into the ship's saloon; women screamed and children started to cry; they were told to be silent or suffer the consequences.

When the fireman ran up from the boiler room, one of Beall's men ordered him back to stoke up the ship; when he refused, he was shot between his thighs. He went back below.

Beall ordered the wheelman to proceed. But the veteran seaman explained to him that the vessel had not sufficient fuel to complete the voyage to Johnson's Island. Beall had him return to Middle Bass.

Before docking there, Beall and Burley jettisoned a cargo of pig iron to increase speed; the crew waved their muskets at the shore workers on the pier to bring up logs for the furnaces. The shore workers refused and Beall had his men fire at them; they managed to escape into the trees. Hearing the shots, a small boy, a friend of Captain Atwood's family, ran to Atwood's house to alert him. When Atwood arrived at the dock, the pirates were engaged in carrying the logs aboard; the Captain was seized, gagged, bound and hurled into the saloon where the ship's surgeon told him, "You had better take things cool, or you will be hurt."

At that moment a whistle was heard and the *Island Queen*, a 173-ton popular American Lake Erie cruiser, berthed alongside. Beall and Burley ordered their men to jump from one ship to the other, flung ropes over the bow and announced the *Queen* was theirs.

When the engineer protested, he was rewarded with a bullet through his cheek. Male passengers were hustled unceremoniously into the boiler room, while women and children were taken ashore and released, along with Captain Atwood, on the promise they would say nothing of the matter to anyone for 24 hours—an absurdly naïve request.

The *Parsons*, now fully stocked with logs, continued on her voyage, with the *Island Queen*, stripped of money and possessions, towed ignominiously behind. Beall decided to scuttle her when towing her threatened the *Parsons'* knot speed. He had her seacocks opened but by the time she drifted free she was in unexpectedly shallow water and instead of foundering, stuck on a sandbar and was salvaged three days later.

The Parsons' hard-pressed wheelman was compelled to advise Beall that to take her to Sandusky, now that it was dark, was too risky because of the shoals and quicksands; Beall ordered him to Malden instead. Once ashore at that British port, Beall and Burley had their men carry their loot, for safety, and hid it in a disused lime kiln they had heard about. Some older male passengers were put ashore at Fighting Island along with the *Island Queen*'s stolen piano and some of her cabin furniture.

Now the time had come to stage the attack on Johnson's Island and the U.S.S. *Michigan*. Beall sailed as close as he dared; the island was blanketed in silence, and the *Michigan* rocked gently in the swell, her one gun seemingly unmanned. But the moment the *Parsons'* side wheel was heard slapping the water, the

Michigan came to life. Captain Jack Carter ordered all hands on deck and trained his cannon directly at the approaching ship. He already had Captain Cole, his champagne-and-caviar host, firmly clapped in irons.

Beall grasped the situation at once. He ordered his men to attack the *Michigan* but they would have been wiped out by cannon fire as soon as they tried to board her and they mutinied, sending a hastily-written note with 18 signatures to Beall telling him they had had enough. He made them sign a document that they were Confederate soldiers, to disguise his act of piracy as a legitimate act of war, thus defusing Thompson's entire purpose, which was to make the *Parsons* enterprise seem to be British. But of course it had already been exposed for what it was.

Beall panicked and ordered the wheelman to put on full speed and make haste to Sandwich, where he had the *Parsons* released from her mooring ropes and set adrift; like the *Island Queen,* she, too, was rescued from a sandbar.

Sympathetic with their purpose, the British North American officials who interviewed the raiders at Sandwich let them go with a note of caution and didn't call the police. Beall and Burley managed to escape—but not for long.

SHORTLY AFTER THE JOHNSON'S ISLAND EXPEDITION, AT THE BEGINNING of October, an important Union spy arrived at Windsor, Ontario, which was increasingly used as a Confederate headquarters in preference to the Queens Hotel in Toronto.

His name was Henry H. Hine. A former lieutenant in the 1st Colorado Calvary, he had been dismissed from his post in April 1864 because he had granted passes to slave holders to bring their slaves out of Missouri in violation of military orders. Found innocent at a subsequent hearing, he joined the team of Lafayette C. Baker, head of the National Detectives Bureau, an intelligence operation responsible exclusively to Secretary of War Stanton. Baker sent him to British North America to investigate further plans against Lincoln and the activities of the Confederate Commissioners and the Sons of Liberty.

He stayed at Hirons House hotel in Windsor, where he assumed the name of H. F. Howell, later changed to Carlos J. St.

Vrain and H. C. Carlton, and joined the Sons of Liberty. He found that their plans to sack and burn Chicago were still on Thompson's mind and, as he stated in an interrogatory session in Washington before a War Committee on November 29, 1867:

> At the same time they were to capture, or kill, the President and his Cabinet and whatever officers were here at Washington of any note.

Hine confirmed that the plan was to compel Lieutenant General Grant to detach a large portion of the Army of the Potomac for the purpose of meeting this insurrectionary army (of Sons of Liberty) and thus enable Lee to reinforce General Albert S. Johnston and break up Sherman's march to the sea.

In particular, Hine mentioned as a chief conspirator a certain Dr. Kent, evidently a B. G. Kent (no first name supplied) who was mentioned at the time of the trial of the Sons of Liberty in Indianapolis. Kent told Hine:

> We shall kill the damned old son-of-a-bitch Lincoln, he ought to have been dead and in hell long ago.

Thus it is clear that at least by October (Hine felt sure the plans had been hatched at the Richmond House in Chicago) the Sons of Liberty were committed to Lincoln's assassination, along with Sanders, Clay and Holcombe.

They were soon to find a willing subplotter, who himself was a member of the Sons of Liberty: the actor and medication shipper, John Wilkes Booth.

A passage in a paper found in Booth's effects after his death, and written after Lincoln's re-election for a second term on November 8, 1864, reads as follows:

> Courage: courage still and *wait*. The Ides of March shall come to these states before the month is named . . .

It is clear from these words that the need, expressed to Colonel Ambrose Stevens and Dean Richmond by the Canadian commissioners in August, to have Lincoln killed before the above date, involved Booth and failed; and that Sanders' time-worn refrain, expressed in the first editorial of the *Democratic Review,* to remember the Ides of March, would now assume a new and dangerous significance. Identifying always with Brutus as the slayer of Julius Caesar, and with Hamlet as slayer of King Claudius of Denmark, Booth would now strike at the revised time. Not on March 15, the actual date of the Ides on the Roman Calendar, but on Inauguration Day, March 4.

JOHN WILKES BOOTH WAS BORN ON MAY 10, 1838, WHICH MADE HIM just 26 years of age when, in the summer of 1864, he first got wind of the Canadian plot against Lincoln. Like Judah P. Benjamin, he was of Sephardic Spanish-Jewish descent; through his genes ran the pain of centuries of oppression under successive Spanish kings. He was thus an ideal recruit for Sanders; he saw Lincoln as a tyrant in the tradition of the European monarchs Sanders had plotted against in London ten years earlier.

His ancestor Ricardo Botha, while in hiding under unilateral Spanish proscription of Jews, had managed to circulate, in the mid-18th century, inflammatory pamphlets in Madrid attacking King Charles III; ironically, when he moved to London, he found that the hated monarch supported the American War of Independence, of which he most passionately approved. He soon became both neighbor and friend of John Wilkes, the polemicist and rebellious supporter of human rights, who hated all despots. Anglicized as Booth, the family thrived in England, where, just as Sanders would scores of years later, they found willing support for their revolutionary principles.

Junius Brutus Booth, named for the assassin of Julius Caesar and identifying with him, achieved prominence early on the stage. He hated the Hanoverian dynasty that ruled England, and the return of the French monarchy to replace the successors of his admired French Revolution. With fiery eloquence, Junius portrayed in the harshest colors the despots he played—Macbeth, Julius Caesar, King Claudius in *Hamlet,* Richard III—while giving every ounce of sympathy to their opponent murderers. In January, 1821, he inevitably crossed the Atlantic to settle in the nation that had thrown off the Hanoverian yoke; he had urgently supported America's cause in the War of 1812. He arrived at an ominous time: during the unfortunate Presidency of James Monroe.

Under that administration, a threatening series of Supreme Court decisions gave judicial sanction to the doctrine of centralization of power at the expense of individual states' governments, decisions that would in the very long run influence the onset of the Civil War. The spread of cotton culture in the South compelled a policy of slavery, reversing the Southern attitudes that had led to the American Colonization Society of 1816 and the settlement of blacks in Liberia; when Missouri entered the Union it was admitted, over much criticism, as a slave state.

John Wilkes Booth, in direct contradiction of his siblings, was dismayed by the idea of potential emancipation and by dictatorial unionism in Washington. Raised in Maryland, he was influenced by the rebellious elements in that state, particularly in the city of Baltimore, that traditional hotbed of intrigue and revolution. A killer in terms of looks, with his inherited Spanish-Jewish beauty, dark olive skin and classically-modeled torso, bent upon a future on the stage, his hatred of African-Americans was inflamed at the Milton College for Boys at Cockeysville, when blacks were accused of killing the father of a fellow pupil and friend.

Snobbish, authoritarian, egomaniacal, yet liked by many for his vulnerability and charm, Booth even objected to white laborers at Bel Air, the family estate, joining the communal dining table on special occasions when ladies were present. He had a consuming need to prove his manhood, not on the stage, which was not recognized as a manly profession, but as a soldier in arms.

In November, 1859, he impetuously walked out of a rehearsal to enlist briefly in the Militia Company F of the Richmond Grays, accompanying the crack regiment by the Baltimore and Ohio Railroad to Charlestown, West Virginia, where, on December 2, he was among the witnesses of the hanging of the famous anti-slaver John Brown. The railroad official in charge of his troop was a kindred spirit, Louis O'Donnell, who would later be one of those connected to the Lincoln assassination, a Confederate agent along with the B & O's chief operations officer, William

Prescott Smith. Booth would have many opportunities to use the B & O, protected as he was by these representatives of the Confederacy.

On February 18, 1861, when Booth was performing at the Green Street Gayety Theatre in Albany, New York, Lincoln was in town on his way to the inaugural ceremonies in Washington. Booth was a voracious reader of newspapers and cannot have failed to pick up that morning the local *Atlas and Argus* of Dean Richmond, whom the Niagara conspirators would later try to entangle in their murderous schemes. Referring to the President-elect's speeches in terms that echoed the views of a secessionist New York state led by the traitorous Governor Horatio Seymour, Richmond slashed away at Lincoln: "Instead of sparkling champagne there is the frothy rush of root beer, yeast foam, uninspired flatulence, slop and dregs . . ." Booth, the moment Lincoln was elected, told his sister Asia, "[Lincoln is] the tool of the North, to crush out slavery, by robbery, rapine, slaughter . . ."

Booth again showed his colors in June, 1861, when he was performing at Mary Provost's Theatre in New York. Someone mentioned the name of George P. Kane, former Marshal of Baltimore, who had been arrested in June, 1861, on orders from Major General Nathaniel P. Banks, along with his entire Board of Police, and charged with plotting along with Brigadier General Pierre G. T. Beauregard to seize Washington by preventing the passage of Union troops through Maryland on the Baltimore and Ohio Railroad and aiding Marylanders to go to Virginia and join the Confederate army.

Following the Baltimore riots of April 19 on, when crowds of Baltimoreans screamed their support for the Confederacy, Kane had, with gangs of men engaged by the police, destroyed four of the city's bridges and cut off all telegraph wires except one that led to the Confederates at Harpers Ferry. In addition to his other subversive activities, Kane was busy selling arms to the South before Lincoln allowed for that.

Reminded of Kane's arrest and incarceration in Fort McHenry, probably because Kane at the time of the New York play season was being transferred to Fort Warren, Boston Harbor, Booth exploded and revealed that Kane was his friend and that any man who

arrested him deserved a dog's death. John Joseph Jennings, of the
Mary Provost Theatre company wrote, in his book *Theatrical and
Circus Life*:

> It was not the matter of what he said: it was the manner and gen-
> eral appearance of the speaker, that awed us. It would remind you
> of Lucifer's defiance at the council. He stood there [as] the
> embodiment of evil.

In April, 1862, Booth performed at Ben DeBar's Theatre at St.
Louis, a nest of secessionists and Knights of the Golden Circle.
DeBar, of British origin and no lover of Lincoln, had adopted
Booth's favorite niece Blanche, the abandoned daughter of his
brother Junius, herself an impassioned pro-Confederate. DeBar
often introduced seditious or traitorous remarks into his play pro-
ductions, worming them into the texts of Shakespeare.

The fact that Booth was especially welcome in the DeBar
household is explained by a report filed by the Provost Marshal
of St. Louis with the War Department on April 24, 1864, ten days
after Lincoln's assassination. It read:

> [Miss DeBar] is an unmitigated rebel, as indicated by her papers, by
> poetry addressed to her rebel officers, by correspondence received
> from her by the same parties, and by various expressions of senti-
> ment found in her writings. The two first portraits in her album are
> those of Jeff. Davis and [Captain Raphael] Semmes [marauder of
> Union shipping as skipper of the Fraser, Trenholm blockade
> breaker *Alabama*], and an exact and minute map, sketched in pen-
> cil, of Island Number 10 [a Union camp on the Mississippi] with
> explanations of the positions of Federal gunboats and fortifications.

In St. Louis that season, Booth played with inspired force,
based upon his inherited hatred of tyrants, the roles of the mad
and despotic Richard III and Count Pescara, the violent assassin
and torturer in Richard Sheil's popular melodrama *The Apostate*;
in his performance of Hamlet, he brought out that same hatred
his father had shown in Hamlet's attacks on King Claudius of
Denmark. In a lighter mood, he brilliantly portrayed the twin

stalwarts who dominated Charles Selby's adaptation of the Paris hit farce *The Marble Heart.*

He formed a friendship with a fellow actor, Thomas L. Connor, who shared his hatred of Lincoln and support for the policy of slavery. At a St. Louis hotel bar, Connor listened without demur as Booth, in his cups, yelled, "This whole damned government can go to hell!" Arrested and hauled before a magistrate, the two men were told to swear the Union Oath of Allegiance or to go to prison for sedition. His career at stake, Booth gritted his teeth and signed; Connor, more bravely, did not, and served a term behind bars as a result. In Chicago, in December, Booth was quoted as saying, "What a glorious way for a man to immortalize himself—by killing Lincoln."

It wasn't long before he was busy telling his sister Asia that he had been able to master the secret box code devised under the aegis of Judah P. Benjamin and Brigadier General John H. Winder of the Richmond Signals operation, and thus had become, like Blanche DeBar, a Confederate agent. He found a convenient cover for his movements across the borders of war in that he began trading in quinine, calomel and morphine, a trade winked at by both sides since medical supplies were useful for wounded or diseased soldiers and sailors. Edward A. Pollard wrote in his monumental *Southern History of the War* (1866) that the very inception of trading with the enemy began with:

> Paltry importations across the Potomac. It was said that the country (the South) wanted medicines, surgical instruments and a number of trifles and that trade with the Yankees in these could do no harm.

Thus, from the outset, Booth needed no permit to travel across the boundaries of conflict; as a well-known actor, thought to be neutral, he also had free movement. Therefore, he was able, as the war progressed, to lay out plans and routes for any and all his activities, none of which were favorable to the Union and most of which were dangerous to Lincoln.

His chief opponent in the matter was the controversial Lafayette Curry Baker, special agent of the Provost Marshal's branch of Washington D.C., who became a Colonel in May, 1863. On the principle of it takes a thief to catch a thief, Baker, who was not above corruptibility, was skilled in exposing corruption in others. Powerfully built and of medium height, he weighed 180 pounds of muscle; a man of violent temper, his face sported a formidable brown beard joining company with a shock of brown, seldom-combed hair; his gray eyes changed from jovial to piercing when he had a criminal in his hands. He was known as the best shot in the North, and a horseman of rare accomplishment.

A devoted family man, he knew all the thieves, cutthroats and double dealers in his adoptive city of Washington. In that respect, and others, he took his cue from the French criminal detective known as Vidocq.

Nothing would have pleased Baker more than to expose such a figure as Booth for trading with the enemy, but like his immediate superior and friend, the former hotshot editor of Horace Greeley's *New York Tribune*, Assistant Secretary of War Charles A. Dana, he was handicapped by the fact that three women close to Lincoln were involved in the same trade. Should Booth be arrested as a spy, he could reveal to an unsuspecting public that these ladies were trading with the enemy. Eliza Violet Gist, of the distinguished Maryland family that moved on both sides of the war, was married to the President's intimate friend and adviser Francis Preston Blair, Sr., father of the Postmaster General, whose offices were used as Confederate maildrops without interference; arrested by Baker, Mrs. Blair was let go after a brief and unreported prison term by orders of the Chief Executive; 600 ounces of quinine were found in her skirts. The President's sister-in-law, Mrs. Clement White, was also busy shipping quinine; her own sister, Mrs. Benjamin H. Helm, traded in cotton. Thus, Booth was able to travel with encoded messages, and legalized contraband, throughout the war and neither Lafayette Baker nor Dana could do anything about it; in January, 1864, Lieutenant General Grant issued him a license.

Booth's most serious commitment occurred in April, 1863, when he was performing at Grover's Theatre in Washington as Richard III in a performance attended by the President on the 11th; and in *The Marble Heart*. Robert Fleming, a member of the company, was present with Booth, as he reported to the Provost Marshal of the 20th District of Pennsylvania at Meadsville after the Lincoln assassination, at a meeting of the D.G. Lodge (Demoralizing Government) a secret society offshoot of the Sons of Liberty. During an initiation ceremony, a member picked up a sword and pointed it at Booth's heart, saying that Booth must take a sacred oath to assassinate Lincoln or that same sword would be used to stab him to death; Booth took the oath.

The story was confirmed by Fleming's mother, to whom he reported it immediately after it happened, and by the oilman Simeon J. McKay, to whom Booth himself spoke of it; further confirmation came from Major Samuel J. Wayman of the 10th New York Cavalry stationed at Elmira, who also heard of it from Fleming. A man who was close to Booth that same week was later his aide in assassination, David E. Herold, who may well have been present at the ceremony.

In a sworn statement to the investigating committee on the presidential murder on April 25, 1865, Henry C. Higginson of Pekin, Illinois, a private in the 19th Illinois Volunteers, stated that on September 20, 1863, he had been taken prisoner at Chickamaugua and transferred to a jail at Richmond, in charge of Brigadier General John H. Winder. In conversations with his fellow inmates, Higginson had learned that a very good friend of theirs was an actor named John Wilkes Booth; they mentioned the benefits the South was receiving every day from the North, a direct reference to the trading with the enemy in products in which Booth took a significant part. One of the prisoners, identified by Higginson only as Ritchie, showed him a letter from Booth dated December 12, 1863; it had been written from Louisville, Kentucky, where Booth had evidently gone after completing an engagement in Cleveland. The letter stated that a man whom Booth knew by the name of Perkins had started with him south down the Kanawha Valley, through three small townships, with a wagon-load of medicines. The Kanawha Valley was a popular route for Confederate agents as well as for medicine traders.

On March 24, 1864, while playing the part of Romeo in *Romeo and Juliet* at the St. Charles Theatre in New Orleans, a popular city for trading in supplies between North and South, Booth sent a contribution to a fund raised by the Sons of Liberty in aid of the family of Phineas C. Wright, a leader of the Sons and, until recently, editor of Benjamin Wood's New York *Daily News*. Wright had been arrested for sedition and imprisoned at Fort Lafayette, New York Harbor.

DURING MUCH OF THAT SUMMER, BOOTH WAS INVOLVED IN THE Pennsylvania oil business with the warm-hearted and naïve Joseph H. Simonds, whom he had met in Boston in 1861, when Simonds was a teller at the Mechanics Bank. In January, 1864, staying with Ben and Blanche DeBar in St. Louis, Booth had heard of oil discoveries in Franklin, PA; he joined forces with Simonds and two Cleveland friends, John Ellsler, manager of the Cleveland Academy of Music, and a gambler, prizefighter and boxing promoter named Thomason Mears, who proved to be a dangerous and unreliable partner.

Booth formed, without legal documents, an oil company and bought for spudding three and a half acres of the Fuller farm at Franklin; Simonds set up a real estate operation, handling not only Booth's investments but other properties as well. They found strong political support in the local Venango *Spectator,* whose pages were filled with articles such as "Lincoln's Double Dealings" and "Lincoln will never win the war." Any local who worked against the neighborhood's treasonable mood by opposing the South suffered the consequences; when a carpenter working on a ferryboat made an anti-Southern remark, Booth pulled a gun on him and made him apologize.

In mid-August, Booth was staying at Barnum's, the popular Baltimore hotel; sometime in the previous weeks he had hatched a plan to carry out the promise he made at the ceremony of the sword of the D.G. group in Washington the previous year. It is clear that he intended to cloak his purpose in a pretended plot to abduct Lincoln only; his excuse would be, to those besotted enough to believe him and follow his dictates, that he simply wanted to hold the President hostage. His purpose was, ostensibly, to secure the exchange of war prisoners, officially suspended since the spring of 1863; but he very well knew that individual prisoners were being exchanged—if they were ill, or had an ailing

family member, or simply had influence and money. A simple survey of the manifest records of such prisons as Johnson's Island
that summer of 1864 shows many such exchanges. But Booth was
able to announce to anyone prepared to follow him in his murderous plan that, on August 10, following a widely printed request
by Robert Ould, chief of the Confederate Bureau of Exchange for
officer-for officer, man-for-man interchanges, Union Secretary of
State Stanton had adamantly refused it.

That Booth had no charter from Richmond to execute his
scheme is clear from the correspondences of Jefferson Davis late
in life. Davis told those who asked him that he never believed
Lincoln could be kidnapped without killing him, and that therefore, even though his own life had been attempted, he would not
retaliate in kind. According to Professor William C. Cooper, the
dean of Davis biographers, Davis knew of Booth's "kidnap" plans
but there is no evidence he gave them his blessing. Indeed, to
have done so would have been a contradiction of his belief that
killing Lincoln was not desirable—if only that it would bring lasting disgrace on the South, and would turn Lincoln into a martyr.
But just the same, he did nothing to stop those plans.

Booth needed naïve young men who would become his tools
in a kidnap plot without realizing they would be involved in murder, and presumably without realizing that they would hang for
kidnap as surely as they would hang for killing. He needed men
whom he had known for years and had measured for lack of cun-
ning and cupidity; men who needed money and were located in
his native state of Maryland.

They would be fit, personable, and—a touch of narcissism—
rather like himself in dark and sultry good looks. His first choice
was an old chum, Samuel B. Arnold, a fellow pupil at the rigidly
correct St. Timothy's Hall, Catonsville, Maryland, who was living
conveniently in Baltimore at the time.

Arnold was, like Booth, handsome, muscular and moody,
with black wavy hair, intense, dark eyes, and a well-trimmed
beard enhancing rather than hiding a stubborn jaw. He was stur-
dily built and finely-proportioned, with an air of quick intelligence; he had early abandoned his parents' plans for his entry to
the Protestant ministry and had instead chosen the life of the

soil, working at the time of Booth's arrival at a farm near Hook-
stown, Maryland, as harvest hand and wheat thresher. Booth sent
him a letter in schoolboy code and a sum in greenbacks; when a
fellow worker asked Arnold what the note meant, the young man
replied, with theatrical emphasis, "You will know all about it one
of these days through the newspapers." Then he took leave to go
to Baltimore.

Booth received him warmly at Barnum's. Handing the youth
a cigar, he reminded him of incidents in their school days. The
doorbell rang, and, in the midst of this calculatedly nostalgic
reminiscence, in walked a second potential recruit: Michael
O'Laughlen, another darkly handsome and brooding youth who
worked as a feed and produce worker part time at his father's
Baltimore firm. Like Booth, O'Laughlen, a passionate hater of
Lincoln, had joined the Knights of the Golden Circle at the outset of the war, with its blood oath to destroy the President; there
can be little doubt that he quickly cottoned to Booth's true purpose, although Arnold may have been unaware of it. All three
men had been connected, Booth in a semi-civilian capacity, with
Virginia regiments that were riddled with members of the
recently-named Sons of Liberty; all three were alike enough to be
brothers: athletic, well-made, highly-charged, with strong tastes
for flashy suits and expensive imported cigars.

Over wine, the dangerous trio discussed the matter of Lieutenant General Ulysses S. Grant's suspension of prisoner
exchanges of the past 16 months. Boldly, and risking exposure
should either young man turn informer for a price, Booth outlined his invented scheme of carrying Lincoln from his favorite
summer residence at the Soldiers' Home in Washington to the
Potomac River and thence to Richmond. The idea found no
demur in Arnold and O'Laughlen, youthful hotheads both,
though undoubtedly they expected support from the Sons of
Liberty for so audacious a plan, and money from Booth as well.
He told his friends he would go to New York and sell his interest
in the Pennsylvania oil business; an idle promise since that business had already proved to be a flop. He was not prepared to
name the most likely source of funds, the Confederate clique in
British North America.

He needed a cover—a reason to go to Montreal, where
Sanders was resident, in case Federal agents were on his trail;
and that cover was easily found. He had long been approached
by Montreal managements to perform in that city, now he could
pretend that he intended to answer their call. So he packed up
his stage clothes in three trunks and traveled to Montreal by
train, arriving at the beginning of October.

To save money, he didn't check into the expensive St.
Lawrence Hall or the similar Donegana Hotel, which anyway was
about to be closed for renovations, but a modest hotel on Côté
Street known as the Royal, which stood next door to the Theatre
Royal. Both were owned by the high-powered impresario John W.
Buckland, who wanted Booth as star of the next season. Booth
entered into his discussions with Buckland, knowing full well he
would never perform in the city, and that in fact he was booked
for November 25, in New York, to appear with his brothers Edwin
and Junius in *Julius Caesar* at the Wintergarden Theatre to raise
money for the new Shakespeare statue in Central Park.

The Royal Hotel was a vespiary of Confederates and their
British sympathizers and Booth, once he was installed there,
was too excited by drink and across-the-board approval to show
even an ounce of desirable caution. When one night a rebel living in an upstairs room sang "Maryland, My Maryland," the
secessionist anthem that burned with anti-Union feelings, it
soon found an echo in every man and woman present, Booth
included, until the rafters rang from attic to cellar with its
famous strains.

Booth formed an intimate friendship with a smart youth
named George Iles, who never forgot him. Iles acted as a messenger boy for John W. Buckland and for the dry-goods merchant and Confederate sympathizer, the Scottish James M.
Baillie. Booth had an unnerving habit of raging about the mis-
eries of the South and pulling a dagger from his belt, telling Iles
what he would do to Lincoln when the time came—and he wasn't
referring to a kidnap.

Iles saw Booth often visiting St. Lawrence Hall, throwing caution away as his drinking increased. The actor attended demon-
strations of billiards by the French-Canadian champion Joseph

Dion, a handsome womanizer like himself, and doomed to an early death from syphilis. Booth, after enjoying the only mint juleps sold north of the Mason-Dixon line, at Dooley's popular 100-foot hotel bar, would walk unsteadily into the billiards parlor, with its candelabras in green shades hung over the green baize tables, and join in bouts with Dion.

On one occasion, as Dion wrote to the Canadian *Hamilton Times* eighteen days after the Lincoln assassination, Booth bragged that he was playing his "own game," and that it was "to bag the *biggest* game this side of hell." Booth added, referring to a stroke in which a player hits one ball with his cue and that ball hits another, driving both into a pocket, "You'll hear of a double carom one of these days," a sure indication that he had another target, apart from the President, in mind. When someone mentioned the up-coming November election, he snapped:

> It makes damn little difference who wins, head or tail. Abe's contract
> is nearly up, and whether he is re-elected or not, his goose is cooked.

At the end of the game, which Dion won, Booth slapped him on the back, congratulated him, and said:

> By God, I like your Canadian style, I must post myself on Canuck
> airs, for some of us devils may have to settle here shortly.

This was, of course, a reference to the fact that Booth planned to flee to Montreal when he had killed Lincoln. And all of his statements again make clear that he did not have mere kidnap on his mind; that he had deceived Arnold and O'Laughlen completely, as he would deceive the others who followed them.

Nervous at Booth's presence and anxious to avoid him, Thompson and Clay left that week for Quebec on the feeble excuse that they needed to see Governor General Monck on some form of official business. What they didn't know was that Monck was staying at the St. Lawrence Hall itself, for meetings with Lord Arthur Cecil from London and Lieutenant General Sir William Williamson, and had been there from October 8th. Told he was unavailable, but not where he was, on arrival in Quebec,

the visitors felt snubbed; Clay blamed Sanders' excessive prom-
ises of support from the British government for what was in fact
an absurd oversight on his part. Booth, working on Confederate
business with Sanders, Montreal blockade runner Patrick C. Martin and former Florida founding senator, James D. Westcott,
whose suite he used, met with George Augustus Sala, to whom
Sanders had told his plans of assassination in August.

Sala, whose presence at the hotel in the first two weeks of
October indicates that he was still, as at Niagara, combining work
for the London *Daily Telegraph* with spying for the Union, remembered Booth in his memoirs, published in 1895:

> He was a strikingly handsome man, dark, with a piercing gaze; but
> to me he appeared to be a chronic case of "whiskey in the hair,"
> and verging on delirium tremens.

Another who met Booth at the time was a New Hampshire
businessman, Hosea B. Carter, who stayed at the St. Lawrence
from early September to February 1, 1865. There he met the various commissioners, Sanders, Beverley Tucker, ex-General Carroll and ex-Senator Westcott but not, of course, Thompson and
Clay, who had so nervously absented themselves. He also met a
certain Clark, identified elsewhere as Marshal Clark, who may
have been a Clark, associated with an equally mysterious Johnston, who would afterward be connected by the authorities with
Lincoln's assassination. Carter told the court at the trial of the
conspirators in May, 1865 that he had frequently observed
George N. Sanders in intimate association with Booth, and others, in Montreal.

One statement Carter made was deliberately omitted from
the trial. On June 1, 1865, he told the War Department Committee that he had seen a treasonable but authorized cotton broker
he knew named David S. Ogden of Nassau and Pine Streets, in
New York, in company with Booth at St. Lawrence Hall the previous October; and that Ogden had said, after the assassination,
that it was the work of "Sanders and Co." The connection
between Booth and Ogden, a key figure in cotton trading with
the enemy, was, of course, by agreement between prosecution

and defense, to be eliminated from the hearings at all costs. A check of the St. Lawrence Hall guest register shows that Ogden was indeed there from October 7, 1864.

John Deveney, formerly a lieutenant in Company E, fourth Maryland Regiment, was in Montreal at the time; he is likely to have been spying for the Union, since so long a leave (from July until February) and in a luxury hotel is incomprehensible, especially in a foreign country. He said at the trial of the assassinations in May, 1865, that he had known Booth well before he saw him in Montreal; spotting him in the pillared lobby of St. Lawrence Hall, he asked him if he were going to perform in Montreal; Booth, foolishly giving away the fact that bringing his theatrical wardrobe north was a blind, said that he was not; that he had come to the city on a pleasure trip.

Deveney saw Booth in intimate conversation with Sanders; the two men stepped into Dowley's Bar for drinks. At the trial, Deveney let slip that he recognized Sanders and knew that Sanders had been Navy Agent in New York; this again suggests that Deveney may very well have been a Union spy.

At the same trial, William A. Wheeler, a liveryman of Chickopee, Massachusetts, stated:

> I was in Montreal when I saw John Wilkes Booth, who was standing outside St. Lawrence Hall. I spoke to Mr. Booth and asked him if he was going to open at the theatre there. He said he was not. He left me, and entered into conversation with a person who was pointed out to me as George N. Sanders.

It takes no leap of the imagination to see what Booth and Sanders were talking about. Since August, when he had laid his cards on the table to Colonel Ambrose Stevens, Sanders had needed a man bold enough to kill the President at close range. Sanders had not forgotten that the most serious attempts on Napoleon III by his friends Hippolyte Magen, Victor Frond and (later) Felice Orsini had been given a theatrical setting. What could be better than having an actor kill Lincoln in a theatre? It would be the culmination of dreams frustrated long before in England and France.

Proof of Sanders' intent can be found in a statement, also made at the trial, by a reliable witness, Captain Henry Finegas, an Irish-born Bostonian soldier who commanded the African-American Union regiment, the Third Louisiana Native Guards. Finegas said that early in February, 1865, he was sitting in the St. Lawrence Hall lounge when Sanders and William C. Cleary, Jacob Thompson's long-suffering young secretary, came in through the lobby door. Finegas heard Cleary say, "I suppose they are getting ready for the inauguration of Lincoln next month." And Sanders replied, "Yes, if the boys have any luck, Lincoln won't trouble them much longer." Cleary asked, "Is everything set?" And Sanders replied, "Oh yes; Booth is bossing the job."

Cross-examined by a defense counsel, who was greatly angered by this account, Finegas proved to be an expert and unshakeable witness; he correctly described Sanders as "low, thick set, with grayish curly hair, a grayish mustache and very burly form," omitting only the beard. Cleary he caught to the life: "Middle sized, with sandy hair; carried his head a little to one side."

That Booth had, at the time of his conversations with Sanders, confidence in certain members of the staff of Ford's Theatre in Washington that they would support any plans to kill at that location, is established by an incident that had taken place in February, 1864.

The story only surfaced 23 years later, when John W. Nichols, who at the time had been First Lieutenant in the 105th Pennsylvania Volunteers, Company K, which was part of the Presidential bodyguard, wrote in the Wheeling, West Virginia *Record,* on April 6, 1887, that he had been acquainted with Lincoln's regular coachman, Francis Bourke, who had served in the same capacity for James Buchanan.

Bourke was on leave—Nichols remembered it was sick leave—and was replaced with a certain Patterson McGee, who proved so domineering and irritating that he was let go; soon after his dismissal, he was seen skulking near the White House stables. Not long after that, the stables caught fire; McGee was believed to be the incendiary. Company K under Nichols was called out at once; they managed to save the Presidential coach, but not young Tad Lincoln's two ponies, or Secretary John M. Hay's beloved pair of carriage horses.

It emerged that the purpose of setting the blaze was to cause so great a distraction that Lincoln could be assassinated in a White House that would be deserted as the staff ran out to fight the flames. But McGee overlooked the fact that Lincoln had a backwoodsman's love of fire engines and had rushed to the scene as soon as the warning bell was sounded, thus saving his life.

Not a word of this episode appeared in the press at the time, undoubtedly because yet again Lincoln managed to suppress it. The most significant detail Nichols added in his article was this: McGee gave as his alibi that he was at Ford's Theatre on a job that night; and the staff there, to a man, unhesitatingly supported his assertion. The fact is that they were lying, Nichols made clear in his statement; it is easy to conclude that, as always, Lincoln wanted no arrest, trial, or questioning of these witnesses. Soon afterward, McGee went to British North America, and when, in late 1865, Beverley Tucker saw off his co-conspirator John Surratt to England, he also saw off McGee. Since the staff of Ford's had proved helpful before, surely at least some of them would be helpful again—indeed, their help would be essential if Booth were to carry out his plans.

Booth moved into St. Lawrence Hall on October 18. That he could now afford to do so is not surprising; nor is the fact that he dared an open association with Sanders. The Ontario Bank of Montreal remained a principal source of money, and of deposits, at the time; but so was the Niagara District Bank of which Clement C. Clay was the supposed chief clerk as J. Bevins Giles; and it is clear that Booth did not only receive money from the Montreal institution, as he had considerable sums when he left British North America.

In testimony at both the trial of the conspirators and the Surratt trial, the Ontario Bank chief teller, Robert A. Campbell, who didn't personally handle Booth's account, let slip a fact that was overlooked in both hearings: that he saw Booth a dozen times, which means that Booth was in the bank drawing or depositing moneys under other names than his own.

The amounts Campbell admitted him drawing only called for two visits and were comparatively modest; none of them was the equivalent of greenbacks or other negotiable currency, including local pounds, but rather sums drawn on the Merchants Bank, an American institution, for $425 (about 85 pounds) and a bill of exchange for 61 pounds (about $305), and some shillings, usable only if drawn on the Confederate Bank, Isaac Campbell's, in London. Booth's oft-quoted statement to Robert A. Campbell that he would "run the blockade" was absurd; he had no reason to run the blockade when his medical shipments were authorized. The implication that he intended going to England was also a blind; he never cashed the bill of exchange, which proves he didn't travel there and was far too well off to need the money.

THE DAY BEFORE BOOTH LEFT MONTREAL FOR FURTHER DEALINGS IN New York, and for rehearsals for a one-night benefit appearance, with his brothers Edwin and Junius, of *Julius Caesar* to raise funds for the new Shakespeare statue in Central Park, a group of letters was taken from the St. Lawrence Hall to Richmond. The carrier was the somber, good-looking spy, Richard Montgomery, who was, in fact, though trusted by the Canadian commissioners, an agent of Charles A. Dana, U.S. Assistant Secretary of War and of the National Detective Bureau leader, Colonel Lafayette C. Baker. He used the code name James Thompson, as if to suggest he was related to the Confederate commissioner.

Montgomery maintained the practice of taking the letters sent by Clay, Thompson, Tucker or Robert E. Coxe to the War Department in Washington, where they were steamed open and examined. Their contents copied and filed, they were resealed with an expertly fabricated copy of the original wax stamp, the envelopes replaced with identical ones; the paper, because it was of English make and watermark, was skillfully matched by a firm in London and shipped over for use.

On November 12, Major General Christopher Columbus Augur, commanding the Department of Washington, who reported directly to Dana and Baker, received several such letters from Montgomery via Colonel Horatio H. Wells, provost marshal of the region south of the Potomac. The first envelope contained two sheets of thin paper; the second contained three. Much of the letters concerned shipments of personal items to the South; amid some complaining from Clay about his isolation from his family, Clay wrote to his wife Virginia that he had sent to her, via a British ship, the *Ellen,* sailing from Halifax, and reaching the not yet fully blockaded port of Wilmington, various items of clothing, including dresses, stockings, gloves, collars and cuffs, and a "magnificent fan" from George Sanders. He went on to emphasize Robert E. Coxe's dealings on both sides of the war by telling her to send mail to Coxe's wife at Poughkeepsie, New York, signing her letters Caroline V. Tracy, an agreed-upon code name.

The most interesting and unsettling letter which his wife was to give to Benjamin, undoubtedly proved of interest to Augur, Dana, and Lafayette Baker, all of whom opposed Lincoln's trading with the enemy; it was composed by Beverley Tucker. It wasn't signed, but it can easily be determined as his because it contained a reference to his injured thumb, which he had accidentally almost cut off when in transit to British North America from England some months before.

In contrast to the fiery attacks on Lincoln in Clay's letter ("No people of Anglo-Saxon blood can long endure [his] usurpations and tyrannies") and threats of upheavals should he be re-elected ("[Democrats] must yield to a cruel despotism or fight. They feel it and know it."), Tucker's note was written with a more practical intent.

It referred to a plan to supply one half dollars and one half meat, for all the cotton that the Confederate government might feel inclined to dispose of; the trade, on both sides of the Mississippi, would be of advantage to Brigadier General Edmund Kirby Smith, commanding in that region:

> After this delivery, the way is perfectly clear to deliver anywhere within General [sic] Butler's department:
>
> It must of course be obvious to you (me) that a concession so great was made only with the understanding that it should be kept with the sacred secrecy; and although it presents upon its face a general rule for the sake of protecting the Executive (Mr. Lincoln,

to whom alone we are indebted), the main intention is that it
should be carried out by my (his) own friends and such others as
only will be useful to us. In order, then, that we may have the benefit from the arrangement, I would suggest that what may be done
shall be done in the name of a single individual, or his agent, so
far as the delivery of the supplies and the receipt of the cotton are
concerned; touching the disposition of the portion paid in funds,
this can be received and deposited as you [Benjamin] may determine—whether in the United States, or in Europe, or in the
Canadas, by instant conversion. To show how thoroughly the
enterprise has been arranged, there are now 10,000 barrels of
pork purchased and ready for shipment . . . it was proposed to get
me a pass to go through the lines, but in this I fear (we) have
failed, and the alternative course has been adopted, to wit, sending the goods by the hand of Mr. D. Preston Parr.

David Preston Parr was a Confederate agent, owner of the
Preston Parr China Halls in Baltimore, who would later, using
authorized trading with the enemy as a cover, engage as his special agent the Booth associate assassin, Lewis Powell (also known
as Lewis Paine.)

The letter went on:

The programme submitted commends itself to favorable consideration, as that it is endorsed by the highest official in the United States
government. Certainty of execution and expedition are thus secured
. . . where are we to look for these indispensable supplies, if not
through the cupidity and avarice of our enemies? . . . I have made a
contract with a party by which supplies of meat will be furnished at
Mobile by written permission of the President of the United States to
the free passage of the blockading fleet at that port . . . my contract
with the party is for the delivery of five million of pounds . . . *the President authorizes the breaking of the blockade.* (emphasis added)

When Montgomery handed over the note to Colonel Wells,
Wells in turn handed it to Dana and Baker. It was decided by all
concerned that immediate action must be taken. Not to stop the
trading itself; in view of the President's collusion, that would be

impossible. But they could, they were sure, kidnap Beverley Tucker, and after bringing him across the border on the false pretext of arranging for him a permit to travel in pursuit of his pork-for-cotton arrangements, grill him on the dangerous plans of the Canadian conspirators, and what he knew from spies of Union troop movements.

They embarked on an ingenious scheme. Posing as a sympathizer with trading with the enemy, Baker arranged meetings with some of Tucker's principal co-intriguers at the Astor House in New York, including Thomas C. Durant, wealthy pioneer head of the Union Pacific Railroad. At these meetings, held in Durant's luxurious suite, it was agreed that Baker would bring Tucker to Manhattan to conduct the North-South treasonable operation as he wished, on the permit he so strongly desired, and in return for this arrangement Durant would pay Baker $1,500 up front ($17,000) or more than three times his annual salary) and $10,000 ($113,000), on Tucker's guaranteed delivery. In addition, Durant promised that Dana, whom he thought they also had in their pocket, would arrange for Baker a Brigadier Generalship, a promise that must have caused that whimsical opportunist a great deal of amusement.

Baker decided he might as well make a feast of his mission and abduct not only Tucker but Thompson, Clay, Sanders and Cleary as well. In early November, Tucker arrived with one of his detectives in disguise at Niagara, and checked into the American House on the Union side of the Falls. He sent a messenger from the hotel to St. Catharines, to invite Coxe to come, with all of his associates, to a meeting, for which he would arrange the necessary permits. But already the Commissioners had smelled a rat; cannier than Durant and his colleagues, they knew what Baker was up to and had gone by train to Montreal.

Baker proved surprisingly naïve. He believed, on his return to Washington to obtain further instruction from Dana, that the reason the Commissioners moved to the St. Lawrence Hall was that Alexander Hamilton Stephens, Vice-President of the Confederacy, was stopping there, and they must meet with him at once. Actually, Stephens wasn't; he was in Georgia, exiled from Richmond because of his virulent criticism of the Administration.

Dana told Baker to waste no more time and go at once to Montreal, where he was to lure Tucker to North America, at the New York town of Rouse's Point. When Tucker arrived at St. Lawrence Hall, he checked in under a pseudonym and without further ado sent his card, with his real name, up to Tucker's room. Tucker replied in writing that he was still in bed, but Baker should go to George Sanders' room and await him there.

When Tucker appeared, Baker asked him if he was willing to cross the frontier, where he would be taken as promised to his friends in New York and Washington to run the trading-with-the-enemy operation with Lincoln's cooperation. Tucker hesitated; clearly, the temptation was great, but the risks of being double-crossed were equally great. Sanders walked in and asked Tucker to step outside.

Baker cooled his heels for over an hour while Sanders clearly advised Tucker, who must have put up an argument, not to go to New York. Finally, Tucker returned and told Baker that on "the advice of friends" he would not make the journey. Asked why, he used as an excuse that certain funds Thomas C. Durant had promised him had not materialized. Nevertheless, Tucker didn't want to close the door on the deal if there was the slightest chance Baker was on the level. He entertained him at a lavish dinner with wine, proudly handed Baker (who scarcely needed to see them) documents that showed him how trading with the enemy was enthusiastically supported in Richmond and Washington and that (referring back to his January 1864 contract) he was the authorized agent of the Confederate government and that he could guarantee a shipment of half a million bales of cotton. He told Baker that 60,000 bales were ready at that moment for shipping north across the Tombigbee River.

Tucker's bragging gave Baker more information than he had ever had before on treasonable trade, but he was unable to overcome Sanders' cautionings. Tucker stayed where he was, with David Preston Parr in Baltimore taking over as his North American agent.

Baker was powerless to arrest Parr because of an executive order from Lincoln issued on September 30, 1864 to Major General Edward R.S. Canby, of the West Mississippi army, and circulated in the War Department for all including Dana and Baker to read:

> Frequent complaints are made to me that persons endeavoring to bring in cotton in strict accordance with the trade regulations of the Treasury Department are frustrated by seizures by district attorneys, marshals and provost-marshals and others, on various pretenses, all looking to blackmail for spoils. I wish, if you would find the time, you would look into this matter with your department, and, finding these abuses to exist, break them up, in your power, so that fair dealings under the regulations may proceed.

Canby, a correct and dignified moralist, was appalled by this instruction and made sure that such regulations were circulated to Dana and other War Department officials. It shocked him that the Confederate army to which he was militarily opposed should be fed pork and bacon when otherwise they could have been starved into submission. He had written to Secretary of War Stanton on September 30 that:

> [Confederate Lieutenant General] Kirby Smith's army would have been disbanded six months ago were it not for the exportation of cotton made through [New Orleans] and other ports on the Mississippi River.

In November, while Dana was trying to figure a way to kidnap Beverley Tucker, Canby took to his bed in agony, not just from a war injury but from horror and shock at his President's misbehavior, which by now had resulted, as Lincoln admitted in a note to him on December 12, in the draining of the Union's entire gold supplies, which were now in George Trenholm's treasury in Richmond as a compensation for Fraser, Trenholm's loss of trade in the blockade. Max L. Heman Jr. wrote, in his family-authorized biography of Canby and with their expressed approval:

> The whole business was enough to make an honest man want to take to his couch in exasperation and disgust.

James P. Holcombe returned to Richmond with guarantees of substantial help in England; help which was supplied in plenty by Lord Wharncliffe, the Earl of Salisbury, and by Alexander Beresford-Hope MP. and James Spence; but he was lucky to survive the journey home. His ship foundered before she could make landfall through the blockade and his companion of the journey, the Confederate spy and hospitably received guest of the British aristocratic establishment, Rose Greenhow, drowned because of the heavy burden of gold coins she had placed inside a money belt around her waist. Holcombe spent the rest of the war trying to have the North Western states secede from the Union.

Clement C. Clay, despite his colleague Beverley Tucker's commercial collusion with the Union, wanted to best Thompson's ill-fated effort on Lake Erie; like Thompson, he fancied that an onslaught across the border would be seen by Secretary of State Seward as provoked by British interests, and that he would declare war as a result; if this seems a contradiction of Tucker's purpose, then it is to be considered that war would finally upset any possible exports to Britain of cotton, since the blockade would be doubled or tripled and the North would need more cotton than ever. Furthermore, Clay was sure that England would win, and restore to the South its appropriate power; once the blockade was raised, cotton could be sold not only to the North, but all over the world.

Clay therefore embarked, quite without support or approval from Thompson, Sanders, Benjamin or President Davis, on an ambitious plan to attack, rob and burn several cities of the North East. Richard Montgomery knew of the general details, but not of the specifics, since these were not conveyed in the messages he carried South. So Stanton, Dana, and their associates were uncertain which cities to defend.

After much research, Clay settled on his first target: the small town of St. Albans, population 3,000-odd and situated south of Montreal, near Lake Champlain, Vermont. It was an ideal objective because of its proximity to the Canadian border; it was within easy riding distance for experienced horsemen. Once the raid was completed, the brigands could escape to Montreal with the

Confederate figures *(beginning at the top, left to right)*: Judah P. Benjamin, Henry A. Wise,
R. Barnwell Rhett, Alexander H. Stephens, James M. Mason, Jefferson Davis, John B. Floyd,
John Slidell, William L. Yancey, Robert Toombs, and Isham C. Harris. 1864.

Scene of the great conspiracy, St. Lawrence Hall, Montreal (photograph circa 1865–70).

Jacob Thompson of Mississippi

Clement Claiborne Clay

Beverley Tucker

George Nicholas Sanders

Ward Hill Lamon

Thurlow Weed

Ulysses S. Grant,
Lieutenant-General, U.S.A.

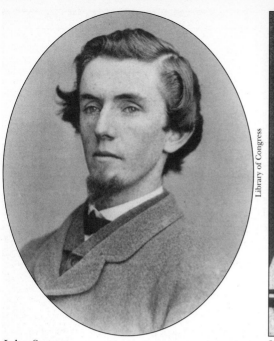

John Surratt

Mary Surratt

Surratt House: The boarding house of Mary Surratt, where the final assassination, or "kidnapping" plot was discussed by Booth.

The assassination of President Lincoln at Ford's Theater, and John Wilkes Booth's escape. 1865.

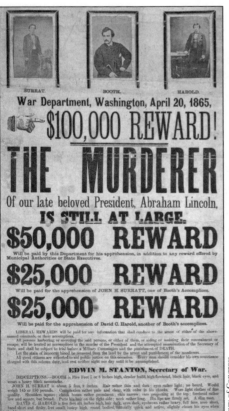

"$100,000 Reward! The Murderer of Our Late Beloved President, Abraham Lincoln, is Still at Large." Broadside including the photographs of John Surratt, John Wilkes Booth, and David Harold.

Illustrated eulogy for Abraham Lincoln.

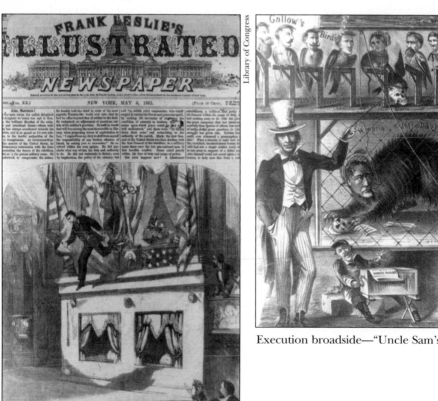

Execution broadside—"Uncle Sam's menagerie."

Illustration of Lincoln's assassination.

loot, then travel by easy stages through Copperhead or Confederate agencies to Halifax, where Benjamin Wier and Alexander Keith could send them by British blockade runner to Richmond. Quietly puritanical, St. Albans in 1864 was a sleepy, God-fearing little town. While the women folk churned and cooked and cleaned house and laundered, the men worked hard all week and, at weekends after church, went out hunting rabbit and partridge in the surrounding woods or fished or shot duck from skiffs in Lake Champlain's waters, rain or shine.

Clay, nervous as ever and half-afraid of his piratical enterprise, was certain it would meet with approval in Richmond; he chose his old friend Bennett H. Young to carry it out. Young would be given his second chance to demonstrate his virility by burning and robbing and killing. The stripling who had so notably failed in his attempt on Chicago in August would, Clay hoped, clean up his record with a display of piracy that on this occasion would actually work. From their first meeting in Halifax in May, Clay had believed in the young man's possibilities.

For Young, the opportunity was exciting; after meetings with Clay in Montreal he instantly reassembled his twenty-odd Confederate Retributors, the same sinewy cavalrymen, all but one from Kentucky, who could be relied upon to shoot to kill and ride till their horses dropped. There were the rich temptations of St. Catharines' square brick banks with their treasure of gold, silver and greenbacks; to youthful soldiers of fortune posing as authorized military men, the prospect was indeed exciting. Officially and for the record, Clay urged no killing or burning; hypocritical as ever, he knew perfectly well no town with healthy male citizens could be invaded without both destructive acts.

In his case, hypocrisy was matched by inefficiency, since he engaged, for use by his Retributors, a malodorous substance called Greek Fire concocted and bottled in cellars in Windsor, Ontario by a scientist with delusions of grandeur. Its namesake and precursor had been used in Ancient Greece, and after that at least until Napoleonic times; the Union had devised an effective version, used most conclusively in the fall of Vicksburg. But this new concoction, an addled and watered-down mixture of phosphorus, sulfur and naphtha, placed in bottles that could be

smashed in rooms or against buildings, was as useless a destructive agent as soda water. Since Windsor was a vespiary of Union
spies, it is likely that the manufacturer, a certain Richard C. Bock-
ing, was also serving the enemy.

Bennett H. Young arrived in St. Albans in early October,
when the leaves were turning gold and there was an autumn chill
in the air. This overgrown militant choirboy with china-blue eyes
and a hefty athletic physique, caused female hearts to flutter as
he took rooms as the Tremont House Hotel, a noxious hostelry
which George Augustus Sala, who had stopped there the previous December, described in terms scarcely to be found in a
newspaper advertisement.

The smell of smoke permeated the place, from the common
furnace and the kerosene lamps in the rooms; the cooking was
appalling in a restaurant which the miserly owner Samuel B.
Skinner opened seldom, and then only to serve meat as indi-
gestible as what Sala called fried ear of Ethiop; instead of paint-
ings on the walls of public rooms and corridors there were
recruiting posters and announcements of a resident prophetess
and clairvoyant complete with turban and crystal ball, who on
this occasion proved unsuited to her chosen profession: she
smelled no rat in Bennett H. Young, nor saw any prospect of
what he might do to her town.

In a hotel where Vermont Prohibition rules reigned, and the
female guests were not seen toying with anything more interesting than a goblet of lemonade, Young provided an instant tonic.
Sexual arousal disguised behind fluttering fans, the female resi-
dents listened, entranced, to Young's *ex tempore* Bible readings,
and to his interpretations based upon a religious college training, while they drank in his square shoulders and well-muscled
arms and legs.

One young lady was so carried away by his pretentious
charms that she allowed herself to walk with him hand in hand
on the village green. He used the opportunity to make a survey
of every foot of the town, from banks to stores to stables from
which horses could be stolen. And all with a view to seeing how
they could be robbed or burned with the optimistic use of Greek
Fire.

Soon, Young's Retributors arrived, by stagecoach or train, or boat across the lake, and all proved popular with men and women alike. They posed as members of a hunting, shooting and fishing Sportsmens' Club in Montreal, an egregious invention calculated to put everyone at ease. Nobody questioned why they didn't bring flybait and tackle and well-tested rods; why they didn't carry rifles but .36 Navy Colt revolvers scarcely suitable for shooting ducks, and why they cleaned out the two gunshops in town within days of their arrival, when there were better and cheaper weapons available in Montreal.

For Young and his men, impatient to start their day of arson and pillage, there was the question of an appropriate date for the attack. Young soon found that the day not to strike was Butter Day, October 18, the Wednesday mid-week market day when the town was filled with visitors eager to snap up bargains of meat and milk and lard, kitchen utensils, garden implements, cows and pigs. The day to attack was Thursday, when the Vermont Governor J. Gregory Smith, who lived there, and older men not fit for war, were in attendance in larger towns like Burlington at meetings on New England legislative issues.

Armed with Colts and rifles, and with bottles of Greek Fire, Young and the Retributors had an early morning meeting on strategy at the Tremont House on October 19. As sunlight faded early, and black cumulus clouds fat with autumn rain filled the sky, Young told his team to strike the banks first, a few seconds before 3 P.M., when the managers would be in the process of closing the doors.

By mid-afternoon, a cold breeze blew down the unpaved streets and there was a speckle or two of rain on the puddles that survived from a recent storm. As three o'clock struck, Young stood on the front porch of the American House and fired his Navy Colt revolver twice, with a loud announcement that the city was now in Confederate hands. The passers-by thought it was a young man's folly, because nobody stopped to challenge him. While several of his team began hustling citizens at gunpoint onto the Village Green, others had invaded the banks in twos and threes.

Tipsy from bootleg alcohol to give them Dutch courage, two men marched into the St. Albans Bank as teller Cyrus T. Bishop was counting up the deposits. They pulled out their Colts and told him their purpose, showing him their Confederate uniform buttons sewn for identification into their gray civilian topcoats.

Bishop was no piker. Instead of obeying the demand for money, he ran to the back room containing the safe and tried to slam the door. The invaders pushed it open and lyingly announced that they were soldiers in the "army" of Major General Jubal A. Early, of North Virginia Valley District. They said they had come to avenge the South for the scorched earth policy of Sherman and Sheridan. ("If you stir or make resistance we will blow your brains out.")

Neither Bishop nor any member of his staff wanted to lose their brains; they had the common sense to use them instead. They sat meekly while the Retributors stuffed their Morocco leather saddle bags with silver and greenbacks to the tune of at least $75,000 ($853,000 and up).

A second team burst into the Franklin County Bank where they announced an identical military excuse as they bundled cashier Marcus W. Beardsley and his staff into the vault along with a last-minute customer; they made off with $80,000 ($910,000.)

The third detachment of raiders invaded the First National Bank, where Major General John N. Nason, an 82-year-old veteran of the War of 1812, was sitting next to the stove immersed in a newspaper. While the intruders held the staff at gunpoint and rifled the safe of some $55,000 ($626,000), the old man continued reading: he looked up only once to remark, succinctly, "This isn't fair." One raider was prepared to shoot him for the comment, but another said he was too ancient to be bothered with. When the Retributors left with their saddle bags stuffed, the military veteran observed coolly, "Seems to me those men are rather rude in their general behavior."

Up at the Governor's mansion, Mrs. J. Gregory Smith, first lady of Vermont, got wind of the raiders and searched her house from attic to cellar for guns. She could only come up with a single empty pistol; she stood on her front porch holding it in an attitude of defiance. At the same time she told her staff to intercept any attempt to take horses from her stables, and to make those same steeds available to any posse that might be formed.

When portrait photographer Leonard L. Cross asked a raider jovially, "What are you trying to celebrate?" he was rewarded with a bullet through his hat. Jeweler Collins N. Huntingdon refused to let the Retributors rob his store. Undeterred, his assailants shot him through the cheek. He recovered, but Elinus J. Morrison, who was building a new hotel, did not. Shot in the stomach as he sought the unreliable shelter of Miss Beatty's Millinery Store, he died two days later.

One spinster, holding her hooped skirt firmly down as best she could, climbed up an apple tree and refused to descend. At St. Albans' Academy for Children, Principal Dorsey Taylor assembled his pupils from their rooms and addressed them in the main hall with the scarcely necessary words, "Little dears, wicked men are doing very bad things here."

A visitor, the 47-year-old but able-bodied Captain George P. Conger, recently retired from the First Vermont Cavalry, had just arrived by buggy to visit his brother who kept a bootleg saloon, when he stumbled into the siege. By coincidence, the first raider he ran into was Bennett H. Young himself. When Young asked him his business, he refused to answer; Young grabbed him but he broke free, raced all over town and managed to whip up a posse from the few men available. He armed them with everything from ancient muskets to pitchforks and somehow rustled up a few stable horses that Young had overlooked.

It was time for Young to get out of town. As the thin fall drizzle slowly increased to rain, and there were distant rumbles of thunder, he and his Retributors, their saddlebags filled to bursting, mounted their horses and threw the bottles of Greek Fire to smash uselessly against buildings. Young had mapped out the escape route thoroughly but the rain increased and the road soon turned to mud; and now their pursuers were busy firing through the storm.

The journey was difficult. The horses Young had stolen were not used to being ridden hard and by cavalrymen; they were work or recreation horses, accustomed to trotting, not sustained galloping and the brutal thrust of spurs. Tree branches from recent winds strewed the ground and the river bridges were narrow and rotted with age. The hard-pressed mounts, foaming at their bits, soon had to give up, and Young lost precious time replacing them in villages and farms.

The pursuers had no better a time of it; their own horses were in a worse state and had also to be replaced, albeit with the locals' willing co-operation.

Once the bedraggled posse, drenched to the skin and fractious to a degree, reached the border of British North America, in obedience to general orders issued by the War Department and issuing from the President, they should have stopped right there. To cross with armed men was in a breach of neutrality, but Conger insisted on going on, swimming his horses across a boiling river and dodging bullets all the way to Frelighsburg.

Young took shelter in a farmhouse; as he was warming himself by the fire, a dozen of Conger's team burst in and carried him into a wagon. Young broke free, seized the reins and drove the wagon down the road, spilling off any of the men who were still aboard. But the posse recovered, overtook him on horseback and held him down; pleading neutrality to a British officer who turned up at that moment, Young escaped being taken back for hanging in St. Albans and instead went under British warrant to Phillipsburg and St. Johns, where he and his companion highwaymen received a warm welcome from the pro-Confederate militia.

As soon as news of the raid was telegraphed to Washington, Secretary of State Seward used the occasion as Clay had hoped, to threaten England with retaliatory action. Similarly, for the first time since the *Trent* incident, the British government made serious warlike noises and sent contingents to strengthen the Canadian border. It was now most urgent that Clay make sure the British North American authorities find the Retributors innocent of any wrongdoing, so as to exacerbate the ill feeling between Whitehall and Washington.

He must make it clear that the raiders were authorized in Richmond and given the support of the Canadian government, even though they most emphatically were not. In order to bring this off, he engaged the services of the man with whom he still had the least rapport either temperamentally or politically, George Nicholas Sanders, while he himself made plans to head for the South as soon as possible.

Sanders, leaving Booth at St. Lawrence Hall, took the train to St. Johns with Charles Coursol, the judge he would bribe in short order to clear the Retributors. Thompson was furious. Not only had Clay upstaged him by bringing off a theft of $88,273 (or one million dollars today) but he hadn't bothered to inform him so he could share in the loot. As for Clay, he had to make sure that Judah P. Benjamin and Jefferson Davis supplied documents lying that they had authorized the raid. To this end, he sent Richard Montgomery south; to make sure the message did not reach Richmond, Montgomery in November, while still in delayed transit, was subjected to an artificial arrest and placed in jail in Washington, only to stage a fraudulent escape soon afterward.

Clay cooked up a fake order signed by himself and backdated to October 5, which could be used as evidence in Court. Money was forthcoming for the raiders' defense, not, of course, from the infuriated Thompson, but from Clay's Niagara District Bank in St. Catharines, courtesy J. Bevins Giles, namely himself. More money was raised by ex-Senator Westcott and even more by the chief Confederate supporter in London, Lord Wharncliffe, chairman of the Southern Independence Association.

So large a sum was raised by these helpful friends that Clay and Sanders could afford to engage the accomplished John J. Abbott, former Solicitor General of Quebec and later Prime Minister of the federated commonwealth of Canada, as chief counsel for the defense, backed by an able team not normally accustomed to taking up the cause of piracy. The Judge would be Charles Coursol; he really wasn't a judge at all but a police justice, no more than a stipendiary magistrate, who had risen to his present lack of eminence up a worm-eaten ladder of corruption and incompetence. A barrister who failed to secure a single brief, he was the catspaw of political manipulators who had him wheedled onto the bench where he proved as bribable as he was undistinguished. He was Sanders-fodder; no doubt of it.

Instead of being dragged ignominiously into jail, the Retributors, transferred by private car on the train to Montreal, were greeted by the Mayor and aldermen as if they were important visitors, and crowds cheered them in driving rain from the sidewalks as carriages took them to the city prison, flanked by a full dress detachment of British soldiers. Sanders had made sure they would not be given cells but redecorated visitors' rooms and staff rooms, comfortably or even luxuriously furnished at considerable expense; he had the finest of food and wine brought in from Montreal's best French restaurants; he supplied attractive women who were delighted to provide nights of pleasure for the dashing young cavalrymen. Sanders' next task was to make sure, through bribery and various forms of coercion, that the thieves were treated carefully at any subsequent trial, and would never be found guilty.

On October 26, he published a letter in the Montreal *Evening Telegraph* lying that the raid was ordered by the Confederate government, and that it was conducted "without unnecessary violence." However, he made a slip when he added that "as soon as the fact of Lieutenant Young's demonstration shall be known in Richmond there is no doubt that the Government will take immediate steps to make their responsibility of and approval of the enterprise well known"—thus letting out the fact that they hadn't known in the first place.

As he issued similar manifestoes to the New York press, Sanders was busy counting the spoils: the sum of $88,273 was accounted for; a good deal more had been lost in transit, spilled from the saddle bags to lighten the horses' loads, spent in quantity when farmers refused on pain of death to yield up their steeds. With Coursol taken care of financially, Sanders had to be sure of the French-Canadian police chief, Guillaume Lamothe. Coursol and the local Copperhead John Bruce, a merchant from Baltimore, met with Sanders and Lamothe outside the Donegana and St. Lawrence Hall hotels; Lamothe assured Sanders that, although he must by law temporarily keep the money, he had no doubt that the prisoners would be released, and the money returned.

Sanders accepted the arrangement. He handed over a carpetbag into which he had stuffed the entire amount. Lamothe took the bag to the Ontario Bank at once. The go-between in the arrangements was the Confederate agent John Porterfield, and a dummy agency called, impudently, Davis and Company, that allegedly acted as stockbrokers across the street from St. Lawrence Hall.

After much rummaging through law books, attorney John J. Abbott and his team found a convenient loophole through which the raiders could squeeze. Coursol would state, after much pretended deliberation following rival counsels' opening arguments at a preliminary hearing, that he had no jurisdiction to try the case, since any warrant of arrest had to be signed by Lord Monck as Governor General. Busy in Quebec with Federation meetings, Lord Monck had not thought it necessary to exercise this rule, and in fact, the then British Prime Minister Lord Palmerston, along with Foreign Secretary Lord John Russell, had, in 1861, given Monck an unofficial authority to exercise it or not. It remained only for Sanders to bribe Lamothe, and everything could proceed according to his carefully laid plans.

WHILE THE CORRUPTION OF CANADIAN OFFICIALS CONTINUED APACE, Booth left for New York at the turn of November; clearly under request not to carry out his plans against the President until March, when the Ides should prove happily coincidental, because, at present, Lincoln was more useful to Clay and Tucker alive than dead. However, and unbeknownst to both, the Chicago detective Allan Pinkerton and with him Lincoln's bodyguard Ward Hill Lamon, still benefiting from trading with the enemy, were convinced that assassination was on the minds of certain powerful individuals in New York, and before the election on November 8, which looked to be a Lincolnian landslide.

Those behind this conspiracy were alleged to be the leading Northern Copperheads—those who ironically were shut out by their disloyalty from across-the-war trading deals with the enemy. On October 26, when Lafayette Baker was making plans to take a train to Niagara for the attempted abduction of Thompson, Clay, Sanders, Cleary and Beverley Tucker, George B. McClellan, who still had a stubborn hope of winning the election, called upon his cherished aide, Edward H. Wright, at Wright's father's house in New York City, bringing with him a message from McClellan's former aide, Detective Allan Pinkerton, who had saved Lincoln from assassination in Baltimore in the spring of 1861, asking Wright to meet with him as soon as possible.

Wright was to take the train to Philadelphia and wait in the lobby of the Continental Hotel; someone would appear who would identify himself as Pinkerton's agent. If he did not, then Wright was to continue to Baltimore, where he would await, at Barnum's Hotel, another messenger.

Wright went obediently to Philadelphia where he met with Dr. John McClellan, the candidate's brother, and with the recently-resigned Brigadier General Andrew Porter, former Provost Marshal of the Potomac, who was due shortly to leave for Paris, and greatly disliked Lincoln. Nobody turned up at the Continental Hotel, so Wright proceeded to Baltimore where, after a long wait in the Barnum's lobby, a man met him and took him to the back of the building; Pinkerton was waiting for him upstairs in a small house.

Pinkerton told him that a group of McClellan's friends and supporters, including August Belmont, the Wood brothers and the writer George Tincknor Curtis, had plans afoot to assassinate Lincoln and that he, Wright, was with them in that intent. Furious, Wright hurried to McClellan's home in Orange, New Jersey, and told him what Pinkerton had said. McClellan dismissed the idea out of hand.

What Pinkerton hadn't revealed was that the plot was known to the Marshal of the District of Columbia, Ward Hill Lamon in Washington, who was scarcely likely to have made it up; McClellan's dismissal of the idea undoubtedly stemmed from Pinkerton's overestimation of Confederate troops that had earlier stumbled McClellan's military career. On October 24, Lamon had seen Pinkerton in Washington by the detective's urgent request; the two men had met at Willard's Hotel, and had gone for a carriage ride along 14th Street. Lamon told Pinkerton that there was a plan in place to kill Lincoln and seize the government. Pinkerton at first refused to believe in the scheme, which had just been exposed by Lafayette Baker, but Lamon assured him that it did exist, and that Lincoln was aware of it.

Lamon made clear that leading Democrats at the Chicago convention (that meant Belmont and the Woods) were implicated and that Pinkerton must act to expose them, even though he was a McClellanite Democrat. Pinkerton insisted on seeing

Lincoln to receive orders in person but Lamon, who knew only too well the President's antipathy to disclosing assassination plans to anyone, would not allow it. But Pinkerton went ahead with his warning.

That the group of Copperheads being investigated by Lamon and Pinkerton saw a willing instrument in Booth is clear from a convincing report filed by an anonymous party, and sent to Secretary of War Stanton after the Lincoln assassination (May 15, 1865). It read:

> General McClellan, A. Belmont, Fernando Wood, Charles A. Haswell [ship designer and secessionist], and Jeremiah Larocque [law partner of the Copperhead Samuel Barlow], were all cognizant of the conspiracy to murder President Lincoln, yourself, and Secretary Seward. These parties, I learn through a servant in Belmont's employ, were all together at a supper at Belmont's house with J. Wilkes Booth in November last.

And what of the guest list? What evidence is there that these men could have discussed with Booth over wine and cigars the proposed murder of the President? Each, certainly, had a motive.

McClellan's airy dismissal of Pinkerton's warnings and denunciations of Belmont speaks for itself; it was his duty to at least report the matter to Washington and to take it up with Belmont and Curtis. But Belmont had backed him to the limit in the election and he had taken a massive bet McClellan would win; certainly McClellan, after his dismissal by Lincoln from his beloved army, would have no motive to refuse to attend so conspiratorial a meeting.

Jeremiah Larocque was senior partner in the Copperhead New York City law firm of Shipman, Barlow, Larocque and Choate; he was among the financial group, along with his prominent partner Samuel Barlow, controlling the Copperhead New York *World*, whose youthful editor, Manton Marble, had been privy to the Niagara conspiracy discussion of August last, and had done nothing about reporting it, even unofficially, to Washington, simply advising McClellan of Dean Richmond's warnings to the conspirators to stay where they were. Larocque, Barlow and Marble had invented a non-existent newspaper, *The Essex Statesman,* to reprint in the *World* a report that Lincoln had exulted in the field of death at Antietam, had slapped Ward Hill Lamon on his knee and had joined Lamon in a tasteless ditty named "Picayune Butler." The fraud almost earned Marble a jail sentence and resulted in the *World's* offices being temporarily closed on Lincoln's personal instruction. Larocque had every reason to see Lincoln dead.

As for Haswell, he suffered greatly from Lincoln's blockade; he was unable to export his ship designs to England or France, and his merchant vessels and their cargoes were hampered by similar restrictions. The same North Atlantic Blockading squadron under Rear Admiral Lee until November, 1864, that allowed trading with the enemy, stumbled almost every enterprise in which he was involved.

In various testimonies under oath at the trial of John Surratt, the informer Louis Weichmann stated that Booth had mentioned being entertained in New York at "an elegant mansion," certainly not a proper description of the merely comfortable townhouse where he normally stayed with his brother Edwin, and that he mingled with "senators and congressmen." This lends support to the picture of his being entertained at August Belmont's house on Fifth Avenue, arguably the most exquisitely appointed residence in the city.

David Black, the world authority on Belmont, and author of the best available biography, *The King of Fifth Avenue,* cast some doubt on the story in his 1981 book, but now regrets that he did. He today believes unequivocally in the anonymous report's authenticity; he points out that Belmont suffered greatly from Lincoln's blockade against exports; the Belmont tobacco lay rotting on the New Orleans wharves. One might add that while prohibited from shipping to England and France, Belmont was handicapped by the uselessness of the Rothschild-owned Alabama State bonds and the fact that he could not ship cotton North, as his Copperhead position precluded him from sharing in the spoils.

Further, one could mention that Lincoln supported Benito Juarez, Mexican revolutionary, who threatened Rothschild's interests in Mexico, as well as the life of the puppet emperor

Maximilian, whose backer, Napoleon III, was very much in the pockets of the Rothchilds in France.

If Booth was indeed at this summit meeting, how did he enter so elevated a circle? The only explanation is that Sanders got wind of its plans, and sent Booth to Belmont, his old friend, who owed him so heavy a debt, going back to the days of Belmont's consulate at the Hague.

That by now the War Department under Stanton was fully aware of Booth's trading in medical supplies as a cover for his activities is clear from two cryptic entries in the Department's letter book indexes, designed to give a picture of correspondences which, in this instance, were either stolen or suppressed. On November 14, the day before Major General Butler left for New York, and Booth was headed from Manhattan to Washington, the following entry appeared:

Doctor J. W. Booth appeals.

The reply, from British North America, appeared on November 17:

J. Thompson. Referring to physicians.

By mid-November, Booth was more easily able to travel on preliminary plans for his escape after Lincoln's proposed March assassination since the Governors of Massachusetts and Western Virginia, both useful crossing points, were involved in trading with the enemy.

Whether through Allan Pinkerton's discoveries or not, there was no attempt on Lincoln's life before Election Day on November 8. An additional deterrent was supplied by the ever-reliable Major General Dix, who summoned reinforcements to prevent any possible uprising in New York City in repetition of the Draft Riots of July, 1863.

Dix summoned to his aid Major General Benjamin Franklin Butler, that chief beneficiary of trading with the enemy, who had nothing to gain by supporting Governor of New York Horatio Seymour, but it was already clear that Seymour would lose the

November 8 gubernatorial election to Congressman and former logger and merchant Reuben E. Fenton, who in fact did win on November 8, and was an eminent member of the trading-with-the-enemy clique. Butler first set up his headquarters, as he surrounded New York by water, at the Astor House, but this was a mistake; it was the center of the trading with the enemy, the meeting place, just days earlier, of Lafayette Baker with Thomas C. Durant. Sagely, Butler moved to the Hoffman House, whose owners could be trusted.

He stayed in place until Lincoln was re-elected, leaving on November 15, when a peculiar episode occurred.

That same afternoon, a young widow, Mary Hudspeth, who had recently moved into town and had taken up a small store in Harlem, boarded the Third Avenue streetcar near her home with her nine-year-old daughter, heading south for her brokers at Nassau Street, which intersected with Wall Street, to deposit some gold earned from sales to customers, and to stop and mail some letters at the Nassau Street General Post Office.

After settling her hooped skirts and preparing for the journey, Mrs. Hudspeth overhead two men talking next to her. One man was clearly a gentleman; his one ungloved, small, white hand and general demeanor indicated that.

The other man was shorter and stouter in build; he had the rough, unrefined look of a man who labored for a living. The refined man said he was leaving for Washington next day; the roughneck, whom the first man addressed as Johnson, said he was leaving for Newburgh, or Newburn, Mrs. Hudspeth wasn't sure.

Then she saw something peculiar. The streetcar jolted at an intersection, and the gentleman was jarred back against his seat. At that moment, his hair moved; it was obviously a wig; and it showed a white forehead. His beard also appeared to be false and moved with it, so insecurely had it been affixed to his chin. She saw he had a scar, invisible to her at first because of the beard, near the jaw bone.

The two men continued in words they knew would be overheard, and couched in tones scarcely suitable for those with dangerous thoughts who wished to keep them a secret. Johnson was angry because he had not been allowed to perform some unnamed violent act, but had instead been asked to convey the plans for such an act to a third party ("I wish it had fallen to me to do what had to be done in Washington.")

Talk of danger to the newly-elected President was very much in the air, and Mrs. Hudspeth was on her mettle to catch every word, especially since she was now convinced the elegant man was the famous John Wilkes Booth. The two men left the street-car at different stopping points; as Johnson got up, he dropped the letter his companion had handed him and it landed on Mrs. Hudspeth's hooped skirt. She didn't notice it, but her daughter observantly did; it was sticking out of the hem.

Mrs. Hudspeth, thinking it was one of her own and not notic-ing the envelope was blank instead of inscribed in her hand, tucked it into her pocket with the rest of the correspondence to be mailed. It was only when she and her daughter reached Nas-sau Street that she noticed the discrepancy and, rather oddly for a well-brought-up lady, instead of taking it to the streetcar com-pany's lost-and-found department, opened it—it was unsealed— and read it. It didn't, of course, occur to her, after she perused its remarkable contents, that the missive would, if it were indeed dangerous to the President, have surely been written in code. And would the great Booth be riding on a streetcar?

The letter was, she saw, written in a shaky, odd, round hand-writing, as if by a sick person using a pen with thick black ink. Clumsy and hastily-done, it suggested that its author was either drunk or disturbed or both.

It was signed Charles Selby; unless Mrs. Hudspeth was famil-iar with the British theatre it is unlikely that she knew Selby, who had died the year before, thus rendering his signature invalid, was the adapter of *The Marble Heart,* in which for years Booth had delighted audiences.

The letter, addressed to a certain person named Louis, read as follows:

> The time has at last come that we have all so wished, for upon you
> everything depends. As it was decided before you left Memphis we
> were to cast lots; accordingly we did so and you are to be the Char-
> lotte Corday of the nineteenth century. When you remember the

awful solemn vow that was taken by us, you will feel there is no drawback—Abe must die, and now. You can choose your weapons. The cup, the knife, the bullet. The cup failed us once and might again.

Johnson, who will give [you] this, has been like an enraged demon since the meeting because it has not fallen upon him to rid the world of the monster. He says the blood of his gray-haired father and his noble brother call up on him for revenge, and revenge he will have; if he cannot wreak it upon the fountainhead, he will upon some of the blood-thirsty generals. Butler would suit him. As our plans were all concocted and well arranged we separated. And as I am writing, on my way to Detroit, I will only say that all rests upon you. You know where to find your friends. Your disguises are so perfect and complete that *without one knew your face* no police telegraphic dispatch would catch you. The English gentleman, *Harcourt,* must not act hastily. Remember, he has ten days. Strike for your home, strike for your country; bide your time, but strike sure. Get introduced, congratulate him, listen to his stories; not many more will the brute tell to wealthy friends. Do anything but fail, and meet us at the appointed place within the fortnight. Enclose this note together with one of poor Leenea. I will give the reason for this when we meet. Return by Johnson. I wish I could go to you, but duty calls me to the West; you will probably hear from me in Washington, no good in Canada. Believe me, your brother in love, CHARLES SELBY.

Mrs. Hudspeth turned to the second letter. It read:

Dearest Husband, Why do you not come home? You left me for ten days only and you have been from home more than two weeks. In that long time you sent me one short note—a few cold words, and a check for money, which I did not require. What has come over you? Have you forgotten your wife and child? Baby calls for papa till my heart aches. *We are so lonely* without you. I have written to you again and again, and, as a last resort, yesterday wrote to Charlie, begging him to see you and tell you to come home. I am so ill—not able to leave my room; if I was, I would go to you, wherever you are, *if in this world.* Mamma says I must not write any

more, as I am too weak. Louis, darling, do not stay away any longer
from your heart-broken wife. LEENEA.

Mrs. Hudspeth in her innocence evidently didn't think that
not only do would-be assassins who were famous actors not normally convey their intentions in conversations on streetcars, but
they wouldn't as a rule drop vital evidence of their intentions on
ladies' skirts to be picked up by enterprising daughters with better eyesight than their mothers'. No doubt with pulses pounding,
Mary hastened, as soon as she had deposited her gold and posted
her mail, to the Hoffman House hotel which, as an assiduous
reading of the newspapers must have told her, was where Major
General Butler was stationed. The fact that he was mentioned in
the Selby letter as a target was sufficient reason for her to make
the unscheduled journey.

Once arrived, she was told that Butler had left the city with
his military entourage on the late morning train. Undeterred,
and remarkably well-informed, she asked to see another guest of
that elegant hostelry, the venerable Virginian Old Fuss and
Feathers, General Winfield Scott, who lived there on full retirement pay and unchanged rank, consoling himself in luxury for
being too heavy and too old to any longer get onto a horse.

Mrs. Hudspeth was advised that General Scott would be
pleased to see her. Moments later, she was in his suite of rooms
and more than ready to tell her exciting story. Intrigued, the
Grand Old Man asked her to read him the two letters she
brought with her. The afternoon light was fading and his eyes
weren't what they used to be. She dutifully obliged; the General
urged her to take them, without further ado, to Major General
Dix. And so, obediently, she did; it had been a full day, and she
and her daughter returned to the humdrum life of Harlem.

Dix examined the two letters carefully. The first, he was sure,
was a hoax got up for one of the Sunday newspapers, but the
painful and sentimental accompanying missive gave him pause.
He took the notes by train to Washington, where he handed
them over to Edwin Stanton, who in turn took them to Lincoln.

Lincoln's response remained unknown to all but those present until it was mentioned in a letter sent to the State Department

by Minister to Japan John A. Bingham, former Congressman and prosecutor of the assassins of the President, on June 27, 1878, and published in the Diplomatic Records after that. The Chief Executive's response, as he added the letters to the bulging file marked ASSASSINS that now replaced an overcrowded pigeon hole in his desk, was that if it was decreed he should die by the hands of an assassin, then it must be so, whatever precautions might be taken to avert that purpose. Once again, not a word of that response appeared in the press; and Booth was not even questioned.

Who could have engineered so elaborate a hoax, designed to frame Booth and whoever Louis was—"Louis Napoleon" Thompson perhaps? Or Louis O'Donnell? Or George Sanders' son Lewis, or son-in-law Louis Contri?—but none of these four had wives in St. Louis. A clue can be found in *Lincoln in the Telegraph Office,* the Civil War memoirs of David H. Bates, assistant to Thomas T. Eckert, head of that office, who was in collusion with Lafayette Baker.

Bates, while omitting any mention of the Hudspeth affair, unwittingly let the cat out of the bag on page 298, in the chapter headed Conspirators in Canada. He wrote that on November 26, while on his way to the Cortlandt Street Ferry, at the southernmost point of Manhattan Island and among the sites replaced by the ill-fated World Trade Center, he was riding a streetcar when, to quote Bates directly:

> He found an unsealed envelope containing, among other papers, a letter, giving directions, evidently referring to a kidnapping plot, and also a picture of Lincoln, with a rope around his neck, and red ink-marks on the bosom of the shirt. These were afterwards found to belong to Payne (Lewis Powell, alias Paine, Booth's later co-assassin.)

That this was an outright fraud is clear, and links Eckert directly (with Baker, who was in New York) to the Selby hoax as well. Lewis Powell was in Virginia at the time, just about to leave the command of Lieutenant John Singleton Mosby, and shortly to turn up in Richmond. There is no evidence that Eckert was in

Manhattan making his way to a ferry that would only take him to the uninteresting location of Governor's Island, when the President insisted on daily meetings in Washington. And again, such threatening letters are scarcely to be found conveniently on streetcars.

At the trial of the Lincoln assassins in May, 1865, and two years later at the trial of John Surratt, Bates, more telegraph clerk than calligraphy expert, despite his reputation to the contrary, testified that the handwriting of the Charles Selby letter was Booth's, although altered for the occasion; Booth had several styles of script but the note does not sufficiently resemble any of them, and was clearly an imitation of the form he used when writing hasty memoranda not pitched in Confederate box code. Thus, Bates was a party to the conspiracy.

Eckert, in a skillful move, made himself Paine's sole guardian when Paine awaited execution in prison the following summer. He was thus able to concoct the story that Paine told him, *in extremis,* that the letter had been lost at the time; that he was supposed to have helped set fire to the city; that he had refused and instead had gone to see Booth on stage in *Julius Caesar* on November 25, the day before the note so conveniently appeared. And what was that fiery plot?

SIX

HOW TO BURN NEW YORK

Jacob Thompson had shown signs of mental disturbance for months; his mishandling of the Chicago and Lake Erie incidents had left him in feverish spirits; the burning of his plantation in Oxford, Mississippi had devastated him; his long separation from his family and lack of written support from Richmond had weighed him down; and now there was the blow that Clay had upstaged him by bringing off the St. Albans Raid. Worse, he obtained no financial benefit from the raid; greedy as ever, he must have fumed that the loot, to which he was not personally entitled, was locked up in a carpetbag in a vault in the very bank in Montreal in which he deposited his payments from Liverpool, London, and the South. And he enjoyed no share of Beverley Tucker's trading with the enemy.

So now he must make one desperate last fling, with the Confederacy starting most seriously to crumble after the fall of Atlanta, to prove his manhood—that mid-19th century obsession. He would, in short, set fire to Manhattan.

What he hoped to achieve by this, except establishing himself as an arsonist and mass murderer, is unclear. To infuriate the people of New York by destroying their public buildings and places of amusement could only alienate them from any possibility of seceding, as the Wood brothers had so dearly wished.

Once again, he enlisted hotheaded young men of the same stripe as Bennett H. Young to carry out his purposes. These young and dashing soldiers, smarting from the death of Brigadier General John Hunt Morgan, their beloved Commander of East Tennessee, who had been surprised and killed at Greeneville in that state on September 4, dearly wanted revenge. To them, no doubt, the threat of disrupting trade with the South or annoying major collaborators in Manhattan never occurred. Unlike Young, who disguised his piracy behind a mask of patriotism, they wanted to destroy the city in order to show the North a thing or two.

Their names were Lieutenant Colonel Robert M. Martin, and Lieutenant John W. Headley; to their number, Thompson added a third and still more fanatical recruit: Captain Robert Cobb Kennedy, the most interesting character of the three.

A Georgian by birth, son of a respected doctor who traveled great distances on horseback speculating in land, Kennedy entered West Point as a cadet in May, 1854; he was discharged for drunken and abusive behavior after already flunking his written finals. A failure in life, he sought compensation by joining the 1st Louisiana Regiment Company G on April 30, 1861, and rose to his current rank. He served under Major General Joseph Wheeler, Commander of the Cavalry Division of the Army of Tennessee. Arrested in an attack on a Federal supply train, he was sent to Johnson's Island as a prisoner on November 14, 1863.

After the failed attempt by Beall and Burley in September of the following year, the frustrated stripling decided to escape on his own initiative on October 4. Using a ladder cobbled together from stolen lumber, he scaled the wooden wall and stole a ducking skiff. He managed to reach British North America unmolested; there he was contacted by Confederate agents as a likely recruit. He soon found himself at the Queens Hotel in Toronto as the guest of Jacob Thompson, who showed his usual weakness for handsome hotheads who could carry out his disruptive purposes.

Thompson promised him, Headley, and Martin the support of the fiery Copperhead James M. McMaster, editor of the New York *Freeman's Journal,* and of the always indispensable brothers Benjamin and Fernando Wood; he told the young men with unreasoning optimism that some 20,000 members of the Sons of Liberty were waiting in Manhattan to strike; and that arms, no doubt paid for from the fund he had handed to Benjamin Wood in August, were already supplied for the uprising.

Martin, Headley, Kennedy, and five others arrived in New York City at the beginning of November, registering at several hotels; Kennedy jokingly assumed the name of Stanton when Seddon would have been more appropriate. The huge, bald, Roman-nosed McMaster met with the arrivals at his newspaper office; he laid out plans, authorized by Thompson, for fires to be started all over the city to create a distraction so that the Sons of

Liberty could sweep in and take it over in the name of the Confederacy; McMaster guaranteed the support of Governor Seymour, who had just lost the November election but would remain in office until January, in this terrorist action against his former metropolis. He said that after the raid was concluded, New York, as long planned, would become a seceded city; a convention of delegates from New Jersey and other New England states would help to form a grand Northeastern confederacy.

Even though it soon became apparent that, as at Chicago, the Sons of Liberty would not appear, but would act with their customary cowardice, the trio of firebugs continued apace. They decided to start by setting ablaze the city's 19 leading hotels, starting, with a foolishness that stemmed from ignorance, with the sumptuous Astor House.

This popular hostelry continued to be the headquarters of the single individual who was most valuable to the Confederacy at the time: Union Pacific Chairman Thomas C. Durant, who still lived there and conducted his meetings in his suite. Others who were frequently in collusion at that address were the traders-with-the-enemy Leonard Swett, Thurlow Weed, Orville H. Browning, and James W. Singleton. Perhaps, because these men were friends of Lincoln, they were not considered unsuitable targets; the raiders evidently knew nothing about trading with the enemy.

These treasonable figures would scarcely have appreciated having their favorite hotel burned to the ground; nor would the Peace Democrats, who sympathized with the South, have enjoyed having their own headquarters, the St. Nicholas, reduced to ashes. That hostelry was revered as the former favorite of the Little Giant; Stephen A. Douglas always stopped there and an oil painting of his stubby face and form hung glowingly in the palm court rotunda.

Growing more nervous by the hour, faced by the enormity of the task Thompson had set them, the firebugs, having abandoned plans to strike earlier, particularly on Election or Thanksgiving Day, which would have driven New York to frenzy, settled upon Evacuation Day, November 25, the anniversary of the departure of British troops from the city at the end of the War of Independence. The raiders, like Thompson, were not sophisticated enough to see, as Clay and Sanders would have done, that this choice of date might indicate a fine British hand in the enterprise. From the beginning, they had never seen the attack on Manhattan as a device for bringing about war between the Union and England.

The folly of choosing Evacuation Day was that Booth was due to perform in *Julius Caesar* that very evening. Arsonists targeted the Lafarge House hotel, which contained within its structure the Winter Garden Theatre, where Booth and his brothers would perform the one-night gala. If the Lafarge burned down as they planned, and the theatre with it, then the most celebrated thespian supporter of the Confederacy, and the most likely assassin of the Union's chief executive, would perish in the flames.

Armed with 144 bottles of Greek Fire, the gang embarked on their harebrained plan. They poured the malodorous contents, and bottles of phosphorus as well, onto beds in the hotel rooms they occupied, having first piled spare linens, pillows and even furniture on top of the same beds to create a bonfire. And, as at St. Albans, Greek Fire turned out to be a damp squib. Richard Montgomery had alerted Washington to such a contingency, albeit very late, and most hoteliers, already prepared for fire, added to their supply of buckets and hoses, and so did theatre, museum, art gallery and store owners.

In each and every case, the pathetic potion sputtered and faded, hampered by lack of oxygen because room windows were closed; it created large amounts of smoke instead, smoke that acted as a warning and sent hundreds of guests running headlong into the streets.

At the Lafarge House, the smoke was particularly alarming; gray-brown billows spewed through the lobby of both hotel and Winter Garden Theatre, and penetrated the auditorium where a number of ladies, greatly panicked, fled, stumbled by their hooped skirts and in one case almost trampling on the hapless theatre critic of *The Brooklyn Eagle*. What John Wilkes thought of this can only be conjectured; but Edwin Booth seized the occasion, as Act Two began, to step out front and urge the rest of the audience to stay. Having paid the present-day equivalent of some $60 a ticket, stay they did.

Robert Cobb Kennedy, in what he later declared to be no more than a display of mischief, targeted Barnum's Great American Museum, which boasted an Evacuation Day special. Barnum bragged in his advertisements that he offered the "tallest, shortest and fattest specimens of humanity" living at the time; three mammoth fat girls paraded before the eager crowd weighing "one ton, 2000 pounds and one ton respectively, accompanied by two 17-pound dwarfs," an "entire tribe" of Okenawa Indians, an albino boy, otters, kangaroos, and a trained seal. Barnum had been warned about the firebugs; he had 11 men on patrol, armed with fire hoses; buckets were placed at regular intervals along the corridors.

Kennedy crept in through an open exit door and broke his two Greek fire bottles on the stairs. Since the stairs were made of stone, this was a futile gesture at best but the smoke succeeded in upsetting the customers. Women and children fled, headed by a giantess, who ran amok through the crowd outside; it took six policemen to subdue her in her seven-foot fury.

The enterprise a disaster, Kennedy, Martin and Headley gave up and fled to Toronto to report their failure to Thompson, who in turn would have to make yet another shamefaced report to Judah P. Benjamin. Meantime, Benjamin Wood used his *Daily News* to pin the arsonist effort on Lincoln, whom he claimed was behind it because New York City defied the Administration.

To save face, Thompson should have fired his hotheads on the spot. Instead, he sent them off on yet another crazy adventure. A double agent in Sandusky, Ohio, never named, told him, and he believed it, that a special train was shortly to leave that town for Detroit, Buffalo and New York City, to transfer a group of imprisoned Confederate generals from his old target, Johnson's Island, to Fort Lafayette. The agent identified several of these men as "Lee's Lieutenants," among the elite of General Robert E. Lee's commanders in the field. They were Major Generals Edward Johnson and Isaac R. Trimble, and Brigadier Generals James J. Archer, Meriwether J. Thompson, John R. Jones, William N. R. Beall and J. W. Frazier.

In fact, this was a Union spy-trap: none of these military figures was at Johnson's Island at the time, and James J. Archer was dead.

Thompson, given this false information, decided to have Martin, Headley and Kennedy derail the train, with his other firebrand, John Yates Beall, acting behind the scenes.

In heavy snow on December 15, the three principal highway-men left from various points in order to intercept the train before it reached Buffalo. They would slow it to a halt by placing an iron bar across the rails, then board it and hold the crew and passengers at gunpoint while they carried the Generals out in irons, and handed them over to associates in the Buffalo suburbs for transfer via Halifax and blockade runners to Richmond.

They waited in the dark near Buffalo at the appointed hour, freezing at their posts, until at last the express came roaring through the darkness, its funnel pouring smoke, its wheels pounding the snow-threatened rails. The engineer saw the bar ahead of him, but knew it was no more danger to the train than a straw in the wind; he ploughed into it at full speed, driving it some 200 yards down the roadbed, then had his men jump out and carry it away. Two other men, holding their kerosene lamps high, walked back along the rails, whereupon the would-be inter-ceptors fled into the night, but not before they were seen, for later description, even in the bad light.

A team of New York detectives infiltrated the British North American Confederate network, posing as extremist sympathiz-ers; they shouted against Lincoln in public places, spat on the Stars and Stripes and made their sentiments known to as many Canadians as would listen, although in some cases, given the British sympathy for Richmond, the result was a serious brawl.

Manhattan detective John H. Young, who had helped defuse the burning of New York, was able by this method to worm his way into the Toronto headquarters run by Jacob Thompson and his associate William Lawrence (Larry) McDonald; there, the secessionist Stars and Bars hung from the walls and in the coun-cil room, a large and impressive chamber; pride of place was occupied by handcuffs worn, in one of his early adventures against pirates, by Admiral Franklin Buchanan.

Young embarked on the bold idea of talking to Larry McDon-ald in the guise of sympathizer, to learn details of the various incendiary plans still being hatched by Thompson; he fixed up a

Christmas night meeting at the town of Lewiston, but a driving snowstorm delayed McDonald's train for several hours until Young received a message at his residence, the Central Hotel at Niagara, that McDonald had purportedly arrived there; and to avoid being followed by Union spies, Young and his men walked through the blizzard to Lewiston.

At the meeting, McDonald revealed every detail of who was behind the attempt to burn New York and the effort to derail the train to Buffalo. As a result, Kennedy and Beall were caught, and both were hanged the following year. When Kennedy begged, in a display of cowardice that belied his manly airs, ex-Governor Seymour, Benjamin Wood, and above all Jacob Thompson, to help him bribe his way out of prison, they failed to answer his pleas. His and Beall's usefulness had expired; and Kennedy, sobbing and screaming in his extremity, knew that only too well.

ONE DAY BEFORE THE ABORTIVE ACT OF BANDITRY ON THE RAILS, CLAY and Sanders once again triumphed over Thompson—in the matter of bribing the officials in charge of the St. Albans raid. With Judge Charles Coursol and now Police Chief Guillaume Lamothe firmly in his pocket, Sanders was in high spirits on the day of the preliminary hearing on December 14, 1864. The handful of Retributors now at large, led by Bennett H. Young, were equally chipper as they, not in irons, but well fed and satisfied by their nights with women of the town, strode confidently into the limestone–and-gilt splendor of the Montreal Court House and took their seats in the largely remodeled, and now much more comfortable, dock.

John J.C. Abbott, for the defense, and prosecutor Bernard Devlin, who had his Irish up, appeared in their wigs and gowns; Judge Coursol, that empty vessel, sat primly on the bench.

Outside, in the limestone corridor at the back of the courtroom, Sanders, more grizzled and growling than ever, lurked with the smooth Confederate agent John Porterfield, fat with wealth and corruption, and the stubby Lamothe, who should have been in court in charge of the prisoners. All three men were waiting for the only possible verdict.

Devlin addressed the Judge at such length and with such eloquence on the issue of the prisoners' guilt, and the need to
export them for summary punishment in Washington, that he
forced a recess until after 2 P.M. Sanders, and the others waiting
irritably outside, had to bide their time, but as two o'clock struck,
they at last had their reward. To a tumult of cheers from the
Canadian audience, which loved the raiders to a man, Coursol
declared that he had no jurisdiction to try the case. Abbott
almost threw his wig in the air; Devlin almost ate his. The freed
prisoners ran headlong into the corridor, where Sanders and
Porterfield, while Lamothe wisely stood back, shook their hands
and sent them off laughing to await them at the Donegana
Hotel, where there would be wine, women and song.

Wasting no time, Lamothe handed Porterfield a written
authorization to collect the money-stuffed carpetbag he had
deposited at the Ontario Bank. Porterfield ran to his sleigh,
which was parked in the snow outside, and had his driver whip the
horses all the way to the bank, where chief cashier Henry Starnes,
who was happily ready and waiting, handed him the loot.

While Sanders enjoyed the pleasures of the evening celebra-
tion with Young and the Retributors, Bernard Devlin and his
team raced by sleigh all over town trying to whip up a new judge's
warrant that would put the Retributors back behind bars, and
based upon the fact that Coursol had acted out of all possible
order in the matter. They finally succeeded after most judges
turned them down; they bearded Lamothe in his domestic den,
but he wouldn't budge; they got the head of the Water Police to
co-sign the warrant instead. And they managed to pull together
a Police Court of Inquiry the next day at which Sanders lied and
lied again, stating that he wasn't a Confederate agent.

Devlin won the battle, but not the war; Lamothe was let go,
but two years later returned to office, and with the bribery
money in his overstuffed pockets; Coursol was removed from the
bench but lived well on his share of the loot and resurfaced later
in the legislature; the prisoners returned to their luxury jail but
all were finally acquitted. It was a sad time indeed for British
North American justice, and Devlin knew it when he told the
Police Court:

If murderers and thieves can find protection in Canada (through) our mistaken and ill-judged sympathy with the wily agents of the South who are plotting and planning how best to subserve their purposes then we in Canada will be made to feel and suffer no inconsiderable part of the horrors which [a conflict between us and the United States] would be certain to entail.

SEVEN

WINTER

PLANS

FOR

DEATH

In the wake of his triumphant performance as Marc Antony in *Julius Caesar* on November 25, Booth had a most serious concern. Having gone through the elaborate masquerade of bringing his theatrical costumes in three large trunks to Montreal to cover his true purpose in going there, he needed now to ship the clothes to Richmond. Lafayette Baker, under orders from Charles A. Dana and Major General Dix, was sure to be on the lookout for any such shipment by land and would search the trains for secret messages sewn in silk into the linings, or for medical supplies hidden inside Elizabethan ruffs and furbelows. So Booth had to take the extraordinary risk, with ice forming on the St. Lawrence River and storms threatening the Seaway, of having his precious wardrobe sent by ship through the blockade. Of all the Southern ports, only Wilmington was not totally cut off.

Normally, of course, the collusion of Rear Admiral Lee of the North Atlantic Blockading Squadron and his father-in-law Francis P. Blair might have helped, but Lee had been moved to the Mississippi Squadron on October 12, and there were no guarantees where so flagrant and dangerous a secessionist was involved. Booth evidently didn't dare risk Halifax as the embarkation point because of investigations into Benjamin Wier and Alexander Keith by the American consul in that city. So he chose the less heavily-policed Quebec instead; Federation meetings preoccupied the local authorities completely.

Even then, the procedure was dangerous, especially since, in addition to the three trunks of clothes, he was committed to sending a fourth trunk, under another name, that contained materials intended for blockade running—unspecified in the available reports, this shipment must surely have been of quinine, morphine and calomel.

Booth engaged the services of the young and deeply committed Montreal Confederate agent Patrick C. Martin, who had met with him in Montreal at St. Lawrence Hall; Martin was in

161

partnership with Alexander Keith, and had, with backing in Richmond, been involved in the early pre-Beall efforts to relieve Johnson's Island. A Baltimorean of Booth's own stamp, he had worked closely with the city's former Police Chief, Marshal George P. Kane, who had been involved in the Baltimore plot against Lincoln's life in April, 1861, and frequently visited British North America.

Martin took an extraordinary step. He painted out the name of an ocean-going barque, scarcely suited for a long and arduous voyage when sidewheelers and propeller vessels were standard, and illegally renamed her the *Marie Victoria.* He instantly invalidated her by refusing to register her with Lloyds of London for insurance purposes, so deep was his fear of discovery, and thus broke the law of the sea; no record of her appeared in Lloyds or any other register of shipping to this day, a unique instance of protective folly, since Lloyds was sympathetic to the Confederacy.

With a copy of Hardee's *Infantry Tactics,* (a sure sign of Booth's frustrated interest in becoming a soldier), plays, photographs from female fans, clothing for some 30 works of the theatre, and the contraband items in the fourth trunk, the precious cargo was taken aboard at Quebec on November 18; for a week the ship lay at anchor, apparently because of fear of boarding, seizure and confiscation of an unregistered vessel under law. When at last the pseudonymous vessel did sail, she set out for Nassau, only to founder in a storm. A salvaging vessel managed to rescue the trunks, which were impounded; it was not until June 7, 1865, that they were examined by William H. Ginley, United States consul in Quebec. Ginley found no incriminating materials, but he had not the knowledge or skill to look for silken messages sewn into the coats or trousers or see that saltwater would have washed away the special inks the Confederacy used. But he did take note of contraband in the fourth (he called it the third) trunk.

Booth had his consolations. He received $1,500 ($17,000) from Confederates which, on November 16, he deposited in Jay Cooke's private bank in Washington. Cooke, then and later (he became official Treasury Agent in January, 1865), was, despite protestations by his family-authorized biographers, deeply involved in trading with the enemy, starting from 1862, when his brother Henry Cooke, manager of the Washington branch, began shipping cotton across the lines; as the most powerful banker in America, supplier of funds for Lincoln's armies and navy he had raised through patriotic bond drives, Jay Cooke was in a sense the Treasury itself. Thus, he worked with such figures as Treasury Secretary William Pitt Fessenden and the authorized trader with the South, special agent Hanson A. Risley, to oil the wheels of treasonable trade in Washington, New York and Richmond.

Assistant Treasury Secretary George Harrington, who had been in that office since the Polk administration, was a partner in E. Parkman, Brooks and Co. of Memphis, Tennessee, cotton brokers. General Edmund Kirby Smith of the Confederacy received guns and ammunition through Harrington to help his army of the Tennessee and Trans-Mississippi.

Thenceforth, protected by Risley, Harrington, Henry Cooke, and his staff, Booth could make his medical and financial transactions more easily than ever. He enjoyed other protections as well; now that Beverley Tucker had appointed the China merchant David Preston Parr of Baltimore as his conduit for trade, he could operate even more freely. In addition, he had in his support the cadre of powerful Confederates in charge of the Baltimore and Ohio Railroad, where he could travel without fear of interference or search.

From top to bottom, the B & O was a Confederate operation, and every time the Union put troops aboard, there could be little doubt their movements would be reported to Richmond. Certainly, the B & O was essential for Parr's operations in espionage, covered by shipments of medical supplies by Booth, and by the agents Robert E. Coxe, John Surratt and (later) Lewis Paine, since the railroad ran a clear line from Baltimore (by branch) to Washington and to St. Louis, where Confederate military interferences could be guaranteed to be suspended by orders from Richmond.

William Prescott Smith, master of the B & O's civilian and military transportation operations, was a Confederate agent, whose special emissary was Lieutenant James H. Fowle, formerly of the 17th Virginia Infantry, who worked closely with Secretary of War Seddon. Early in the war, Smith's special assistant had been John Williamson Palmer, a Confederate spy who leaked vital Union troop movements which the ever-treacherous Horace Greeley published in the New York *Tribune* over Palmer's pseudonym, Altamont.

Chief Receiving Clerk on the same railroad, and directly responsible to Smith, was the aforementioned Louis O'Donnell, nephew of the wealthy New York Copperhead Columbus O'Donnell. He lived at Mrs. Boardley's Baltimore lodging house, a nest of Confederates and Copperheads, owned, like its neighboring lodging house, by Booth's friend, the former Baltimore Marshal and Southern sympathizer George P. Kane.

O'Donnell, young and dangerously outspoken, was a friend of Sarah F. Hayes, whose husband was assistant medical director of Baltimore's Fort McHenry Prison, and assumed the full directorship in January 1865. When, that winter, Mrs. Hayes asked O'Donnell what he thought of Sheridan's victories for the Union in the Shenandoah Valley, O'Donnell replied, "There is one thing; Lincoln will never see Illinois again." Mrs. Hayes asked him, "Why do you talk that way? You must know nobody can injure him, surrounded as he is by guards and hundreds of soldiers." O'Donnell repeated his threatening statement. Later, investigators found a link with Booth; O'Donnell had, in his official capacity, been aboard the same Baltimore and Ohio train that took the Grays regiment to John Brown's execution; Booth would have had to register with him on that occasion.

It was William Prescott Smith and Louis O'Donnell who took Booth's late December acquisition, and long-term Confederate agent John Surratt, on his journeys north and south; in sworn statements after the Lincoln assassination, Smith confirmed that another Booth associate, the Prussian George Atzerodt, took the messages and legalized contraband north and south by his boats on the Potomac River near Washington; another contact in the Union capital was Chief Superintendent of the Statistics Bureau, John A. Jones. If the heat was on from Federal agents, messages were concealed in hollowed-out tree stumps on the river's banks and Smith picked them up.

The most popular route was to or from Great Goose Point, Matthias Point and Port Tobacco, which last became Atzerodt's nickname. A witness of the trade was the New York merchant Edward Martin, a colleague of Thomas C. Durant and Robert E. Coxe, who on one occasion met Surratt in a local inn, waiting to make the crossing; after Surratt left, on an Atzerodt boat, Martin had to wait until escapees from a Union prison had been ferried over. In his last hours, freed for once from the mendacious and menacing presence of Thomas T. Eckert, Lewis Paine, awaiting execution, told Dr. Abraham Dunne that he had, in the secret service for Judah P. Benjamin, "journeyed back and forth from Richmond to Washington and had conference in Baltimore with powerful men." That, of course, was while working for Beverley Tucker and D. Preston Parr, and traveling by the Baltimore and Ohio Railroad.

Yet another contact for the conspirators was the dangerous Willard Saulsbury, Copperhead Senator for Delaware, who told the Provost Marshal of Georgetown in December that he knew Lincoln would be assassinated on or about March 4, the exact date Booth presently envisaged; and that the streets would "run with blood."

Especially helpful in such matters was Francis Harrison Pierpont, Governor of "restored" (i.e. Union-controlled) Virginia, who had long worked as legal adviser to the Baltimore and Ohio Railroad, and represented the carpetbagging New York company of P. H. Whitehurst. As Union governor of a divided state, he operated out of Alexandria, a way station for authorized contraband. With full military and governmental support, he was a useful cover for trading in medical supplies and information, and Lincoln liked him for his emancipatory stance on slavery.

Of all these colleagues high and low, none would be more useful to Booth after they met in late December than the subtle and devious John Harrison Surratt, who had enlisted in Richmond with Benjamin and with the Provost Marshal of Richmond, Brigadier General John Henry Winder, whose treatment of Union prisoners at Andersonville makes his name infamous in history. When Surratt joined Winder, the latter was in the divided position of running a Signals Secret Service Bureau while riding roughly over rules of war in running his various camps. On February 7, 1865, worn out with his responsibilities and hated by most, he died unmourned; after that, Surratt would be working for Judah P. Benjamin and Booth exclusively, commuting from Richmond to Washington to Baltimore, New York and Montreal, always with the cover of his medicines, and often in the company of a lady spy, Sarah Antoinette Slater.

Slender, pallidly good-looking and fine-boned, Surratt was far from the typical corn-fed farm boy his Maryland rural origins might suggest. Like Bennett H. Young, he was intended for a religious career; his father, an alcoholic unsuccessful farmer, wanted him to be a priest. He was raised in the belief, based on racism, that the former family home had been burned down by slaves; the pattern of his own racism was firmly set. As a Marylander, he was typically in support of the Southern cause, a brother-in-spirit of John Wilkes Booth.

At age 15, Surratt was entered at the Jesuit St. Charles College at Ellicott City, where boys were trained for the seminary. The training was repressive and harsh; youthful impulses must be permanently quashed in expectation of lifelong celibacy. Surratt's love of the South increased when Southerners paid for his education, when his struggling mother was unable to do so.

In July of 1862, he quit St. Charles and took over his father's post office at Surrattsville. As William Prescott Smith revealed in secret testimony in 1865, post offices, run by Postmaster General Montgomery Blair, whose immediate family was, of course, trading in medical supplies, were used to deposit messages and run trading items in canvas bags supposedly containing mail; Surratt's older brother Isaac, who conveniently acted as a Pony Express messenger between Santa Fe, New Mexico, and Matamoros, was indispensable in the matter.

It was essential that the Surratts, mother and son, be friendly with the mailmen who traveled between Washington and Surrattsville, to keep an eye on documents and treasonable items and make sure that nobody carrying the post was a Union spy. One such man was John T. Tibbett, with whom they felt safe, since Mrs. Surratt had known him from his childhood.

They were so sure of him, in fact, that they made dangerous statements right in front of him. At the beginning of March, 1863, the time Lincoln signed the Federal Draft Act, Tibbett, bringing mail into the parlor, heard Surratt say, "The damned Northern army and its leader ought to be sent straight to hell." That same week, Tibbett swore, Mrs. Surratt said she would give $1,000 ($11,300) to anyone who would kill Lincoln.

Significantly, as Tibbett recalled during the Surratt trial in June, 1865, the Surratts would ask anxiously whether Tibbett had seen blockade runners; they would scarcely have asked a mere mailman, who would not be privy to such activities, unless he knew the traders with the enemy by sight.

John Lee, Captain of Detectives in the office of Washington Provost Marshal James R. O'Beirne, was under orders to obtain information on shippers of quinine, calomel and morphine across to the South. One of those he singled out for inspection was John Surratt; he traced his movements from the Baltimore depot, the terminus of the Baltimore and Ohio branch line in Washington, across the Eastern Branch Bridge, but did nothing to stop him. Clearly, the Presidential-level protection that also aided Booth considerably aided Surratt, since under normal conditions he would be subject to arrest as a blockade runner.

While the transportation of intelligence and vital supplies moved smoothly via Beverley Tucker in Montreal, David Preston Parr in Baltimore, and John Surratt at both locations, via the Confederate-controlled Baltimore and Ohio railroad, through George Atzerodt and his Potomac river boatmen, and thence through the Red River Valley or the Florida-Georgia border courtesy of David Levy Yulee, the relative of Joseph Holt, safehouses became essential. The reason was that, though stymied at every turn, Lafayette C. Baker, Charles A. Dana and Allan Pinkerton might find a way to disrupt the entire underground operation.

Such a place was found in the Washington home of Thomas S. Green. Green was a wealthy carpetbagger with real estate and business interests in Western Virginia, protected by the trading-with-the-enemy Governor, Francis Harrison Pierpont. Green was married to the equally wealthy Anne Corbin Lomax, sister of Major General Lunsford Lindsay Lomax, of the Confederate Army of Northern Virginia. She was a close friend of David Preston Parr, whose two sons were serving under Lomax at the time.

The Greens owned a colonial mansion that filled an entire block on Constitution Avenue between 17th and 18th Streets in Washington. Underneath it was a dungeon complete with shackles and a maze of twisting corridors that defied anyone to escape. There the President or members of his Cabinet could be hidden and tortured; meantime, Booth, Surratt, or any other traders and spies, could also be hidden there if the heat was on.

Surratt himself found another, if far more modest, safehouse when his mother, after renting out her property at Surratsville, took possession of a three-story structure with attic and cellar, at 541 H Street, Washington, moving in at the start of October, 1864. The establishment, which had few boarders but proved to be a useful meeting place for conspirators, was flanked by a filthy alleyway, the stench of unswept horse manure and overflowing drains scarcely quelled by early falls of snow.

Surratt's dislike of blacks was not decreased when, three weeks after he moved in, Maryland freed the slaves; in short order the streets were filled with African-Americans, augmented by others pouring in after abandoning the South, and the shouts and fireworks made sleep difficult. To add to the Surratts' paranoia, the black encampments near the City were ravaged with smallpox, and the victims, if not dead and thrown haphazardly into the Boundary Street Cemetery, were thought to be abroad. Soon, the Washingtonians began attacking the African-Americans in their midst, and the Surratt boarding house was surrounded by crowds throwing bricks, stones and garbage.

WITH SURRATT ON HIS TEAM FROM DECEMBER 23—WHEN DR. SAMUEL A. Mudd, a useful medical contact on the quinine trail, introduced them—Booth enjoyed the further protection of an expansion of the cotton ring. A leader was Judge James Hughes, who had stepped down from the bench of the Court of Claims where, ironically, he had failed to help those loyal citizens whose cotton had been seized by the Confederacy. Now he could ship these same failed claimants' cotton north and put money in his pocket as well from the sales. The equally corrupt Secretary of the Treasury William Pitt Fessenden made him Treasury Agent in charge of cotton, and with him, as overall agent in January, 1865, Booth's banker Jay Cooke.

Equally important was the aforementioned operator James W. Singleton of North Virginia, adviser and friend to Lincoln, gentlemen planter and financier and member of the Sons of Liberty, now about to be renamed the Order of the Star. Like that other trader, Francis Preston Blair, Sr., Singleton, from his visit to Niagara in August, 1864, remained a supporter of supposed peace negotiations, and declared the war unconstitutional; his reason was still the inconvenient interruption of commerce, disguised in conciliatory doubletalk. Hardliners in the Union knew his Southern sympathies and burned the outbuildings on his farm when he attended a peace conference in Peoria.

On November 22, Singleton was in Montreal, boldly conferring with Clay and Beverley Tucker on the trade-plus–intelligence operation; he traveled to report his findings in Richmond. Another ringleader was the leading Washington lawyer Orville H. Browning, former senator from Illinois, of whom it was said (by Theodore C. Pease, in his introduction to the published two-volume Browning diaries) that "The President's office and the President's secrets opened as they opened to no other." Others still were Republican power broker Thurlow Weed and Illinois Lawyer Leonard Swett, both old and close friends of the President.

Like David Levy Yulee, Swett had pushed for Joseph Holt as Vice President in 1864 and later, when that effort failed, helped him to become Advocate General, a post as useful as Salmon P. Chase's as Chief Justice of the Supreme Court when it came to securing immunity. He was protected from charges of treason by the Lincolnian Henry J. Raymond of the *New York Times,* a friend he had supported in peace moves after the failure of the Niagara conference.

On September 6, 1864, Swett had shrewdly arranged for the President to appoint his former law partner, William W. Orme of Bloomington, Illinois, as cotton agent, acting for the Treasury and William P. Fessenden in Memphis, Tennessee, a main point of shipment.

Orme was no mere speculator or businessman on the make. He was a former Brigadier General who carried his influence to the top of the Union army. Ironically, it was he who ran Camp Douglas, Chicago, so cruelly that he provoked Jacob Thompson to attempt his action in August; although he resigned that post on April 26, 1864, he left instructions that his policy of brutal suppression be continued by his successors.

Another major figure involved in the cotton conspiracy was John Albion Andrew, governor of Massachusetts, the most powerful political figure in that state. He had thrown his considerable weight behind Lincoln in the 1860 campaign as chairman of the state delegation to the Republican National Convention, but by 1864 he had lost confidence in the President and had backed Salmon P. Chase as Republican candidate. But he still shared, through Chase, the benefits of Lincoln's trading with the enemy.

A fellow conspirator was George Ashmun, also from Massachusetts, who presided over the Republican National Convention in 1860 with Andrew's full support. In 1864, Lincoln rewarded him with the post of government representative on the board of the Union Pacific Railroad of which Thomas C. Durant was chairman, a handsome sinecure that he supplemented with arrangements with merchants in trading with Richmond. Thomas Corwin was no less a strong supporter of Lincoln. A former governor of Ohio and Secretary of Treasury in the Fillmore Administration, he had just resigned as Minister to Mexico, crucial for anyone involved in trading with the confederacy via Matamoros, and was now an influential lawyer in Washington. Yet another trader was William Helmick, an Ohio man like Corwin, and former Congressman from that state, who now occupied the post of chief clerk of the Pension Office, which gave him access to Union military records.

Browning and Singleton brought the direct representative of and co-financier and host of Sanders, Clay and Tucker, Robert E. Coxe of St. Catharines and Poughkeepsie, into the circle and soon had Lincoln sign permits for him—despite the fact that he was at the heart of the plot to kill the President hatched at Niagara in August, and conveyed to Lincoln by Major General Dix.

AT THE END OF 1864, DESPITE THE FACT THAT HE WAS STILL LIVING much of the time at the expensive National Hotel in Washington, and was able to buy weapons, afford good food and wine and enjoy the company of at least one high-class prostitute, Booth, always a sponger, wrote to his partner in the oil business, the hard-pressed and struggling Joseph H. Simonds in Pennsylvania, begging for money and lying that he wasn't doing well. The naïve and unsuspecting Simonds scraped up $500 ($5,690); he wrote that he had thought (Booth must have boasted of this earlier), the actor was taking in greenbacks to the tune of $1,000 ($11,300) a month—and this was probably true, but from his New York Copperhead sources. Simonds urged him to give a benefit performance—for himself. In adding up the accounts he stated that Booth had invested $5,624 ($64,000), in the oil firm; he referred to Thomas Means, a drunk, thief and con man whom Booth had brought into the firm, and who had repudiated all his debts ("I wish while you have been doing nothing you could have come here and we would have taken good care of you and you would not have been sick and could not have lived fast.")

An expensive item on Booth's agenda was a new woman friend, the plumply appealing Lucy Lambert Hale, daughter of the New Hampshire Senator John P. Hale, the Free Soil party's noisy stump orator who had failed as presidential candidate against Franklin Pierce.

Senator Hale was a strong opponent of slavery and a sworn enemy of Governor Seymour of New York. That Booth would have become involved with such a man is a clear indication that he wanted a strong contact in government; he would be able to determine details of government activities among groups that were not involved in trading with the enemy, as Hale was above reproach in that respect.

Booth now secured another recruit, the stagestruck fan named David E. Herold, whom as we know he had first met in one of the most charged weeks of his life: the second week of April, 1863, when he took the blood oath of the D.G. Society at the point of a sword while performing at Grover's Theatre in Washington. The young man was perfect Booth fodder: fit and attractive, darkly good looking, like Booth himself he was a Marylander;

his father, who died in 1864, had friends who were well placed for medical shipments in the Washington Navy Yard, where Herold senior had worked. David Herold knew the trading-with-the-enemy-courier routes south of the federal capital extremely well; he was a passionate duck shooter, familiar with rivers and inlets. He also worked for a Washington pharmacy, always useful for buying morphine, calomel and quinine—William M. Thompson's Drugs, at 15th and New York Avenue. He had known John Surratt for some time. Among his varied talents was skilled musicianship; he played trumpet part time in the brass-and-flute band of the United States Marine Corps, and in March, 1863, serenaded Mrs. Surratt and her daughter Anna at night, outside their combined post office, tavern and family home at Surrattsville. In an authenticated confession after the Lincoln assassination, George Atzerodt stated that one of Booth's plans was to kill Lincoln during such a serenade, a note in the music timed to indicate when the President should be shot.

At the turn of the New Year, 1865, Booth was busy recruiting others to his murderous purpose. He wasn't always able to succeed; caution, if not patriotism, stopped his fellow actor Samuel K. Chester from complying with his plans. When Chester refused, Booth made a direct reference to the powerful group with which he was involved; it could be taken either as the D.G. group of Washington, the Order of the Star, or the clique of Copperhead business and political leaders in New York, or perhaps all three:

> You will at least not betray me. You dare not. I will implicate you anyway. The party are [sic] sworn together and if you attempt to betray us you will be hunted down through life.

Chester, for whom Booth would get a job in Ford's Theatre's repertory company, would be engaged to open the back door as a signal, and then help out in what Booth incorrectly described as a kidnapping plot; Booth kept pressing for help and promising money; he also offered, at various times, the same employment to the actors John Matthews and Matthew Canning. Neither wanted to be involved.

Also at the turn of 1865, Booth met with Surratt for the first time; odd, since both were on the same trade-plus-espionage agenda, but it was often thought advisable in Montreal and Richmond to keep secret agents apart. The encounter happened by chance, through the imprudent action of Dr. Samuel A. Mudd, the secessionist physician on the quinine trail.

They met outside the Odd Fellows' Hall, on 7th Street in Washington, when Mudd was out walking with Booth; Surratt was accompanied by Louis Weichmann, a former schoolfriend whom Surratt was unwise to trust.

Booth invited the three men to his rooms at the National Hotel. Apparently, a man he called a "congressman" who would scarcely have left important government documents lying about, had placed them in a cupboard for Booth, who told the others they would provide "a nice read" when he was left alone.

It is clear that the same "congressman" (Booth must have meant James W. Singleton) saw danger ahead for the whole cotton trade. Surratt told Weichmann at the time that an "elderly gentleman" (probably Browning) living in the neighborhood of H Street had given him $3,000 ($34,100) to enable him to get involved in cotton trading with Europe, a restored prospect for those at the top of the trading with the enemy enterprise when the North might cease and desist. Surratt said he intended sailing shortly for Liverpool and London through the blockade and then returning to the South via Matamoros, where his brother Isaac of the Pony Express would help him complete the journey home with his loot.

What precipitated so drastic a plan? It was the action taken, for several weeks now, in secret sessions of Congress, by Maine Congressman Elihu B. Washburne of the Committee on Commerce, a disappointed and embittered old friend of Lincoln, and a man of impeccably upright moral character, who was exasperated by the President's involvement in what amounted to trading with the enemy.

The view was shared by commander-in-chief Lieutenant General Ulysses S. Grant, who was maddened by the constant pressure to let through arms, pork, beef and gold to the south and cotton, turpentine, and rosin (much as he needed them) to the North. Washburne was chiefly responsible for pushing Grant to the top of the military machine; he had helped legislate the Lieutenant Colonel designation, which had been long in disuse, for Grant's particular benefit.

Throughout the turn of the year, and into January, the Committee on Commerce, with Washburne's unstinting support, assembled a mass of information on trading with the enemy. It concluded that the trade had demoralized and corrupted the army and navy, prolonged the war, and cost the Union thousands of lives and millions of treasure; that it was, in essence, treasonable; that the amount of supplies needed for support of the rebels through New Orleans, Memphis, Norfolk and other places almost surpassed belief.

No doubt getting wind of the Washburne investigation (since his colleagues, including Thomas C. Durant, gave evidence to the Committee naming him), Beverley Tucker on January 2, 1865, wrote an anxious note to Francis P. Blair, Sr., who was involved in a phony peace mission to Davis and Benjamin in Richmond, to check on his cotton deals, asking him to contact Secretary of State Seward and set up an interview with Lincoln in person. His letter fell on barren ground; having Robert E. Coxe in Washington as emissary for the Canadian commissioners was risk enough, and Tucker's letter went unanswered.

Three days later, Lincoln personally signed a pass for Coxe, who went to Richmond with Singleton for another fraudulent peace discussion, like Blair's held with Davis and Benjamin, and putting forward, as Blair had, an absurd idea of joining the Union in conflict with Napoleon III's puppet Emperor Maximilian, in Mexico, when Maximilian was protecting Benjamin's investments in the Tehuantepec Isthmus. During this preposterous discussion, and despite threatened action from the Washburne committee, Coxe made a deal for 50,000 bales of cotton, 10,000 boxes of tobacco, 10,000 barrels of turpentine and 10,000 barrels of rosin, for Sanders and Tucker's benefit with Lincoln's approval and paid out of the dwindling Treasury holdings in greenbacks since by Lincoln's own admission the Union had sent all its gold to the Confederacy.

A subsequent "peace" conference took place with Lincoln at Hampton Roads at the beginning of February, between a curiously ill-assorted trio of politicians and Lincoln to continue the nonsensical discussions. Alexander Stephens, Vice President of the Confederacy, was, of course, opposed to Davis, and as we know a long time absentee from his official duties in Georgia; Senator Robert M. T. Hunter, precursor of Benjamin as Secretary of State, had been among the peace emissaries to Jacob Thompson in July, 1864—a contact of Beverley Tucker, he was clearly in sympathy with the Confederate Commissioners; and Assistant Secretary of War John A. Campbell was no better than a Confederate spy. While the conference continued, Singleton secured seven million dollars' worth of cotton, rosin, turpentine and rosin. However, the days for this kind of operation were numbered.

While the three Commissioners were on their way to Hampton Roads, the Confederate agent Reverend Stephen Cameron arrived from Montreal after a perilous journey and Judah P. Benjamin handed him a fake and backdated authorization for the St. Albans raid; Davis insisted that Cameron fold the instructions in tissue paper and conceal them carefully on his person. In Montreal, Cameron produced the documents in court, at a new trial of Bennett H. Young and his Retributors, and, backed also by lying statements from Sanders, they were, with the exception of Young, acquitted. Another who brought false confirmation just in time from Richmond was Kate McGruder, a girlfriend of Lewis Sanders, whose entire team of female agents was dressed entirely as nuns.

By late February, Clay had had enough. With the Washburne committee hearings hanging over him and his circle, and no doubt acting on warnings from Beverley Tucker, he decided to return to Richmond without official instruction from Davis or Benjamin. That he was directly linked to Singleton is shown in a letter sent by his brother, Colonel Henry Lawson Clay, to Clement's wife Virginia, from Richmond to Beech Island, on January 17, 1865, forwarding a message from Singleton, which stated that Clay would be returning soon, not risking the blockade but coming via Mexico and Texas, where he had property.

On January 31, he sailed from Halifax to St. Georges, Bermuda, aboard the British steamer *Old Dominion,* then changed ships to the appropriately named *Rattlesnake,* a Fraser, Trenholm blockade runner. Three days later, the vessel ran into

a storm off Fort Moultrie, South Carolina and foundered, ironically, on the wreck of Liverpool Mayor Edward Lawrence's
Fraser-Trenholm pirate ship *The Night Hawk.*

Clay and the other passengers took to the lifeboats; Clay's boat
ran aground and, with secret messages for Benjamin slung in an
oilskin bag around his neck, he struggled up the rocks in the rain.
Much of his luggage lost, the hard-pressed and bedraggled emissary went via Macon to Augusta, Georgia, to see his wife and family, then proceeded on a prolonged and painful journey to report
to Davis and Benjamin in Richmond, arriving on February 18. It
was an embarrassing meeting: for all the success of his authorized
raid on St. Albans, he had not a nickel to show for it.

WHILE THE WASHBURNE COMMITTEE CONCLUDED ITS FINDINGS,
Surratt abandoned all caution.

William E. Cleaver, a quack doctor and abortionist, owned a
livery stable on Sixth Street in Washington, not far from Mrs.
Surratt's boarding house. He, with his partner Samuel A. Rainey,
acted also as a veterinarian. He had known Surratt for many
years.

On January 1, Booth had brought him a one-eyed bay horse
to keep and feed; 10 days later, Booth brought in a light bay mare
for the same purpose. Samuel Arnold also made visits to the stable. On January 25, at 4 P.M. by Cleaver's record book, Booth
arrived with Surratt, who hired the bay mare to be ready by 7 P.M.,
with Booth's permission.

At 7 P.M., he returned to pick up the mare; it was raining very
hard. In Cleaver's office, Surratt said that he and Booth had
some bloody work to do; that they were going to kill Lincoln, the
damned old scoundrel; that he had ruined Maryland and the
country. Surratt said if nobody did the job, he would do it himself, and he pulled out a pistol and placed it on Cleaver's desk. It
is clear that he saw Lincoln's usefulness, following Washburne's
exposures, as on the very verge of expiration.

Sometime that winter, Surratt again showed his hand. He
spent a night at the home of a friend, E. L. Smoot, near Surrattsville. Smoot asked him about his trips to Richmond and Surratt said, with a smile, and arching his neck theatrically, "If the

Yankees knew what I have done, and what I am doing, they would stretch this neck of mine."

DURING THE LAST WEEKS OF JANUARY AND THE FIRST DAYS OF FEBRUARY, 1865, Surratt spent much of his time traveling between Richmond, Washington, New York City and Montreal, on Confederate intelligence missions cloaked by medication trading and by, at this stage, some trading in cotton as well. He had in mind extending his activities to run the blockade to England and Booth, showing all too clearly the sums to which he had access, talked to him of buying a ship to that purpose. In this respect Charles A. Haswell would be indispensable (years later, in Italy, Surratt told an informer named Henry de St. Marie that a New York shipping concern was in the background of the Lincoln conspiracy).

He and Booth formed a connection they would soon have cause to regret. The aforementioned Louis J. Weichmann (whose name was originally Wiechmann) was tall, hefty, bespectacled, an avid reader running to fat at the early age of 22; as a native Baltimorean, he encouraged confidence in his new friends; like them, he had learned the devious arts of religious and social intrigue that resulted from training by the Jesuits. Son of a tailor, he had attended the Washington Seminary from the age of 13; he then entered the less cloistered world of Philadelphia Central High School, from which he graduated on February 10, 1859. Clever, smooth and persuasive, he mastered seven languages as well as shorthand. Like Surratt, he studied for the priesthood, in his case at St. Charles College in Maryland, where he first met St. Marie, his would-be nemesis, but failed his vocation. In Washington, he taught at the distinguished St. Matthews Institute.

His value to Booth and the other conspirators was that he held a job in the most crucial of government departments for leakages of inside information and for making contact with inmates of Union jails who might be enabled to escape and help the Confederate cause. As a clerk in the Commissary General of Prisons, which was part of the War Department, he was in charge of vital records; he knew which prisons were poorly guarded, which were offering exchanges, where Confederate military leaders were housed, and which camps were ravaged by disease and would not therefore be suitable for intervention and breakout.

Better still, it would only take limited snooping, and Weichmann had all the instincts of a boll weevil, to find out what Secretary of War Stanton, Assistant Secretary Dana and Lafayette Baker might be up to in any further attempts to disrupt trading with the enemy or to bring Beverley Tucker or George Sanders back from Montreal as captives. From his point of view, he could use the information he gathered either for the benefit of Booth and Surratt, or against them, should he, as it was almost inevitable he would, turn informer at the price of his own immunity. The plump stoolpigeon pressed on; and soon he became embroiled.

Weichmann's greatest advantage was that he had access to Brigadier General William N. R. Beall, the namesake and possible relative of John Yates Beall; the latter was due for execution as a collaborator in terrorist activities in British North America. One of those military figures whom Jacob Thompson's agent in Sandusky lyingly stated was on the train to Buffalo whose hijacking John Yates tried to arrange, Brigadier General Beall was the ultimate exponent of trading with the enemy.

With the joint approval of both Union and Confederate governments, he had been released from Johnson's Island in July, 1865, and had been allowed to open, of all things, a Confederate store in the heart of Manhattan, into which he was permitted by both William Pitt Fessenden and George A. Trenholm, opposing Secretaries of the Treasury, and by Abraham Lincoln and Jefferson Davis besides, to ship cotton North across the lines and sell it in bales to acquire money for clothing for military prisoners of the Union. In fact, as the condition of those prisoners all too clearly showed at the end of the war, the arrangement resulted in his own comfort, not theirs. And Louis J. Weichmann was certainly his contact at the War Department in Washington.

Surratt formed a friendship with Weichmann so deep that they shared the same bed. Heterosexual men, especially if pressed for money, often shared beds in those days, but Weichmann and Surratt were scarcely short of cash and Mrs. Surratt's boarding house, where they lived in the same room and between the same sheets, was not usually crowded to the rafters since she made sure that the guests were either political innocents or sympathizers with the Confederacy. Both men married in later life and Surratt had seven children.

Some time in January, Surratt talked to Weichmann of moving to Richmond permanently, perhaps to deceive his bed-mate of his plans to kill the President; he talked of being in close touch with the Very Reverend John McGill, Roman Catholic Bishop of the Confederate capital, who corresponded with him by boat across the Potomac on the all-purpose white flag of truce used by ferryman George Atzerodt to cover contingencies. From Surratt, Weichmann learned that Booth was mingling with sympathetic states' representatives, both Senators and Congressmen—the reference could only be to Singleton, Benjamin Wood and Willard Saulsbury, that fiercest of Lincoln's opponents.

From the end of December, Booth and Surratt had secured a strong ally in Montreal. Weary of Jacob Thompson's failures at Chicago and Lake Erie and the failed train interception near Buffalo, Benjamin had ordered him to step down as leader of the British North American Commission and make room for a younger and brighter man with military experience—a decision Davis and Benjamin should have made many weeks before. At 28, Brigadier General Edwin G. Lee was second cousin to Robert E. Lee and, on another side of the family, to Rear Admiral Samuel P. Lee, who now was running the Mississippi Blockading Squadron, which was even more useful for trading with the enemy than the North Atlantic squadron he had previously operated.

Aristocratic in appearance, Edwin G. Lee belied in every aspect of his being his exalted military rank; he would have looked improbable even as a private. He had neither the presence nor the physique of a military commander; he suffered from tuberculosis, which gave him a faintly greenish, sickly pallor; his shoulders were narrow and sloping; his chest weak; he had the thin white hands of a Bohemian attic poet. But he wasn't weak in spirit; his direct stare and haughtily jutting cleft chin partially corrected the picture of fragile, recessive weakness.

He was a member of the military unit that arrested John Brown at Harper's Ferry and he stole that prominent captive's telescope. He cast in his lot with the South at the outset of the war; the Hamtramck Guards became Company B, second Virginia Infantry of the Stonewall Brigade; an ardent if underweight and consumptive figure in uniform, he rose rapidly through the ranks, inspired by his mother's instruction to "Kill the abominable Yankees."

Brigadier Generalships were common in those days, when beardless boys led other beardless boys to the slaughter; but Lee's health undermined his efforts and, instead of Jefferson Davis and War Secretary Seddon feeding him to the Union cannons, they sent him to British North America under Benjamin and Winder's secret service banner. It was an attempt to humiliate the failed Thompson, whose resignation Benjamin asked for by letter but did not, in fact, receive.

On December 5, 1864, Lee and his wife Susan sailed for Nassau aboard the blockade runner *Virginia* under orders from Rear Admiral David Dixon Porter, with cotton, rosin and turpentine for use in England. Chased by Union ship captains, who had instructions to protect cotton from leaving the country when it would be of use in the North, the Lees arrived safely in the Bahamas and transferred, like Thompson, Clay and Holcombe before them, to the British ship *Alpha,* for transfer to Halifax.

They arrived on December 30 and, like their predecessors, made contact with the inevitable Benjamin Wier and Alexander Keith, and with the still hospitable Archbishop Thomas L. Connolly, who gave them his traditional welcome dinner for Confederates in exile; they also met with Jane, Mrs. Beverley Tucker, and two of her children, Margaret and Ellis, who had just arrived on another blockade runner.

The Lees and the Tuckers traveled 536 miles by sleigh through snowstorms and 30 degrees below zero temperatures across the frozen St. Lawrence River to Quebec and Montreal, moving into a comfortable suite at the St. Lawrence Hall that had become Sanders' and Tucker's headquarters, along with ex-Senator Westcott's rooms. Another contact there for Edwin was his cousin Cassius Lee, who had fled to Montreal as early as June, 1863, after two stays in prison as a Confederate spy.

Brigadier General Lee set up a full-scale operation in Montreal in collusion with John Porterfield, the Virginia cotton broker William Corse, his brother John, and the spy and courier Sarah Antoinette Slater; top of the agenda was making sure that Bennett H. Young and those of his Retributors who were still in prison would obtain acquittal at their upcoming new trial through documents obtained by Mrs. Slater from Richmond which would lyingly confirm that they were on official military orders to raid St. Albans; and there was much talk in that circle of Lincoln's imminent murder.

Another major contributor to the Booth-Surratt-Beverley Tucker axis from January on was the aforementioned David Preston Parr, aged 46, of Baltimore, whose china shop maintained a raging bull in the person of Lewis Thornton Powell (Lewis Paine), a tall, strapping, glowering but well-educated Mephistopheles; a soldier, trader with the enemy and potential murderer. Parr was short by contrast, barely five-foot-six, and slight, with blond, receding hair and a fair complexion; he looked just the kind of delicate aging epicure who would be appropriate for dealing in figurines and English porcelain vases favored by the rich ladies of Baltimore. But, in truth, he was very far from that image. He was a determined and ruthless operator on Beverley Tucker's behalf, and his wife was an ardent and committed secessionist. Mother of his eight children, Anne Gregory Loane was the daughter of the prominent British merchant and collaborator with the South Joseph Loane, who had been at the St. Lawrence Hall as early as August, 1864, in contact with the Canadian commissioners.

Parr was ideally placed to run the Tucker network of spies, traders and traitors. He had twice been reported by anonymous informers as running the blockade, but so great was his money and influence, and his assistance to the Lincoln trade routes so valuable, that nothing was done about him. He was especially well connected to Tucker's New York clique; his contact there was with the well-to-do businessman and carpetbagger John Patts Brown, whose enterprising daughter, Josephine, specialized in spying for Richmond while shipping—what else?—medical supplies. Her uncle, and her father's brother–in-law, was one of the most powerful figures of Baltimore, Robert T. Banks, who would become a notably corrupt pro-Southern Mayor of that city after the war was over.

The Parrs' son, David, their eldest boy and second child, was enlisted at 19 years of age in Company A, Second Maryland Infantry Regiment, and then seconded as Sergeant to the Signal Corps, the intelligence branch of the Confederate army, under a Lieutenant General who had strong Canadian connections, Jubal A. Early; and then as an employee of the War Department in Richmond when Major General John C. Breckinridge, his commander, became the Confederate Secretary of War, replacing James A. Seddon in February, 1865.

Lewis Powell became Parr's chief operative with the usual cover of trading in medical supplies and gifts of china. Powell's other contact, Charles G. Heim of Baltimore, and Heim's father of the same first name, also traded between north and south with Powell's landlady and girlfriend Margaret Branson, of Branson's Boarding House, a buzzing vespiary of Confederates, as their reliable protector.

As Beverley Tucker's contact in Baltimore for trading with the enemy, Parr linked directly to the next stage of the secret network with the Greens in Washington, and then to Senator R. M. T. Hunter, in Richmond.

On January 26, 1865, William C. McDougall, Secretary of the Province of Quebec, issued to Surratt in that city a passport under the name of John Watson, merchant, a citizen of Great Britain; this helped Surratt to overcome border restrictions which had been imposed following the St. Albans Raid by Union Secretary of State Seward. At the same time, Booth obtained a pass, which he showed to his associate Samuel Arnold later on, at Vicksburg, now under Union occupation, and signed by Lieutenant Colonel Theodore S. Bowers, Adjutant General to Lieutenant General Grant; this provided him with an equally reliable cover for his activities which now extended to shipping cotton across the lines. Armed with this useful cover, he began to intensify his plans against Lincoln. He formed an association with James Lamb, who worked as a painter and handyman at Ford's Theatre and was overheard by witnesses, who reported to theatre owner John T. Ford, making dangerous threats against Lincoln's life.

Booth went to the point of hiring another Ford's employee, Edman ("Edward") Spangler, a hard-drinking carpenter he had known for many years. The coarse, muscular artisan had built a cottage on the Booth estate at Bel Air, Maryland, in 1854; he had been engaged because he had worked on theaters in which the Booth brothers performed.

Spangler's friendship with Booth began when the actor performed at Ford's in the fall season of 1863. They caught up again during the winter of 1864-5 when he conferred with Booth closely on the internal structure of the theatre, showing him strategic (useful for kidnap and murder) elements that he might have overlooked in his performances and visits between seasons. A man of all parts, Spangler also took care of Booth's horses; while working overtime as a voluntary nightwatchman, he slept on the premises, ostensibly to be available in the event of burglary or fire.

During those weeks of January and February, the Elihu B. Washburne Committee on Commerce conferred in secret sessions of Congress on trading with the enemy while Booth, Atzerodt, Surratt and his mother and Lewis Paine continued to exemplify that dubious activity with Tucker, Edwin G. Lee, David Preston Parr, the Greens, Judah P. Benjamin and R. M. T. Hunter. The figures the Committee came up with were staggering: Thomas C. Durant, Tucker's accomplice and railroad tycoon, had obtained 4,100 bales of cotton, Leonard Swett 50,000 bales, Ward Hill Lamon, acting with his brother Robert, 55,000 and Robert E. Coxe, acting for Beverley Tucker and D. Preston Parr on specific Lincolnian license via Orville H. Browning, who was now their lawyer, 50,000, as well as 10,000 barrels of turpentine and 10,000 boxes of tobacco, making this St. Catharines plotter against the president the biggest profiteer of all. The Governors of New York, Massachusetts and Union-controlled Virginia were listed as busy engineering arrangements for favored friends and associates.

For Lieutenant General Grant, the report by Washburne, his closest friend and supporter, was intolerable. He had always hated having to allow Lincoln to trade with the enemy and he had a strong personal reason for detesting such commercialized treason. His father, the ebullient and unscrupulous Jesse Grant, had made a fortune with such tradings as early as 1862; Grant Senior had worked with the Jewish carpetbaggers Henry Harmon and Simon Mack, which had provoked the Lieutenant General into the notorious General Order Number 11, barring non-Gentiles from employment by the Treasury and banishing those who were already there.

Grant later saw the unwisdom of his show of racism, and rescinded the order, but the charge of anti-Semitism remained. Once he objected to such shipments, it is clear he was marked down by Booth, Surratt and their colleagues as another target; no other figure presented a greater threat to their trading with the enemy than he did.

By February 7, Lincoln was unregenerate; he sent a directive to Grant that read:

> Singleton, who bears you this [note of License for trading with the enemy] claims that he already has arrangements made, if you consent to bring a large amount of Southern produce through the lines. For its bearing on our finances, I would be grateful for this to be done, if it can be done without injuriously disturbing your military operations *or supplying the enemy* [italics added].

On February 29, when Grant was complaining to Sheridan that 70,000 pounds of bacon (emanating clearly from Beverley Tucker) was going South to feed the Confederate troops, Singleton, with Judge James Hughes, was on his way back to Richmond on yet another spurious "peace" mission. The Richmond *Enquirer* saw through this; on March 9, after Singleton and Hughes returned to Washington with the cotton supply, its editor Edward A. Pollard wrote:

> Cotton, not peace, is what Mr. Singleton is really after . . . trading cotton for bacon is a business that requires no mystery, and if Mr. Lincoln desires cotton and tobacco, and is willing to exchange for them provisions at proper prices, why not send his bacon minister

here openly, and avow his purpose to drive a trade even amid the din of war? The spectacle of two great nations fighting and trading at one and the same time is novel, and Europe must again recognize the giant step made by this country in war trade as well as in war implements. If the United States has outstripped the world in iron-clad ships, big guns and great armies, it has also taken the first step toward a big trade with its enemy. Having blockaded all the ports and effectively shut Europe out from the great staples of the States, it monopolizes commerce by opening a neutral ground for trade. This is said to be Mr. Singleton's and Judge Hughes's business.

That Booth did not believe such trading could continue for long, and that it was time to bring his dream of Lincoln's death to final fruition, is revealed in a report filed by John B. Van Dien, of the War Department in Richmond, in the columns of the Cincinnati *Commercial* on June 24, 1865, and reproduced in the *New York Times* the following day. Van Dien was appointed, through the influence of Confederate Vice President Alexander Stephens and Major General Howell Cobb, a clerkship in which, working for Winder and Benjamin, he was in charge of the secret files of the Confederate intelligence operation. This meant that he dealt directly with Tucker, Booth, Surratt, Parr and the other traders.

He reported on Booth's visit to Richmond in late February:

(I was) introduced to [War Secretary] Breckinridge by Mr. Benjamin . . . Booth commenced by saying that a plan was being formed, by parties in the Northern States and Canada, friends of the Confederacy, to capture or assassinate Mr. Lincoln; that he had a full list of the names, and all they desired was an official recognition on the part of the Confederate authorities, and that then the order would certainly be executed. He further stated that they required no pecuniary assistance from the government, as that was already secured; that they were not after gain but were activated by a desire to render the Confederacy a service, by removing the tyrant who was the cause of so much suffering to the country, and the only obstacle in the way of a speedy peace.

Messrs. Davis and Breckinridge both expressed their hearty condemnation of the plot, and advised Booth to think no more of it, that they felt their cause was just, and that God, in his own good time, would give them the victory, without resorting to anything but the most honorable warfare, and that they were willing to leave Lincoln's punishment for his great crime to the providence of a just God and an outraged people.

Benjamin said nothing. Booth then retired, and the last words he uttered in the room were, "He must die!" After Booth and his friends were gone, Davis said, "Those fellows came here merely to see the Richmond sights, and their assassination plot is mere fudge." Breckinridge and Benjamin laughed, and the latter said, "I think so." The matter received no more attention. All agreed the matter was fudge.

Booth traveled to Washington. The ceremonies for Lincoln's inauguration as President had long been set for March 4, the date on which Willard Saulsbury and other Copperheads had predicted for his assassination, and which Booth and his backers also had in mind. The previous day, Booth and Surratt accompanied Weichmann on a walk to the House of Representatives; Booth noticed a bust of Lincoln on a landing, along with some of the legendary figures of the American past. "What's he doing here before his time?" Booth asked.

He managed to secure a grandstand seat behind the President through the good offices of Lucy Hale, whose father had just been appointed Minister to Spain and was packing his bags to leave. According to a statement made on December 5, 1888, by Brigadier General Henry L. Burnett, who had been a Major in 1865, and sworn out before a notary public, Booth showed signs of making an attempt on Lincoln's life during the great address in which the words "With malice toward none" entered history. At the moment they were spoken, Burnett said that Booth started forward, gripping his knife threateningly, and that Captain John W. Westfall of the Washington police overpowered him.

Officers Otis S. Burton, Robert Strong, Charles C. Cleary, William J. Belshan and John Plants all swore out affidavits for Ward Hall Lamon in March and April, 1876, their contents confirmed in

1887 in a published reminiscence by Lamon, that Booth, acting in a menacing manner, tried to break through the police cordon before the ceremony and was overpowered at the time. No word of this incident appeared in the press next day and some historians have omitted it from the record or expressed disbelief that it ever happened.

But why would five respected policemen, Lamon and Brigadier General Burnett, who had much to lose, risk their reputations by perjuring themselves over a matter that occupied only an obscure margin in the presidential records? The truth is clearly that both incidents took place, but were rendered more colorful in joint and separate memory; it was entirely in character that Booth, held back with other members of the public behind the cordon until seated, lost patience and furiously tried to break through, waving the authorization from Senator Hale; having been let in, he may well have started murmuring threateningly, and as the President reached the phrase "With malice toward none," snapped and pulled out his dagger; on both occasions, Captain Westfall, in charge of security, may well have restrained him, anxious as he was in the excitement of the occasion, the crowd bursting with unrestrained enthusiasm; the incident went unnoticed by the press. Just over a month later, a regretful Booth told the actor Samuel Knapp Chester, "What an excellent chance I had to kill the President on Inauguration Day if I had wished." Wished and lost his nerve is probably the truth.

ON MARCH 12, BOOTH HAD MORE REASON THAN EVER TO COMMIT murder, and to include Stanton in the list. Orville H. Browning, who represented many friends of Booth's including J. Preston Parr, Robert E. Coxe, Mr. and Mrs. Green and Beverley Tucker, wanted to see the Secretary of War to complain of Lieutenant General Grant's ending trading with the enemy, which, he knew only too well, could ruin his clients' chances of further profit, and write a finish to the medicine-cotton-tobacco-rosin-turpentine-espionage network. Stanton exploded at Browning in rage; he screamed that every man who crossed the line of war to buy cotton in Richmond should be shot dead; that it was a case of "trading in the blood of the soldiers," and that it sacrificed the interests of the country to enable "mercenary scoundrels" to amass large fortunes. In this, he echoed his friend Elihu B. Washburne's summary in the report of the Committee of Commerce on trading with the enemy, issued on March 1, and emphatically supported by Grant:

> The trade which has been carried on with the insurrectionary states since the outbreak of the rebellion . . . under the sanction of law . . . has inflicted very great injury upon the public service . . . (it has led) to the prolongation of the war and it (has cost) thousands of lives and millions and millions of treasure . . . (it) almost surpasses belief.

Stanton shouted at Browning:

> I would rather that every pound of cotton in Richmond should be burned than we should buy it and pay for it in greenbacks.

Browning replied in terms which Lincoln sometimes echoed:

> Every note we put in a rebel pocket makes him a friend of our government and will destroy the Confederacy.

Could sophistry go any further?

On March 16, Browning went to Lincoln to grumble about Stanton and Grant's attitude; that his friend James W. Singleton, as an example, could be ruined by a suspension of the authorized contraband and that it would be "an outrage to ruin him." Lincoln responded, according to Browning's diary, by saying, "Oh no! Stanton isn't going to do anything desperate. He has always been as much in favor of the trade as I am." Whereupon Lincoln signed a pass to ship cotton, in defiance of the very authority he had given Grant, for Robert E. Coxe, the instrument of the Confederate Canadian commission, its backer and landlord in St. Catharines, in whose Park Street house a scrap of a letter from John Wilkes Booth was suspiciously found. Stanton proved almost equally reassuring when Browning pressed him on the matter ("We won't ruin Singleton bad.").

THREE DAYS BEFORE BROWNING SAW THE PRESIDENT AT THE WHITE House, Booth contacted Michael O'Laughlen in Baltimore with the words, "Don't fear to neglect your business. You had better come here at once," and then he summoned Arnold. Well-financed, presumably by the Belmont Copperhead business and political group in New York, since Thompson in British North America was never generous with his funds and had no apparent desire, after the failure of his disruptive efforts, to kill Lincoln, Booth put up his colleagues in comfortable quarters and, later, in hotels. On March 14, he also sent for Lewis Paine, telegraphing David Preston Parr in Baltimore to make sure he came.

On March 15, the Roman Ides of March, Booth was surprisingly not quite ready to carry out his plans against Lincoln's life; but he was still busy preparing them. He was increasingly assured of the co-operation of Lewis Paine who, under the pseudonym the Reverend Wood, posing as an ordained minister, was often at the Surratt boarding house on trips to Richmond and Baltimore for D. Preston Parr, and at times occupied the attic room upstairs.

On the afternoon of March 15, Paine walked into the room Surratt shared with Weichmann and asked Surratt, who was sitting on the bed, to step outside as he had something to say to him in private. When they left, Weichmann was amused to find that Paine had managed to drop a false mustache he was carrying in his pocket on the dressing table; instead of taking it to Paine, and perhaps enjoying his potential role of spy, he hid it in a box he used for toiletries.

He snoopily followed the two men up to the attic and found them in Paine's room as he expected they would be; they stood up to hide what was on the bed, but relaxed and sat down when they saw who he was; evidently they thought of him as one of their own, because the bed was piled with a small arsenal of revolvers, bowie knives and riding-boot spurs. In front of Weichmann, the young men began fencing playfully with the knives, as if in rehearsal for a duel, or for a fight against enemies.

Weichmann, the classic sneak, went downstairs and warned Mrs. Surratt what her son and his room-mate were doing. "I don't like this," she said, but added, "Think nothing of it. John often makes his way into the country and he needs arms for his protection."

Early that evening, Surratt showed Weichmann a $10 (current value $113) Presidential box ticket Booth had given him for the night's performance at Ford's Theatre of Nicholas Rowe's popular and harrowing melodrama *The Tragedy of Jane Shore,* about the cruel starving of the adulteress of that name by the future Richard III, the hunchbacked Duke of Gloucester. Weichmann said he would like to be included in the party but Surratt punched him teasingly in the stomach and said that he couldn't manage that. Surratt then had the nerve, after deliberately excluding his close friend and bedmate, to ask him airily for the use of his military cloak, no doubt "borrowed" from the Department of the Army storeroom, as Paine needed to wear it; he didn't say it was a disguise because, remembering the mustache, it is clear that Weichmann put two and two together. He must also have realized that something was afoot that night to which even his friends dared not make him privy.

Surratt and Paine took with them to Ford's two female guests of Mrs. Surratt, the nine-year-old schoolgirl Apollonia Dean, who was certainly too young to be allowed to see the grisly horrors of *Jane Shore,* and 17-year-old Honora Fitzpatrick. Whatever happened that night, they could be sure to suspect nothing.

The foursome settled into the Presidential box, enjoying the all-out melodrama of the play, until Booth appeared, put his head around the door and beckoned Paine to step outside, no doubt to discuss how best the box could be invaded murderously when the President should occupy it. Absorbed in the frenzied action on the stage, the two young ladies didn't try to eavesdrop.

The performance over, Surratt and Paine took them by carriage back to the boarding house; the two men left with a pack of playing cards for Gautier's popular Eating Saloon. From there, they went to the Lichau House, another popular restaurant and bar, where they met with Booth, Michael O'Laughlen and Samuel Arnold, arrived dutifully from Baltimore; and with George Atzerodt, who was taking leave from trading with the enemy in boats across the Potomac. Paine whimsically introduced himself to O'Laughlen, Arnold and Atzerodt as "Mosby," significantly the name of his former commander, Colonel John Singleton Mosby, who had a deep-seated hatred of Ulysses S. Grant, and had once tried to capture him on a train.

Booth began addressing the troop of hard-drinking and cigar- smoking supporters with his usual phony shtick of kidnapping Lincoln and holding him hostage against the release of prisoners, which Weichmann knew was happening anyway from his work at the Commissionary of Prisons. Arnold, impatient and irritable at being dragged from his gainful employment, said that unless the plans were carried out in seven days, he was going back to Baltimore. Booth was furious at the threat; he promised to shoot Arnold unless he complied with his scheme, no matter when he chose to carry it out. "Two can play at that game," Arnold replied; his lack of fear defused Booth's anger, and the meeting broke up. Next day, the 16th, Surratt, Paine, Atzerodt and David Herold met at the Surratt house and rode off on an errand whose purpose is uncertain, but is likely to have been investigating the routes south, with which Arnold and O'Laughlen, unlike the others, were not familiar and on which the so-called "abduction" journey would take place. That night, Mrs. Surratt was in tears; she was frightened, evidently, for her son's safety; her daughter Anna—herself a racist and Southern sympathizer—also panicked. At the dinner table, Anna stabbed the handle of her dinner knife into the tablecloth and cried out, "If anything happens to John though his acquaintance with Booth, I will kill Booth for sure!"

When the actor John Matthews came home to his room opposite Ford's that afternoon, he was surprised to see Booth lying on the bed reading *Julius Caesar*, perhaps to increase his identification with the character of Brutus, who killed the tyrant. Innocently or not, Matthews told Booth that a benefit performance would take place that night at Campbell's Soldiers' Hospital on 7th street on the outskirts of Washington and that Lincoln would be there. Booth was riveted and left at once to alert David Herold and O'Laughlen to pick up a black iron box containing weapons and bullets that Booth had previously sent to the lodgings O'Laughlen shared with Arnold, by the unsuspecting hall porter of the National Hotel.

Herold was to take the box in Booth's buggy to an agreed-upon location, John C. Thompson's Jolly Village Inn at the tiny hamlet identified only as T.B. Arnold and O'Laughlen met with Booth at a livery stable near the Patent Office; they rode to their lodgings on the horses Booth arranged for them, and armed themselves. Then they rode off in a drizzle of rain for the Campbell Military Hospital assignment, stopping on the way for refreshments in an inn to await the others.

They had a long wait. Atzerodt was the first to arrive, and with him Lewis Paine; Booth and Surratt were last. Over drinks, cigars and chat, Booth, after some fudging, had to admit his plan wouldn't work; he had found out at a visit to Campbell's that the President would not be attending the performance that night. The reasons given were various; the real one may well be that *Still Waters Run Deep*, the farce by Tom Taylor, the author of *Our American Cousin*, which the veterans wanted to see, was extremely racy and filled with sexual references almost unheard of in the period, and if Mrs. Lincoln were going, it could shock her severely. Also, Lincoln had been ill and was tired after the day's engagements.

David Herold picked up the trunk filled with guns, rope, and monkey wrench from John C. Thompson and he, Surratt and Atzerodt accompanied it out to Surrattsville on the 18th. Over drinks and cards, Surratt softened up John Lloyd, his mother's continuing tenant, into agreeing to hide the contents. When Lloyd said he couldn't imagine where the small arsenal could be concealed, Surratt had a ready answer.

From his years of growing up in the house, he knew every nook and cranny; an especially good hiding place had occurred to him. He led Lloyd up a back staircase past the liquor store-room and showed him the locked door of a guest room. Lloyd had long wanted to open it up for visitors, but had never gotten round to asking Mrs. Surratt for the key.

Surratt opened the door; he showed Lloyd a gap between the joists that supported the ceiling and Lloyd obligingly hid two guns there. Then, at Surratt's suggestion, he carried the rope and monkey wrench down to the liquor storeroom and hid them in it.

Lloyd, by this action, shows that he had knowledge of Booth's and Surratt's master plan. A former member of the police force, he certainly didn't think all this concealing of dangerous weapons was a child's game.

That evening, Surratt, Herold and Atzerodt took the buggy posthaste back to Washington to see Booth's one-night benefit performance as Pescara, the murderous inquisitor Count of Grenada in Richard Sheil's 1817 tragedy *The Apostate,* in which he menaced a black Moor so terrifyingly that the man might have been Lincoln himself. Soon afterward, uncertain of what Booth required of them, O'Laughlen and Arnold temporarily resumed their humble tasks in and near Baltimore.

And trading with the enemy continued, albeit in a far reduced form. On March 23, Robert, Lincoln's decent and unsuspecting son, had an unsettling experience. He had gone to City Point to visit Grant. He missed him and instead saw his aunt, Emilie Helm, arriving aboard a small boat (which could well have been one of Atzerodt's) flying a white flag of truce from the South, and accompanied aboard by none other than James W. Singleton, who, following the Washburne report, was in disgrace with Stanton, Dana, Lafayette Baker and the War Department. Mrs. Helm acknowledged Robert with what must have been some degree of embarrassment and then took off to the Willard's Hotel to discuss with Orville H. Browning the remaining 600 bales of cotton she was expecting daily on her brother-in-law the President's written authorization and personal cognizance. Soon afterward, Robert Lincoln took her south to the front line at Petersburg, to pick up the cotton.

Mrs. Helm's sister, Mrs. Clement White, arrived shortly afterward, also by boat, on a similar mission regarding an even larger number of bales. In view of the fact that two Confederate siblings of Mary Todd Lincoln were cheerfully negotiating the waters of the Potomac through the likes of George Atzerodt, it is scarcely surprising that, Washburne or no Washburne, John Surratt was able to make plans for a lengthy journey to Richmond.

That week Mrs. Surratt abandoned caution and associated openly with a Confederate soldier, Lieutenant David Barry, who had served for two years under Brigadier General Lee in Virginia;

he worked with an agent and blockade runner, Lieutenant Charles Keyworth of the Signal Corps (the Secret Confederate Service), and with the agents Augustus Howell, Sarah Antoinette Slater, and Josephine Brown; these spies brought regular word to Barry of the activities of his two sons, both under Lee's command.

On March 27, Washington newspapers announced that Lincoln would attend the opera on March 29th, a performance at Ford's of Verdi's *Ernani*. Booth telegraphed O'Laughlen, who was back in Baltimore, urging him to come with Arnold, with the words, "WE SELL THAT DAY SURE." Arnold advised him to cease and desist. He wrote:

> Suspicion rests on me now from my whole family and even parties in the country . . . Times more propitious will arrive yet . . . Do not act rashly or in haste. I would prefer your first query, 'Go and see how it will be taken in R[ichmon]d . . . Do not in anger pursue this . . .'

By coincidence or not, Lincoln cancelled the opera visit and remained at City Point; it was said he was busy reviewing the troops. Booth left on a brief journey to slake his frustrations in a romantic liaison at Newport, Rhode Island, and let off his rage in a furious political argument with his brother Edwin in New York.

On March 30, Surratt visited his old friend Brooke Stabler, who kept his horses, saying that Booth could use them any time as he was about to make a journey south; that he, Surratt, had "women on the brain" and in pursuit of his desires he would be absent for a week or two; he left later that day. His companion of the journey south, as so often before, was Sarah Antoinette Slater, who, wearing a theatrical mask, had turned up that week at Surrattsville and at the boarding house with Augustus Howell, thus proving that Mrs. Surratt was privy to Confederate espionage as well as across-the-lines trading.

After Surratt and Slater left for Richmond, and at this stage of the war it could only be on passes supplied under Presidential license to avoid arrest by Grant's men, Weichmann asked Mrs. Surratt what her son's mission was. She replied that he was seeking a clerkship in Richmond, a curious thing for her to say since to obtain such employment was an act of treason, unless she was sure of Weichmann's Confederate sympathies. Surratt had tried to deal with Weichmann's prying questions on a previous trip by saying that he had no interest in political affiliations and would serve anyone who would pay him best. Certainly, Weichmann failed to report Surratt's trip to the authorities at his Department of the Army offices when he discussed the matter of Booth with his immediate superior, the war veteran Captain David Gleason; he mentioned only Booth's connections to the cotton trade, and attempts to go south; he did not betray his bedmate at that time nor did he reveal the presence of guns, knives, ropes and wrenches in the boarding house attic room of Lewis Paine or at Surrattsville.

On March 31, while Surratt and Mrs. Slater headed south without apparent difficulty, despite the fact that Richmond was under attack and the trains were filled with Union troops, a mysterious visitor arrived in Washington, his path crossing theirs on the way. Benjamin Ficklin, yet another in the chain of Booth associates, was due to be listed along with Booth and his *confrères* and arrested with all accomplices after the April 14th assassination. Ficklin was another example of a carpetbagger who had powerful connections that granted him immunity from prosecution in those days.

Tall, lean and dark, with closely cropped black hair, Ficklin was described by one friend as looking like "a refined pirate." He was involved in cotton trading, and had been associate quartermaster in Richmond at a time when Beverley Tucker made his initial trading contracts there in January, 1864. He acted as a blockade runner to England, a betrayal of the Confederate agreement that all cotton was to go to the Union, and he frequently crossed the Potomac, carrying a white flag of truce to bring, as a cover for any unenlightened troops, letters to and from the Catholic prelates of New York and Richmond. He also brought north (as War Secretary Stanton learned from Orville H. Browning in a memorandum dated May 25, 1865) papers of vital importance belonging to Emilie Helm, and passed them on to her at her Washington hotel—sufficient reason for him to be allowed to travel unmolested, even though he was suspected of murderous intent.

More than any other conspirator, Ficklin grew rich from his cotton deals, richer even than Thurlow Weed, Ward Hill Lamon, Leonard Swett, Singleton, or others of Lincoln's intimate circle. He was able from his ill-gotten gains to buy Monticello, the former home of Thomas Jefferson in Albemarle County, Virginia, and live in it like a Rajah with a flock of African-American slaves.

Surratt arrived in Richmond at the end of March, checked into the expensive Spottswood Hotel under the cheeky name of Sherman, and found that the Union threat to the city was so severe that Mrs. Jefferson Davis and her four children had fled it on the same day; government department staffs were frantically sorting papers, destroying many and piling the rest into trains.

With little time to spare, and cannons booming in the distance, Surratt had been called to a summit meeting with Jefferson Davis and Judah P. Benjamin, with as his companion Henry Hall Brogden, a secret agent who doubled as assistant manager of the Spottswood; when Joseph H. Bradley, attorney for the defense in the 1867 Surratt trial rashly asked Brogden about the meeting, Edwards Pierrepont for the prosecution objected, and the Judge sustained that objection. Pierrepont's reason is obvious: he had to protect the Johnson administration and Lincoln's memory because the conversation would have dealt with trading with the enemy.

Benjamin handed Surratt important documents to be taken to Brigadier General Lee in Montreal along with some $200 in gold and greenbacks ($2,270). The documents were orders of instruction to Lee to obtain any and all sums Jacob Thompson had deposited at the Ontario Bank.

During her son's absence, Mrs. Surratt was constantly sending Weichmann to the National Hotel to summon Booth to secret meetings at the boarding house; showing that she knew a great deal, she told Weichmann, referring to Brooke Stabler, liveryman-stable keeper, "Brooke considers John, Herold and Atzerodt a party of gamblers and sports and I want him to think so." On one occasion she was so anxious to see Booth, but afraid of visiting him herself, that she intercepted Weichmann on his way to church and made him go to the National—a burden, since he was quite devout—and when Booth came to the boarding house she walked with him to the top of the kitchen stairs and whispered, so that Weichmann wouldn't overhear. This was a far cry from her question to him of a few days before: "What are these men (Booth and Atzerodt) doing in my house? What has John to do with all this?" By now, she most certainly knew.

And what they were up to may have included being party to arson. It is unlikely to have been a coincidence that at the outset of April, there was a fire at the headquarters of Major General Christopher C. Augur's headquarters in Washington, which contained many incriminating documents concerning the Canadian operation, including the originals of the all-important letters from Beverley Tucker and Clement C. Clay, regarding plots against the President, and carried to the capital by Richard Montgomery, as well as the extraordinary communication of Tucker dated November 1, 1864 in which he directly stated that Lincoln was his endorsing supporter in trading with the enemy. Fortunately, the appropriate correspondence, handed by Montgomery to State Secretary Seward, had been forwarded to London, to Charles Francis Adams, Minister to the court of St. James, but the documents never surfaced during the trials of the conspirators or of John Surratt, and indeed went undiscovered for many years.

On April 3, Surratt, back from the South, turned up unexpectedly at the Surratt boarding house just before supper. He mentioned only $40 of the sum Benjamin had advanced; when Weichmann told him that Richmond was being evacuated, Surratt angrily snapped back that this was a lie; Davis and Benjamin had assured him that it would not be, ever. Weichmann made no response in the face of such arrogant stubbornness and Surratt went up to the room shared by tombstone mason John T. Holahan and his wife Eliza, and knocked on the door.

Holahan came out and Surratt asked him for $50. Holahan, generous to a fault, immediately fetched the sum required and handed it to Surratt, who pocketed it, and then boldly asked for $10 more. The patient tombstoner fetched the tenspot without a murmur.

Surratt offered him two twenty-dollar gold pieces and Holahan refused to take them; he said Surratt was good for any loan.

Only when Surratt persisted did the generous Holahan agree. Then Surratt whisked Weichmann off to spend some of the money on an oyster supper.

That same day, Union Secretary of State Seward received word from British North American consuls that a plot was afoot to assassinate the entire Lincoln Cabinet; this plan followed a grievous blow to Booth's, Surratt's and others' plans to run the cotton blockade to England. On March 16, Lincoln had issued an order that any non-resident foreigners involved in blockade running in the United States were to leave for British North America or Europe in 12 days on pain of arrest. This meant that many of Beverley Tucker's contacts, hitherto protected by their British nationality, would be disconnected; another proof that Lincoln's usefulness had expired.

Jacob Thompson had had enough. He left for Halifax, to sail to England or to the South, and Lincoln's agents advised the President of this. Lincoln replied that if one had an elephant by the tail it was better to let him go; he must surely have known that if Thompson were arrested and tried he would reveal the facts about the cotton trade; at any rate, Thompson postponed his plans to leave British North America.

That week, two others in the plot against Lincoln thought it prudent to absent themselves. Fernando Wood and George McClellan both sailed for England at the beginning of April. August Belmont had been in Paris and London since January.

Meanwhile, after Surratt left for Montreal, the atmosphere at the Surratt boarding house became a mixture of the tense and the jovial. Weichmann tried to jest with Booth about the fall of Richmond, not a wise or tactful thing to do and Booth, appropriately pricked, replied sharply, "the Confederacy is not gone up yet," produced a Perrine war map of the South and spread it out, showing by his comments that he was privy to the secret movements of Lee, Major General Joseph E. Johnston and their troops. This provides further evidence that Weichmann was by no means the innocent party he claimed to be.

Meantime, friends of Booth went to great lengths to establish his absence from Washington, when in fact he was at the National Hotel plotting the final details of the assassination. On April 4, an ardent Copperhead and draft protestor named William W. McGregor arrived at the Red Lion Hotel in Pittsburgh with a man who looked like Booth; the two men entered their names into the register and "Booth's" signature was perfect.

On April 6, a letter addressed to Booth was sent from South Branch Bridge, Cumberland, Maryland, but not, for some reason delivered to him. Veiled in oil business language, it stated that $8,000, plus another $1,000 supplied by "Lou," would be available for the "job" in hand; that everything depended on "Wilkes" and his helpers; that Booth could get through on the previously arranged route he must go through Thornton Gap by Capon, Romneys and the Branch; Jake would be "at the Greens" with the funds; and so forth in similar vein.

A Union military scout, Robert Purdy, identified the letter as coming from a certain Leonidas McAleer, of South Branch, who acted on both sides of the war; he had reported Rebel movements against Cumberland and New Creek.

Meantime, in Montreal, Surratt had meetings with George Sanders which can only have concerned the assassination plans ("Booth is bossing the job for us," as Sanders had told Cleary in early February). Surratt also met with John Porterfield, who had kept the St. Albans money carpetbag, and John Douglas Corse. Corse was the brother of Brigadier General Montgomery D. Corse, of the army of North Carolina, who was captured by Union troops at Sayler's Creek after the disaster at Five Forks and was now in prison. Among Benjamin's instructions carried by Surratt to Edwin G. Lee was that Thompson must hand over two million or more in pounds, but Thompson refused; on April 14, he withdrew $649,873.20 (equivalent to $7,390,000 in modern dollars) from the Ontario Bank with plans to make off with it to London.

On April 8, Surratt went to the prominent Montreal tailor John J. Reeves and ordered him to make a Garibaldi jacket, known as an Oxford jacket in British North America. To wear it was a political as well as a sartorial statement, since Sanders' idol and dinner guest was still the symbol of hatred of tyrants to whose number Sanders and Surratt had so firmly added Lincoln. Made of gray-green cloth instead of the bright red required and worn by Garibaldi itself, it was caught at the waist by a thick belt and flared out in a skirt at the hips. It took three days to make, and Surratt returned for a final fitting on the 12th. He had just received an urgent telegram from Booth to come to Washington at once.

On April 11, while he was still in conferences with Sanders, Surratt's mother and Louis Weichmann took off to Surrattsville, where she hoped to collect a debt from her neighbor John Nothey for $479. En route, they ran into John Lloyd with his sister-in-law, Emma Offutt, at Uniontown; Mrs. Surratt got out of the buggy Weichmann was driving and told Lloyd in a low voice that he must make sure the "shooting irons," that he had hidden in the joists of the upstairs room, would be available when needed.

Lloyd was shocked: he said he had heard that the house was to be searched, evidently from a friend of his in the police—a colleague in the contraband trade. He added, no doubt from the same source, that he understood John Surratt would soon be arrested; that soldiers were after him; and for the crime of going to Richmond. Mrs. Surratt laughed heartily at the suggestion, lying that her son had not gone there, and how could he possibly get there and back in six days? The question was absurd, because anybody traveling on permits could get to Richmond and back, just 110 miles away, in a matter of two or three days. Weichmann said later he heard none of this conversation, and nor did Mrs. Offutt, but this also was absurd; the location was a quiet village, where many were indoors in light rain and where every sound could be heard; the buggy was not the size of a stagecoach, but a small, narrow vehicle.

Furthermore, Weichmann is sure to have known that Mrs. Offutt had for years been privy to, and approving of, plots against the President.

Mary Surratt discussed with Mrs. Offutt the problems of Sarah Slater's and John Surratt's fellow courier Augustus Howell, who, under the new Grant system of controls, had been sent to prison for trading with the enemy and for intelligence work. Mrs. Surratt showed her complicity with Howell by saying that she would encourage him to swear out an oath of allegiance to the Union, Booth's old ploy to escape arrest in St. Louis, and a popular device of spies and contrabanders then and later. She would also, she said, intercede on his behalf at the judicial level, and talk to a judge on the bench. By now, Orville H. Browning was representing Howell as attorney of record, but she made no mention of his name; later, when she went on trial for murder, Browning arranged her defense.

That night, Booth, Herold and Paine attended Lincoln's speech from a second story window of the White House to a crowd that was somewhat less ecstatic than at the inauguration. Booth whispered to Paine to shoot to kill, but Paine, showing an unaccustomed degree of caution, refused; he didn't want to be torn to pieces. Booth whispered, "That is the last speech he will ever make. Now, by God, I'll put him through!"

EIGHT

BAD FRIDAY AND BEYOND

To cover Surratt's journey south from Montreal in his brand new Garibaldi jacket, Brigadier General Lee concocted a plan for him to make a survey of the military prison at Elmira, New York, through bribing a guard, and thus lay the basis for a general escape. This was an absurdity: the jail, damaged by recent floods and ravaged by smallpox, was in quarantine, in pools of brackish water; prisoners were being shipped off south in exchange or to other jails on an almost daily basis, and since Richmond had fallen and Lee's army was defeated, what possible reason could there be for such a harebrained rescue expedition? At all events, despite later statements to the contrary, there is no hard evidence that Surratt pursued anything along those lines.

He left Montreal at 3:30 P.M. on April 12, arriving at Elmira in the early hours of the 13th, and checking into the Brainerd House hotel, the best and most expensive in town.

In order to establish an alibi, he walked over on the morning of the 13th to Stewart and Ufford's, the best menswear shop in town, and engaged Charles B. Stewart, co-owner, Joseph Carroll, cutter and tailor, and Frank H. Atkinson, bookkeeper, in cheerful conversation, much of which centered upon his Garibaldi jacket. They thought Surratt was a Canadian, and he did nothing to disabuse them of the idea. He asked for a particular kind of dress shirt, which wasn't in stock; he riffled through those they had, and said they didn't suit him; later, Carroll recalled firmly, unlike the others, on the witness stand at the Surratt trial in 1867, that Surratt had come back the following day. In fact the store was closed on Good Friday, a tradition in God-fearing New England towns. Grilled by prosecuting counsel Edwards Pierrepont, Carroll fell apart completely; he talked about promising Surratt that the shirts would be available on the 15th when Ufford, a partner in the firm, would return from a buying trip to New York; but this statement would more likely have been made on the 13th, which would have given him time to telegraph

Ufford in Manhattan to be sure to have them with him when he came back.

Charles B. Stewart only stated that he had seen Surratt on the 13th, and Atkinson, despite desperate efforts by defending counsel Joseph H. Bradley, would not state positively that he was there on the 14th. Thus Surratt was left with only one easily undermined and fragile witness to state that he was there on the day Lincoln was assassinated.

Surratt left town on the 10:30 special train that carried no passengers, except one official on the caboose; it took packages, letters, gravel and stones and timber to the construction crew that was busy rebuilding the Williamsport bridge across the Susquehanna River that had been swept away in a recent storm. In order to prove that no such train existed, Bradley Jr. or some other agent of the defense, went to extraordinary lengths, described in the *New York Times* in an article published on November 1, 1867, and based upon exhaustive research long after the Surratt trial:

> One of the Superintendents erased from the regular report of trains going south the entire column in which was entered the movements of that special train. When this erasure was noticed (by the prosecution team), the original report of the conductor of the train was speedily produced. These officials had even gone further, and in addition to destroying the record of the special, had also altered the report of a train by which Surratt could have reached Baltimore in time to take the forenoon to Washington.

Since the lone official on the caboose saw no sign of Surratt on the journey from Elmira to Williamsport it is clear that the adventurous young man boarded a freight car, no particular feat for anyone of his age and athleticism. He arrived at Williamsport at 12:30, and proceeded at once to the depot office of Ezra B. Westfall, the Pennsylvania and Ohio Railroad trainmaster, who was there to guide passengers to the rope ferry the company ran for the benefit of its customers. Westfall, who identified Surratt in court at his trial, said under oath:

> A man came to see me who was very anxious to get through. He asked me some questions with regard to the trains. He inquired what would be the probable chance of getting over the line. I took him to be either a rebel spy or a government detective. I cut him off very short . . . I did not give him much satisfaction because I thought it was none of his business how we ran our trains at that time.

All Westfall would tell Surratt was that the bridge was down, and that he must take the special rope ferry across the raging and almost unnavigable Susquehanna. Surratt walked at top speed to the hastily improvised ferry pier and saw, much to his relief, that the ferry boat had just arrived and that the ferryman, the Irish veteran Morris Drohan, was tying her up with the rope.

Surratt asked Drohan to take him across so he could catch the next train; Drohan told him it would cost him 50 cents. Surratt agreed; and half-way across the turbulent waters handed him a dollar, and told him to keep the change.

When Drohan testified to the matter in court, he was so convincing, and held the court so spellbound, that defense counsel Joseph Bradley gave up any idea of cross examining him, and walked away from the witness stand with a contemptuous gesture of dismissal.

Luckily, a gravel and wood train from further south was waiting on the other side of the river, empty of its load which had been handed over to the bridge building superintendent, and set at once to return to Montoursville and Sunbury; this time, Surratt rode the caboose alone. He changed trains at Sunbury, where he waited several hours for the Pennsylvania and Erie passenger express in which he left just after midnight, and arrived in Baltimore at 7:25 A.M.; he changed again to the ever-reliable Baltimore and Ohio Railroad, and arrived easily in Washington at 10:25.

Wasting no time, he left his suitcase at the depot and went at once to Booker and Stewart's barbershop, just a short walk away, on E Street. The popular African-American barber Charles H. M. Wood was there to shave him, noting that he was dusty and unkempt from his grueling 24-hour journey. Booth and

O'Laughlen, no doubt by prior arrangement, joined Surratt for haircuts and shaves; Surratt was second in the chair after Booth, telling Wood, "Clean me up nicely. I am going away in a day or two," which was indeed not less than the truth. He had a whispered conversation with Booth afterward that, try as he may, Wood could not overhear; all he could make out was that it had to do with Baltimore.

Wood had been at Secretary of State Seward's house to take care of his tonsorial and shaving needs, and had had breakfast; Seward, injured in an accident, was not an early riser, so Wood's later estimated time of 9 A.M. for Surratt's arrival was wrong.

That morning, Surratt went to Ford's Theatre on a specific, and very important, errand, no doubt assigned to him by Booth. Normally, the door that led from the vestibule where the owner's brother Harry Ford ran the box office was locked, in case of illegal entry in the daytime, but this particular morning it was open for carpenters and because a group of actors in the stock company, who would be performing in Tom Taylor's *Our American Cousin* that night, had been summoned in haste to rehearse, in the upstairs paint room, in the street outside, and later on the stage, a song, composed for an actors' benefit the following evening entitled "All Honor to Our Soldiers." This patriotic ditty was rescheduled at great haste to be performed that same night, because Harry Ford and his staff had just been given the exciting news that the President would be attending the 8 P.M. performance and the song would be sung for him afterwards.

To avoid giving each member of the cast and carpentry crew a key, the door was, despite the management's subsequent denials, open the whole morning. Not only did Surratt slip easily through it but so did a clock repairman and theatre fan named Theodore B. Rhodes, who liked to wander into empty places of entertainment on days he could spare from his work, to imagine the smell of grease paint and the roar of the crowd when buying tickets was beyond his means.

Rhodes, a classic example of a snoop, noticed two things as he crept in: the drop curtain was down, with advertisements on the fireproof steel, not the regular curtain of heavy velvet; the reason was clearly that the singers, once returned from the street or the paint room upstairs, would be able to block out their positions and movements in a fairly limited space.

Exploring the dress circle so he could obtain a full view of the stage, Rhodes saw a door of the State (or Presidential) box open and close. The defense counsel Joseph H. Bradley at the Surratt trial did his best to demolish this statement without success; the fact is that Rhodes certainly could see the door opening and closing if he directly faced the box on the opposite side of the dress circle (today it is called the mezzanine). Normally, it would be too dark to see easily when the house gaslights were off but the windows and skylight were open and the bright morning sunlight more than provided sufficient visibility.

He ran into Surratt, who said, improvising with his customary skill and speed, that since the President was coming that night, he and a carpentry team were busy preparing the box; he was holding a three-foot long stick of North Carolina pine he had abstracted from a music stand used by a member of the Treasury Regimental Band that had performed at a cotillion there on February 22nd.

While Rhodes watched, Surratt fitted the stick into a hole he had drilled in one of the doors of the box, a hole no larger than his thumb. He whittled the stick down to fit the hole and left the shavings on the floor. He explained that the idea was to prop the door closed, because it had a damaged lock, against intruders during the performance that night; actually he was preparing both a peephole and a block to hasty exit, for Booth to carry off his assassination plan.

At the Surratt trial, defense counsel Bradley tried desperately and futilely to discredit Rhodes; he stumbled into a ditch when he asked him to describe the hat Surratt was wearing. Rhodes described it as a black velvet hat; others later confirmed they had seen Surratt in a jockey hat, which was often made of black velvet in those days. No writer then or later has addressed Rhodes' statement, or the proof it provides that the device of drilled peephole, music stand support stick and use of that stick as a bar to escaping the Presidential box were Surratt's—and made Booth's assassination of Lincoln possible. Also, the shavings Rhodes described were still on the floor when the President died in the early hours of the following morning, and were found by investigating Judge A. B. Olin.

James Lamb, the scene painter in the theatre, who was overheard by witnesses discussing Confederate sympathies with Booth on at least one occasion, was less than reliable in his court testimony. He said he was in his paint room the whole morning working on scenery for a play based on Tennyson's *Enoch Arden* but he made no mention of the rehearsal in that same room which would have prevented the cast from seeing Surratt, or Rhodes for that matter; and he lied that he would have heard if the curtain Rhodes described were lowered, when in fact the singing around him, and even echoing up from the street outside or the stage, would have drowned so muffled a sound.

James absurdly added that he would have heard the curtain despite the noise, as a miller heard a drumwheel, forgetting that flour mills are usually tomb-like in their silence. Lamb also lied in saying the cast was rehearsing *Our American Cousin,* which they knew by heart, instead of "All Honor to Our Soldiers;" finally under pressure from Edwards Pierrepont, he had to admit he wasn't sure if the curtain was down or not, thus blowing his entire testimony out of the water; and by admitting to Pierrepont that the theatre was daylit, he destroyed Bradley's contention that it was too dark for Rhodes to have seen the Presidential Box door opening and shutting.

A major controversy blew up in court when witnesses, who couldn't remember the name of the music hall, said they had seen Surratt with Booth and others at one such establishment in the afternoon; Benjamin W. Vanderpoel, a young attorney who had been released from a Confederate prison and had known Surratt for many years, said he saw Surratt watching "a woman— or something" dancing on a stage in an upstairs room at such a place. Bradley dragged one witness after another onto the stand to testify that music hall after music hall had no rehearsal that day; but Vanderpoel and others mentioned no rehearsal; only the solo appearance of what seemed to be an effeminate male.

That individual was almost certainly a man, never named, who, at the barber's shop that morning, and in front of Booth and Surratt, had pirouetted in front of a mirror in long curly black locks that suggested a transvestite, or an actor using drag for comic effect; and the music hall concerned was identified, despite Bradley's attempts to avoid that, as the Teutonia. At 2:30 P.M. David C. Reed, who had known Surratt since childhood, saw him in Pennsylvania Avenue, just below Booth's National Hotel. Surratt recognized Reed also, and the two men nodded to each other; like other witnesses, Reed noticed that Surratt wore smart pantaloons, and had fine spurs on his riding boots; that he also had a stiff-brimmed hat, a proper description of the black velvet jockey hat Theodore Rhodes had noted. Reed saw him head for the Metropolitan Hotel, where O'Laughlen then lived.

Sometime after 3 P.M., John Lee, the detective who had followed Surratt at the beginning of the year to track his movements in trading in medical supplies with the enemy, recognized him also in the street; shortly after that, it is clear that Surratt, his task completed, left town to return to Elmira to give the impression he had never left.

Three soldiers claimed at his trial that they saw him in front of Ford's at 10:15 that night, the time of the assassination, but they had confused him with a lookalike actor named C. V. Morse who was going to appear in "All Honor to our Soldiers," was worried about the time at which *Our American Cousin* would end and that he should be ready for it, and went to his dressing room right after that. Actually, in order to get back to Elmira in time to support his alibi, Surratt had to catch the 3:30 P.M. B & O train; he would be at his destination by 9 A.M. on Saturday morning.

AT 10:30 ON THE MORNING OF APRIL 14, THE EXACT TIME SURRATT left Elmira, Secretary of War Stanton sent word to his staff that because it was Good Friday, he would call for a one-day holiday, and everybody could go home, or to church. Louis Weichmann hurried off to mass at St. Matthew's Church and two hours later was back at the boarding house, where he ate lunch and went to his room to write a letter. At 2:25 or thereabouts, Mrs. Surratt told him she had to go to Surrattsville again and once more try to extract the debt owed her by her neighbor, John Nothey. She said that the well-to-do George Calvert, who had a property nearby, had told her she must repay him the loan her late husband had

raised with him on an I.O.U. to put down the original deposit on
her boarding house some years before.

Anxious to leave as soon as possible—her purpose was not as
innocent as it seemed—and since Booth had sold his horse and
buggy, she gave Weichmann $10 to run out and rent the trans-
portation. As he left for Howard's Stables, Booth arrived sud-
denly and walked into the parlor to talk to her. At the livery
stable, Weichmann ran into George Atzerodt, who was renting a
horse for Lewis Paine. Weichmann noted that, and returned with
the buggy to the boarding house.

As he went up to his room to fetch his letter for mailing, he
noticed that Booth was talking to Mrs. Surratt in the parlor. She was
standing with her back to the half-open door; Booth was leaning
against the mantelpiece. Despite straining his ears, Weichmann
couldn't hear what they were saying, but although Booth must have
seen him, he didn't, perhaps significantly, close the door.

By 2:40 P.M. Booth had left and Weichmann told Mrs. Surratt
he was ready to leave and the buggy was outside the front door.
She was about to climb in when she remembered that Booth had
left something with her and she had forgotten to bring it; she
returned with a round brown paper package that Weichmann,
who placed it on the floor under his driver's seat for safety,
noticed contained something brittle; in fact it was a pair of field
glasses, useful for Booth if he should be in flight after the assassination, to spy out the movements of his pursuers.

En route to Surrattsville, in a sprinkle of rain on an otherwise
brilliantly clear day, Weichmann drew up at a blacksmith's shop,
presumably to water the horse. He and Mrs. Surratt saw soldiers
lolling on the grass, pickets' men on the alert for suspicious travelers. She asked someone how long they would be there—not
the wisest question for someone up to no good. "They will leave
at eight o'clock tonight," was the reply and, knowing she would
be passing by during the trip back from Surrattsville after that,
and Booth would use that escape route, she was greatly relieved.

Thus reassured, she was in a lively and talkative mood for the
rest of the journey. When Weichmann finally reined in the horse
at Surrattsville, she got out quickly and Weichmann handed her
the brown paper package. Once inside the living room, surprised

to find John Lloyd absent, she asked him to figure the interest on the money that Nothey owed her for the 13 years of the debt, then had him draw up a threatening letter.

After he finished writing it, Mrs. Offutt arrived. Asked the whereabouts of John Lloyd, she said he was at the town of Marlboro, giving evidence against a man named Edward Perrie, who had stabbed him in a barroom brawl.

Lloyd turned up drunk at 6.30 P.M., saying that Perrie had been found guilty and that he had been celebrating all the way home. Mrs. Surratt gave him the package with the field glasses and asked him to have the "shooting irons" that her son had him hide in the upstairs room ceiling joists, ready when needed. She said that he should also bring up two bottles of whiskey from the liquor storeroom, when the appropriate visitors arrived.

Lloyd took the package to the storeroom, went to his quarters and threw up.

When he came downstairs, Mrs. Surratt asked him to repair the broken spring on her buggy wheel; he told her he hadn't the necessary tools, but drunkenly managed to tie up the struts with ropes. Then, with Weichmann in the driver's seat, he and Mrs. Surratt took off to Washington.

She was no longer light-hearted now; she was, she said, anxious to be home by nine P.M., and she told Weichmann that he must make sure she did. She said she had to meet some people at that exact time. When Weichmann asked her who they were, either she didn't say, or he later lied that she didn't.

He said he seized the occasion to ask her what Booth was doing when he wasn't acting; this also lacks the ring of truth, since if he didn't know what was going on in the cramped and claustrophobic boarding house, then he would have to have been deaf and blind. Mrs. Surratt was supposed to have replied that Booth was going to New York very soon and would never return; a nonsensical statement at best.

She was also supposed to have asked Weichmann whether he knew that Booth was "crazy on one subject," and he answered meaninglessly that he did not.

The travelers passed the picket point at the blacksmith's shop and noted, no doubt to Mrs. Surratt's satisfaction, that the soldiers

had, as expected, left their posts at eight P.M.; however, she may
have had pause when the very same cavalrymen rode alongside the
buggy for part of the journey home. About two miles from Washington, Weichmann reined in the horse and pointed to the brilliantly lighted city in the throes of celebrating the Union's victory;
the Stars and Stripes had just been raised over Fort Sumter. Weichmann said it was better for the country that peace should return,
and Mrs. Surratt replied, according to him, "I am afraid that all
this rejoicing will be turned into mourning, and all this gladness
into sorrow;" that there would be punishment for "a proud and
licentious people."

As they rode down Pennsylvania Avenue, a torchlight procession came past; the buggy horse shied at the brilliant flash of
lights and they had to make a detour up Second Street. They
arrived at the boarding house on schedule—a few minutes
before nine; Weichmann returned the vehicle and horse to
Howard's Stable. He returned to late supper with Mrs. Surratt,
Anna, her daughter, and Olivia Jenkins, Mrs. Surratt's niece.
During the meal, served as always in the downstairs dining
room, the doorbell jangled loudly—it was often jested that it
was the loudest bell in Washington—and Susan L. Mahoney,
the African-American maid, didn't answer it; this suggests a call
was expected. Heavy footsteps, the footsteps of a strong and
powerful man, were heard by everyone at the table going up
the stairs; two of the guests had different stories of what took
place.

According to Olivia Jenkins, Anna went upstairs to see who
the visitor was; she returned, saying it was a naval officer named
Scott, who had brought with him two documents for Olivia; she
handed them to her. According to Weichmann, the visitor was
actually Booth, and the implication was that it was to discuss
details of the assassination, and not with Anna, but with her
mother, who was really the one who went upstairs.

It would certainly be logical that Booth would drop by to be
sure that the weapons and whiskey would be available from John
Lloyd at Surrattsville; lamentably, Edwards Pierrepont at the Surratt trial failed to push Miss Jenkins to say who Scott was, and
what the documents contained.

Also during supper, Anna said that she and her mother had received word from her brother in Montreal, and that his "board" (the St. Lawrence Hall) was too expensive at $2.50 a night; that he was planning to go to Toronto. Mailed before he left Montreal, this letter was clearly a blind covering his true mission to Washington. To protect his mother, Surratt had made sure she didn't see him that day.

At the same time as the group concluded supper, Booth, at 10:15, had written himself into history by invading the Presidential box at Ford's, where Surratt's stolen music stick and drilled peephole were indispensable and whose assigned guard, John Parker, was absent having a drink. The crowded theater filled with laughter at the inane antics of *Our American Cousin,* the sudden shot so unexpected and so drowned by mirth that at first it was barely noticed; the illustrious gaunt figure of the President slumping forward, Booth's leap to the stage, so carefully thought out to take place in the dark, so ruined by the blaze of gaslight when an accomplice failed to turn off the main; his entanglement in a flag brought in only that afternoon; his 12-day flight with the aid of Surrattsville field glasses and shooting irons to the swamps and woody brakes of a nightmare journey to his death by gunshot at the hands of a mad soldier in the flames of a burning barn—such, along with Lewis Paine's abortive attempt on Seward, and an unknown assailant's effort to break into Grant's private car on the train north, was the stuff of legend, born that night as the Surratt boarders polished off their food.

AFTER DINNER, ANNA WENT UP TO HER ROOM FEELING ILL; ELIZA Holahan asked Mrs. Surratt if she would like to go, as she had indicated earlier, to mass; they started walking past the adjoining houses. Eliza said it was a heavy and disagreeable evening and suggested they go back; she had noticed a dark threat of rain.

Mrs. Surratt joined her guests in the parlor. She seemed desperate to make idle conversation; evidently, Booth's visit had unsettled her. She asked Weichmann pointlessly where the torchlight procession that had startled the buggy horse earlier that evening was heading for; he said he understood it was heading for the White House to serenade the President, and was made up of employees of the Arsenal.

The unhappy landlady was not a criminal by nature, much less a murderess; she had, to help her son, and the Confederate cause in which she passionately believed, been caught up in a web of murderous conspiracy and having given that son and Booth (whom she called "Pet") loving and dangerous help, there was no going back. She showed her agony of mind as she paced up and down, fingering her rosary and saying silent prayers. She was all too aware that this was Good Friday and that she would surely go to Hell for what she was involved in. She asked Weichmann to pray for her intentions; clearly she didn't mean only for him to pray that her son's and Booth's murderous plans would be carried out, but that he must pray to God for her to be forgiven in making them. Weichmann replied, or said he did, "I never pray for anyone's intentions unless I know what they are." "Pray for them anyway," she said.

Mary's nerves were stretched still further when Honora Fitzpatrick and Olivia Jenkins began teasing Weichmann playfully in some kind of childish game; irritated beyond endurance, their landlady packed all three of them off to bed; she herself, of course, couldn't sleep and remained dressed and presumably pacing the parlor.

At 2 A.M. the loudest doorbell in Washington rang again. Eliza Holahan was the first to wake up and put her head out of the upstairs window to see who was there. When she saw police in the street she sensibly withdrew.

Mrs. Surratt was still in the parlor. Weichmann had also been restless; he had been out in the yard taking the night air, and was back in his room without having changed into his nightshirt; the young women were asleep. Weichmann pulled on his trousers, and with his dress shirt still unbuttoned, walked to the front door. He asked who was there. A voice answered, "Government officers. We have come to search the house—for John Wilkes Booth and John Surratt." "They aren't at home," Weichmann replied, rather oddly in Booth's case, since he didn't live there. "Let us in anyhow," the voice said.

With a certain degree of impudence, Weichmann said he would have to ask Mrs. Surratt's permission before he could oblige. When he told her, she said, in stress, "For God's sake let them in! I expected the house would be searched." If anything is needed to prove that she knew what had happened at Ford's, that statement supplies it.

Weichmann opened the door and a posse led by Officers A. C. Richards, J. W. A. Clarvoe and J. A. McDevitt strode in. The first thing they saw was a mud-covered shawl lying in the front corridor.

This was odd, to say the least; Mrs. Surratt was not noted for untidiness, and why would a shawl be covered in mud when the ride out to Surrattsville did not involve it falling off the buggy? The likelihood is that she had pushed it into the back of the buggy which had been sloshed with mud in recent rain due to the broken spring; and that it had been hanging on a peg in the hall, and had fallen down in the night.

The police searched the boarding house from top to bottom. When Clarvoe asked Mrs. Surratt where her son was, she replied, "Not in the city, sir." Clarvoe asked to see Weichmann's room, Weichmann took him there; he put his hand on Clarvoe's shoulder and asked, "Will you be kind enough to tell me the meaning of all this?" Clarvoe told him the President had been murdered and pulled out from his coat the bow of a neck-handkerchief soaked in blood, telling him that it was the President's; that Booth had killed him; and (inaccurately) that Surratt had killed Secretary of State Seward. With McDevitt and Weichmann following, Clarvoe returned to Mrs. Surratt, who had changed into another dress in a matter of minutes. The detectives asked her when she had last seen Booth and she lied that it was at two P.M. the previous day; that she had just received a letter for her son but had no idea where he was ("A great many mothers do not know where their sons are.")

Clarvoe, who had served with John Holahan in the police force some years before, went up to his room and asked him what he knew: Holahan got permission to warn his daughter and Anna Surratt, who shared a bed, that the police would question them, and the detectives, without much ado, walked in and pulled the bedclothes off the two young women, and talked to them.

After the officers left, Anna Surratt cried out in the parlor, "Oh Ma! Just think of that man Booth having been here an hour before the assassination, I am afraid he will bring suspicion upon us!"

Indeed he might; for not only did Miss Surratt thus reveal that the mysterious visitor during supper was not a naval officer named Scott but Booth himself; she also revealed that she knew the exact time of the assassination, which had not been revealed to her by the detectives. Mrs. Surratt then got in deeper by saying, "Anna, come what will, I am resigned. I think that John Wilkes Booth was only an instrument in the hands of the Almighty to punish this proud and licentious people."

At early morning light, Weichmann ran out to get the Washington *Chronicle* with all of its horrifying detail of gunshot and terror. He said to the others at the breakfast table, "It's a deplorable crime. Booth's visits here will be inquired about." To which Anna Surratt replied, "Lincoln's death is no worse than that of any nigger in the army." "You will find out differently," Weichmann sharply replied.

TRAVELING THROUGH THE NIGHT OF APRIL 14-15, SURRATT, POSING AS a British North American courier, complete with dispatch case, Canadian-British accent and Garibaldi jacket, was back at Elmira at 9 A.M. on Saturday the 15th. To make his alibi perfect, he went to another tailor's shop, John Cass's, giving the impression he had never been away. Cass on the witness stand was confused about the time he saw Surratt; he said it was at quarter to eight, or eight o'clock, and that Surratt came in the store and (repeating his performance at Stewart and Ufford's), asked about a particular kind of shirt, and rejected the ones Cass showed him. But Cass didn't open his store until 9 A.M., and word didn't come to close all stores from the mayor's office until 9:30 that morning, when an extra edition of the Elmira *Advertiser* was rushed out to the stands to announce Lincoln's death. The first edition, published at 7.30 A.M., did not contain a word of it (Lincoln had died just minutes earlier) and even for the second edition, the editor was unable to clear the front page. What seems to have happened was that Cass opened his store against the local mayoral rule at between 9.30 and 10 and let Surratt in, then closed it again. Cass did recall that when he mentioned the assassination to Surratt, the response was disrespectful; Cass was annoyed, until he decided that, since Surratt had said he was a Canadian, he would not have strong feelings in the matter.

That afternoon, Surratt took the train to the town of Canandaigua, where he checked into the Webster House hotel, registering as John Harrison, and stating that he was from New York. In an unwise effort to place him in Washington that night, prosecutor Edwards Pierrepont questioned the validity of the signature; and made much of the fact that the night record book, containing details of guests and cash entries for payment of rooms, had been tampered with while it lay in a woodshed of Frank O. Chamberlin, the hotel's new owner, for two years; William Failing, the original owner, explained that children used the shed as a playroom, and often pulled out any paper they could find for infantile games. Pierrepont, with support from the Judge, suggested that this was actually the work of Joseph H. Bradley Junior, who had already had more than his share of tasks to perform; it was far more likely to have been the work of the Pierrepont team, a classic case of the pot calling the kettle black; Surratt went on to Montreal.

ON THE MORNING OF THE 15TH AS INSTRUCTED, WEICHMANN AND Holahan appeared at the 10th street police precinct and reported to McDevitt; with that officer and Clarvoe, the men set off on a search for Surratt on horseback, picking up his photograph from his mother at the boarding house, visiting Herold's mother at the Navy Yard to obtain his picture also, then traveling to Surrattsville, so that McDevitt and Clarvoe could talk to John Lloyd. Clarvoe knew Lloyd, who, like Holahan, had at one time been in the police force. When he asked Lloyd if he had heard the news, and if he knew who had done it, Lloyd joked with a dangerous lack of taste that, "They say it is a fellow named Booze, a circus actor." Clarvoe told him that he shouldn't "play that kind of game" and asked him about Mrs. Surratt's visit to Surrattsville with Weichmann; Lloyd confirmed the details.

Clarvoe told him he was a "made man" financially if he would say where Surratt, Booth and Herold went; he said he didn't know,

but if he were asked what route they would take, it would be by way
of the Piscataway Road; that was a blatant deceit. Clarvoe, McDevitt,
Holahan and Weichmann unwisely took that route, but there was
no sign of the conspirators and McDevitt decided to proceed north
after Surratt, following a tip that he was in British North America.

At Surratt's trial, the family maid, Susan L. Jackson (neé
Mahoney), lied that she saw Surratt in the dining room at nine
that night after Weichmann returned with his mother from Surrattsville; that she saw Mrs. Surratt take up the washing and that
she asked her if it was Weichmann's and she said it was her son's,
who was there in the room, and was he not very much like his sister Anna? There is no question that the prosecution bribed Ms.
Mahoney, since it was absurd that after three weeks in the house
she would not have seen Surratt before as she claimed, and that
the conversation she reported would have taken place after she
had seen him several times. The man she married after the assassination, Samuel L. Jackson, stated, also under oath, he had not
heard his then fiancée make any reference to Surratt being
there; the impossibility of her statement, which she had earlier
made to John Lloyd's servant Eliza Hawkins, is that from the
moment the assassination attempt was known to the police at
10:30 P.M., every train out of town was stopped and there is no
way that Surratt could have been aboard any of them.

McDevitt, Weichmann and Holahan set out for Montreal; at
Burlington, Vermont, Holahan, accidentally or not, dropped a
handkerchief on which the Surratt housemaid had stitched Surratt's name for identification purposes, and which Holahan had
picked up with his laundry at the boarding house in the depot;
the effect of this was to make it seem that Surratt was there and
delayed the investigation. McDevitt then made inquiries at St.
Lawrence Hall.

What the hotel staff didn't tell him was that Surratt had
found shelter at the home of John J. Reeves, the tailor who had
made him his Oxford or Garibaldi jacket, and that he was now
being taken care of, with the full approval of the ecclesiastical
authorities, by a Catholic priest.

Recalled by Secretary Stanton, the pursuing team went home
empty-handed.

NINE

AFTERMATH

OF

THE

TRAGEDY

And what of the principal figures who had so urgently wanted Lincoln's destruction? Benjamin Wood was silent, except for a predictably fake editorial full of praise in his *New York Daily News.* That must have caused the treacherous publisher many a sleepless night; Horace Greeley, smarting from Lincoln's failure to offer him the sinecure of the Postmaster Generalship or any inclusion in trading with the enemy, at first refused to withdraw a scathing attack, due for publication in the New York *Tribune* on the 15th, until warned by his managing editor, Sidney Gay, that the result might be a wrecking of his offices; Gay spiked the article and Greeley walked out, white with rage.

In London, which didn't receive the news for several days, Fernando Wood arranged a mass meeting of Americans in exile to express condolences, then refused to attend it, and left for Paris to avoid a display of hypocritical grief. August Belmont, back in New York after a long absence, wrote to the Rothschilds in London on April 18 with a notably cold detachment, confining his comments to the adverse effect on the marketplace. Horatio Seymour said little, none of it of consequence. For all these men, there was the realization that Lincoln's death was a greater disaster to them and to the South than his life; he was at once enshrined and immortalized, and if any man spoke against him, that man would be lynched on sight.

When Joseph Shaw, editor of the Western Maryland *Democrat,* failed to produce an editorial sufficiently reversing his four years of furious attacks, he was stabbed and shot to death.

St. Lawrence Hall was the scene of rejoicing; the moment the news of Lincoln's death was confirmed, Sanders and Brigadier General Lee contacted every secessionist they knew, Jacob Thompson abstaining, and summoned them to a party of wine, women and song to celebrate the departure of the hated President.

And what of the traders with the enemy? Judge James Hughes warned Orville Browning about greater danger now for Singleton;

he told him that the political figure Britton A. Hill was calling for Hughes and Singleton to be driven out of town, but Hill saw them only as Copperheads, overlooking the fact that they had been in league with the President on their cotton deals.

Nothing was made of the fact that Ward Hill Lamon, who should have been in town to protect the President's life, was in Richmond instead, on what was described as business connected with the reconstitution of Virginia, but was more likely to have been checking on whether the cotton he had bought for greenbacks could still, in a wrecked city, be found in storage and shipped.

Within days, Browning made it his business to do what he could for the assassins, and to press the incumbent President, Andrew Johnson, to continue cotton trade with the South; on May 2, he went to see Stanton to arrange for new shipments across the Potomac, but Stanton refused, saying he hoped the appropriate boats would be seized and confiscated. On May 4, Browning was still at work helping Robert E. Coxe to secure the remaining cotton in Richmond and on May 10, when Coxe was arrested for his part in the Canadian conspiracy, he had him out of handcuffs in 24 hours. He continuously urged Johnson to have Benjamin Ficklin released, and finally succeeded, on June 19. No charges against that treacherous millionaire were preferred.

Browning wasn't done yet. He set up a prominent leader of the bar, Maryland Senator Reverdy Johnson, as defense counsel for Mary Surratt at the military trial of the conspirators. He also set up Thomas Ewing, another one of his law practice partners, as defense counsel for Dr. Mudd. And he himself was never questioned or arrested, for obvious reasons.

In order to find Beverley Tucker's connections to the assassination, Major General Halleck sent troops to his home in Buckingham County and ransacked its rooms; they found nothing; his wife Jane had destroyed all incriminating papers; but that the family was terrified is shown by the fact that Tucker's daughter Annie died of a heart attack after the search. Jane, with her older boys James and Ellis, rejoined, after many setbacks, Tucker and their younger children in Montreal in July, only to find that there were kidnap threats against him; she called in the Queen's

Artillery Regiment and the Mayor of Montreal's special guard to
protect him. It seemed that Lafayette Baker hadn't done with
him yet, but in the end nothing happened.

Though pleasing to Sanders and Lee, Surratt's presence in
Montreal was embarrassing to Jacob Thompson who, like
Tucker, lived in constant danger of kidnap and arrest.

Jefferson Davis's former chief commissioner went to Washington intending to give himself up and throw himself upon the
mercy of the court, but friends sensibly advised him to evade justice at all costs, and he disguised himself as a peddler, selling tin
cans off a cart through the backblocks of Maryland; when asked
for his whereabouts by soldiers at a country inn, he pointed them
in the wrong direction. Back in Montreal, he sent a woman he
knew, Mrs. Loring, the landlady of the Inn of the Seven Gables
where he was hiding, to his family home at Oxford, Mississippi,
to bring his wife Catherine money and documents which she
should read and then burn.

The energetic Mrs. Loring (whose first name is lost to history) hid the documents in her bustle, posed as an ardent Unionist and took a river boat from Cairo, Illinois, to Memphis,
Tennessee, and thence went to Oxford, where Mrs. Thompson
received her in a makeshift office in the burned-out surround-
ings of what was left of the family plantation. Kate obediently
destroyed the incriminating documents and headed north with
her visitor; the enterprising ladies arrived safely in Montreal, and
the Thompsons left for Halifax, to take ship to England, Catherine first because she needed medical treatments for cancer with
a specialist in Germany.

Thompson followed her to London, where the former Confederate Secretary of War, John C. Breckinridge, was already
installed.

It emerged after the assassination that Lincoln's last visitors
were pushing for the cotton states' trade to continue in the wake
of the transfer of prohibitive authority to Grant; James W. Singleton made a call (at a time not recorded), Orville H. Browning
had an appointment but Lincoln was unable to keep it as he had
to leave for the theatre; but George Ashmun, the partner of the
treasonable trader and Beverley Tucker partner Thomas C. Durant

in the Union Pacific Railroad, was with him in the Red Room at 8 P.M., just minutes before he left for the theatre; Ashmun had arranged for a colleague, Charles A. Hawkes, to obtain, on December 27, 1864, 72,000 bales of cotton, 7000 barrels of turpentine, 7000 barrels of rosin, 5000 barrels of tar and 3000 boxes of tobacco from Georgia and Florida for delivery by April 1. Since Grant had ordered much of the supply seized, Ashmun was lodging a complaint against the government to which Lincoln was giving a sympathetic ear; he made an appointment for Ashmun and a friend, probably Hawkes, to return the following day.

Browning, Ashmun and the traders-with-the-enemy Thomas Corwin and former War Secretary Simon Cameron were supposed to be the four civilian pall bearers, but only Browning had the effrontery to appear when called upon. Perhaps the others knew what Lincoln's support of their nefarious dealings had cost him.

On April 18, Weichmann's boss Major Gleason named Sarah Antoinette Slater as "a French woman who carried money to the St. Albans raiders in Canada." Arrested in New York, she was quickly released; D. Preston Parr and Robert E. Coxe were also arrested and released within twenty-four hours, presumably because they knew too much about trading with the enemy, and the actor John McCullough, a loyal friend of Booth who also knew a great deal, was allowed to leave for Montreal.

Augustus Howell was kept briefly in solitary confinement; he reported that Surratt had used his position as employee of the Commissary General of Prisoners to pass on information to him and for Surratt to convey to Richmond; then he was released.

More damaging evidence against Weichmann piled up. Gilbert J. Raynor, a fellow clerk whose desk was in the same office as Weichmann's, said Weichmann had stated he could make as much as $20,000 to $40,000 ($227,000 to $455,000) in a certain enterprise and soon after that had introduced Surratt to him at the office. But Weichmann also knew too much to be charged.

After two days hiding with his tailor in Montreal, Surratt was picked up by Joseph H. Du Tilley, coach-and-handyman for the Reverend Charles Boucher, Confederate-loving parish priest at the town of St. Liboire, some 34 miles east of Montreal.

Du Tilley drove him to Trois Rivières, and thence, with the aid of an Indian scout, across the St. Lawrence by canoe, whence he took him to Father Boucher's house, under the pseudonym of Charles Armstrong.

Surratt contracted pneumonia; he suffered also from a recurrence of malaria picked up during his time of service with the Stonewall Brigade; he took to his bed for months as a semi-permanent invalid.

Throughout those weeks, in the 19th century equivalent of a 17th century priest's hole in England, Surratt was kept in ignorance of the outside world. Not allowed to see a newspaper lest he should suffer an emotional breakdown, he was oblivious of the trial of his mother and the other conspirators.

A hastily conducted military tribunal, scarcely better than a kangaroo court, that trial was very badly handled by all concerned. The defense had no time to prepare its cases; the issue of trading with the enemy was disallowed; the evidence was a shambles in the hands of such perjurers as the journalist Sanford Conover, Dr. James Merritt, and others whom Sanders supplied to exaggerate charges against the Canadian conspirators with a view to discrediting them later; Advocate General Joseph Holt was his absolute dupe in the matter. The result, in view of public feeling, was a foregone conclusion; dragged into court in chains and hoods, except for the veiled Mary Surratt, not able to give evidence for themselves, almost overcome by the heat and prison conditions—Lewis Paine tried to commit suicide by dashing his brains out before the hearing began—they were found guilty and all except Arnold, O'Laughlen and Dr. Samuel Mudd, who were sent to the Devil's Island of Florida, the Dry Tortugas, were hanged in heat so blinding that an umbrella had to be held over Mrs. Surratt's head so she wouldn't faint and thus temporarily evade the hangman's noose.

One curious fact was that, even in prison, she had a connection to trading with the enemy; her best friend among the inmates was Virginia Lomax, the sister-in-law of Thomas Green, trader and owner of the Washington mansion with dungeon and chains.

On July 7, somebody told Surratt the truth at last, and he became hysterical, crying out in agony at the news. Since Surratt suffered from malarial chills, Boucher had workmen break a hole in the wall of his room to make place for a stove. When a maidservant peeped under it to spy on the mysterious house-guest, Surratt was furious and jumped out of bed to startle her. He realized now she might report his presence to the police; Father Boucher, smelling the possibility of scandal, had him return to Montreal.

There he took shelter in the home of a merchant, André J. LaPierre, who lived at the uninviting address of 116 Old Ceme-tery Street, opposite the palace of Bishop Ignace Bourget; Edwin G. Lee came to see him from Quebec and gave him the equiva-lent today of $4,400 in pocket money. It was at that time that Sur-ratt read in the local newspaper that the Vatican was seeking recruits for the Papal Zouave guards. It was a particular interest of Bourget's to send Canadians for that service to Italy.

On April 19, with Booth and Surratt on separate flights from arrest, Sanders sent an open letter to New Yorkers to the *New York Times,* which had dared to state accurately that he was a principal figure in the assassination plot. He said:

> While your country is in the deepest mourning and intensely excited in all its parts, the editor of the *New York Times,* calmly sit-ting in his room, takes cowardly advantage, and satanically charges innocent persons, [his] political opponents, with the highest crimes. His fiendish words are but a degree less criminal than the act of the assassin.
>
> So confident am I of the enlightened and impartial justice of the people of New York City, that I will, with the permission of the authorities of the United States, go at once to that city, and give the cowardly wretch the opportunity to prove his infamous charge.

The letter concluded with a lie:

> We say we have no acquaintance with Mr. Booth or any of those alleged to have been engaged with him. We have never seen or had any knowledge of any wise of him or them and he has never written us a note or sought an interview with us.

On April 25, Edwin G. Lee issued a manifesto denying any complicity in the assassination and charging the ultimate insult to a male in 1865, that Secretary Stanton was "unmanly" in making such charges. ("In denying it indignantly, contemptuously, I only fear that I am, in even my own humble person, condescending too far.")

When Johnson offered a reward at the beginning of May of $25,000 for his, Clay's, Thompson's and Tucker's arrest, a futile gesture that was never acted upon, all extradition rights from British North America were ignored by an administration that was obviously desperate to conceal trading with the enemy.

On May 4, Sanders and Tucker jointly issued an open letter to Johnson, published in many newspapers and marked by a degree of sinister humor:

> Your proclamation is a living, burning lie, known to as such by yourself and all your surroundings, and all the hired perjurers in Christendom shall not deter us from exhibiting to the civilized world your hellish plot to murder our Christian President.

This was the same President whose death had been the cause of celebrations led by Sanders at the St. Lawrence Hall just 19 days before. The letter continued:

> We recognize many of your most distinguished generals, men of honor, and we do not believe their association, even with you, has so brutalized them as to prevent their doing justice to a public enemy under such grave charges. Be that as it may, we challenge you to select any nine of the 25 generals that we name to form a court-martial for our trial, to be convened at the United States Fort at Rouse's Point, or any other place, on the guarantee that you will not have the power to incite the mob to destroy us, en route:
>
> Gens. Scott, Grant, Sherman, Meade, Rosecrans, Howard, Burnside, Hancock, Hooker, Schofield, Wright, Dix, Cadwallader Washburne, Emory, Blair, Pleasonton, Logan, Steele, Peck, Hatch, Franklin, Rodman, Alexander, Carr, Reynolds and Meagher.

The joke had a dark side: as Sanders and Tucker well knew, one member of this distinguished and improbable roll call was dead. Brigadier General Isaac Peace Rodman had been killed near Sharpsburg on September 30, 1862; his namesake, Major Thomas J. Rodman, was merely an ordinance official and could not have formed part of a court martial commission. Not even Benjamin Wood or other newspaper owners dared ask through their editorial columns why a more modest tribunal was not set up to try Sanders and Tucker in Washington.

The manifesto they issued went on to an even more extravagant suggestion:

> We propose that the money that you have so prodigally offered by way of the reward for our capture be paid over to defray the professional and other expenses of our trial, to the lawyers that we shall designate, and who are in no wise to be prejudiced in our defense. Our witnesses are also to have the fullest protection, and upon our acquittal of the charges preferred against us in your proclamation, we are to be permitted to return under safe conduct.

And at the end came a cheery repetition of their earlier lie:

> In conclusion, we say we have no acquaintance whatever with Mr. Booth or any of those alleged to have been engaged with him. We have never seen or had any knowledge in any wise of him or them, and he has never written us a note, or sought an interview with us.

William C. Cleary issued a similar, but feebler, denial in more sober and subdued language; President Johnson, of course, made no response.

Even bolder was Tucker's letter to Secretary of State Seward whom Lewis Paine, his agent through D. Preston Parr, had almost succeeded in killing. It referred back to Tucker's request to come to Washington on the cotton deal; and it contained other details: that Seward had arranged for Thurlow Weed to show the applications to Lincoln and that Lincoln had approved Weed coming to Montreal to discuss the matter, but at the last minute, no doubt suspecting danger from Lafayette Baker, Weed did not travel north. Tucker's letter also revealed that he had telegraphed Seward on the night of April 13, the eve of the assassination, to let him go to Washington, since there was talk of assembling the Virginia legislature in that city to discuss reconstruction. But the "dreadful deed" of Good Friday had interrupted the plan.

The next paragraph read:

> Now I submit [Mr. Seward] when you take all these facts, especially the last names into consideration, and the further one that President Lincoln was fully advised of the nature of the business that brought me here [to Montreal] and that he granted several parties in the North permits, under and in accordance with the Trade regulations of the Treasury Department, to make exchange with me of provisions and merchandise for cotton, you certainly cannot believe that I had either knowledge of, or complicity with, the great tragedy.

With typical impudence, Tucker went on to complain that he had not been court-martialed as he had requested, with the Union military top brass as judges.

The letter to Seward was only published once, in the obscure and unnoticed pages of the St. Catharines *Commercial,* on November 30, 1865. Needless to say, it elicited no response.

On May 12, Sanders and Tucker struck again. They issued a broadside, published, unlike the above-mentioned missive, in numerous newspapers, including the *New York Times.* It read:

> The mendacious and ferocious proclamation from the Federal ruler, maddens and disgraces a page of American history. Thirsting for blood, and uneasy in his new-found power, the semi-elected President of the disorganized "United States", with the harpies that surround him, seeks by the mysterious cloud of concerted calumny to distract the world from a too-ready penetration of his schemes for the murder of a Magistrate elected by a chivalrous people with the highest forms of civil government. The "conclusive" evidence that the Federal organs claim to have been sent to Europe can only be forged papers and suborned testimony, that will shrivel before the fire of truth.

After citing his letter to the people of the city of New York of April 19, Sanders absurdly gave his offer to go there as *prime facie* proof of his non-complicity in the murder plot; and he concluded with another charge against Johnson:

> The real object was not so much (to catch) the persons of certain men in Canada, but the use of their names for the manufacture of a network of conspiracy in which to enmesh President Davis' reputation, and consign him to the hand of Federal detectives at the first moment of his capture, without shocking the public sense of Europe by a formal political execution.

On May 15, based upon incriminating documents showing his dealings in the treasonable trade-espionage network with Beverley Tucker, the Confederate Senator Robert M. T. Hunter, one of the three principal delegates to the Hampton Roads "peace" conference of the previous winter, found himself uncomfortably shipped back in irons to the same location. He was on his way to the prison of Fort Pulaski in Georgia along with his fellow Hampton Roads negotiator, Assistant Secretary of War John A. Campbell. Like the third fake peace proposer, Vice President Alexander Hamilton Stephens, who served considerable time at Fort Warren, they were months in imprisonment. Knowing far too much about trading with the enemy (Stanton was certain Campbell was an actual spy, and he knew about Hunter's Canadian connections), they were paroled at last, and returned to their comfortable lives as men of wealth and position. As a constant critic of Jefferson Davis, Stephens was the least guilty of the three, and in truth wasn't guilty at all.

When Major General Halleck sent incriminating letters to Stanton from Sanders and Tucker, stripped from the ransacked home of Senator Hunter, Halleck wrote, "By composing these documents with others of Tucker's and Sanders', additional links in the chain of events may be supplied." Evidently they were too hot to handle in terms of Lincolnian commerce with the South, because they soon disappeared; Stanton avowing he never received them, although today they exist in the old War Department files at the National Archives in Washington.

Indeed, had they not been released, Hunter and Campbell could severely have damaged Lincoln's memory. Immediately after the Hampton Roads conference, he had reversed his humorous rejection of the Greeley-Sanders-Clay-Jewett proposals of the previous August at Niagara, and had stated, and had Congress secretly approve, the very plans that objectionable quartet had manufactured—namely to not make freedom of the slaves mandatory, in the event of a negotiated peace; that it had never really been an issue with him; and that Sanders' proposed sum of $400 million (or $4,550,000,000) would be paid to the Confederate government in compensation for its losses.

Tucker was still at it on June 1: he directly cited an incident, in a widely circulated letter to the press, linking President Johnson to John Wilkes Booth. He mentioned that some eight hours before the murder, at shortly after 2:30 P.M. on April 14, Booth had dropped by Johnson's rooms at the Kirkwood House Hotel where Atzerodt was staying, with a note asking to have a conversation. Tucker called these "words of a strange and mysterious import," which he took to mean a certain familiarity between actor and Vice President that carried a whiff of murderous conspiracy. His reason for adducing Johnson's involvement was ludicrous; he had been snubbed at the Inauguration Ball. Tucker added that the new President was the only man among 35 million Americans who had motive for assassination of Lincoln—an absurdity at best. Actually, as a fellow guest at the National, Booth could easily have asked Johnson to confirm that Lincoln would be present for sure at Ford's that night; uneasy about Booth's connections, Johnson didn't come out of his room to see him. And Booth, who planned to have Johnson killed, wanted to be sure of his whereabouts.

On June 8, Sanders sent a round robin announcing to newspapers his desire to found a National Opposition Party separate from the Democrats, a desire that predictably remained unsatisfied. He chose the occasion to condemn, as a recklessly "crammed" perjurer at the assassination trial, Sanford Conover, when Sanders himself was the crammer. He turned on his former boss, James Gordon Bennett of the *New York Herald,* who joined the *New York Times* in calling for his arrest; and he condemned

Advocate General Joseph Holt, who was in charge of the trial, as a "Titus Oates," a reference to the seditious forger who had attempted the life of King Charles II of England.

Sanders then declared that a number of witnesses, held in secret session by Holt, and questioned by Holt and his team, had disappeared and "whose singular harmony of style betrays the common source;" he promised them a long life of infamy in a Canadian penitentiary. He avoided the fact that the common source was himself; he would add others to their number later, so that they would be found to have committed perjury and thus cast disgrace on Holt for believing them. The *New York Times* made mincemeat of this latest effusion from Montreal saying, "Mr Sanders so-called plan for an opposition party . . . would be in support of those who oppose punishment for treason and assassination."

Frustrated in his attempts to get a rise out of President Johnson, Sanders decided to embark on a new plan that he hoped would bring disgrace to the American government; he would engineer his own kidnapping, be carried off to Washington, escape trial because of all he knew, and collect a handsome share of the reward money with his "captors." In this, he acted in collusion with his son-in-law, the Italian-American adventurer Louis Contri, who had entered into an ill-fated and ill-advised marriage with his daughter Virginia Sanders.

Beverley Tucker and a team of freebooters, led by Wayne W. Blossom, Carlos E. Hogan and William F. Burns, all of whom had criminal records, entered into the plot. Sanders decided to involve the sacked former Detective Inspector John O'Leary; O'Leary had been dismissed as the right hand man of the heavily bribed Guillaume Lamothe of the Montreal police, who was still in disgrace and out of the force for his corrupt role in the release of several of the St. Albans raiders in December, and for helping them to escape, with the aid of an experienced French Canadian scout, to the frozen North.

Sanders and Contri had managed to come up with $10,000 ($113,000) from the stolen St. Albans money for O'Leary, who would use the bulk of it to bribe Chief of Montreal Police Frederick L. Penton into assisting in the scheme. However, O'Leary changed his mind at the last minute and pocketed the money, telling his former boss what Sanders was planning instead.

On August 8, 1865, O'Leary went to Sanders' house and "arrested" him on a citizen's warrant; he pushed him into an awaiting carriage with Carlos E. Hogan as driver and William E. Burns inside. At a place called Priests' Farm, three men by pre-arrangement flagged down the vehicle at gun point, threw O'Leary out, handcuffed Sanders and ordered Hogan to lash the horse to a gallop all the way to the toll bridge at Côte St. Antoine. The gate was closed, by Police Chief Penton's orders, and the "kidnappers," led by Wayne W. Blossom, told Hogan to charge his horse through the gate, breaking it off at its hinges.

The "kidnappers" dragged Sanders from the carriage and pulled him into the underbrush; the plan was to take him to Lichine on the St. Lawrence River, where Indian boatmen were waiting to ferry him across on the first stage of his journey to Washington. But Penton's men were waiting, also under cover, and fired volleys of bullets into the brush, so that Hogan and Burns were forced to hand over their "captive." When asked for the key to Sanders' handcuffs, they were unable to find it; he shared the police wagon all the way back to Montreal.

On arrival, while a key was made by a locksmith, he announced that he would like to go to St. Lawrence Hall and display his manacled wrists to the guests as an entertainment. The request was denied.

The trial of the fake kidnappers was held in November; they were defended by the St. Albans prosecutor Bernard Devlin. He charged Sanders with collusion, but the jury wasn't interested. Their only concern was that O'Leary, whose testimony was crucial, was both a Roman Catholic and a Freemason; since all were Catholics, and the Church condemned Freemasonry, they were unable to take seriously his statement on the witness stand that the "kidnap" was a put-up job. The jury told the judge that they could not, in the circumstances, reach a verdict; they were excused, but the judge, against Devlin's protests, refused to release the prisoners and committed them to trial the following spring. Once again, in 1866, the Mason-Catholic issue so upset the new jury that they could not reach a verdict, and this time the judge had to let the hoaxters go.

Sanders arrived in England in September; Judah P. Benjamin had arrived on August 30, after many harrowing adventures and a series of disguises, on a long flight through Georgia and Florida, leaving Jefferson Davis and Clement C. Clay, who had rashly given himself up in the hope of being found innocent of Lincoln's death, to face prison terms with very little financial help from him. Accompanied by Brigadier General William Preston and Major General John G. Walker, both of the Trans-Mississippi command, the most popular area of cotton trading with the North, and aided by Rear Admiral Samuel P. Lee of the Mississippi Squadron, Benjamin settled comfortably in London with his loot in gold and took rooms in Confederate-filled Sackville Street, meeting those of his political stripe at rooms in the Burlington Arcade.

Gladstone and Disraeli were his great and powerful friends, along with Lord Wharncliffe, Alexander Beresford-Hope, M. P., and various Dukes and Earls who were sympathetic to the South. Later, when Jefferson Davis was released from imprisonment, they made Davis welcome. Beverley Tucker arrived in England afterward in November as a roving correspondent for newspapers; neither he nor Sanders were persona grata with Benjamin, who refused to give them any financial assistance as he rose to become a leading Q.C. and a legend in his time. Later, Tucker became the popular manager and host of the Stephenson House hotel at St. Catharines, but he went bankrupt and sank into poverty and obscurity.

Jacob Thompson arrived in London with well over $600,000 (or $6.83 million) and refused to give Benjamin more than $12,000 of it.

After pleasant months touring through the Lake District and other appealing English locations, reading Wordsworth and enjoying Paris, Thompson finally took up residence in 1869 in a mansion in Memphis, Tennessee. He threatened to write his life story but, on November 20, 1883, he told the *New York Times,* his former nemesis, that he had decided not to do so since, if he did, it would "utterly ruin" at least one man who had the confidence of the Union government at the time of the Canadian commission and at the same time had aided the Confederacy; that man was still in Congress. He could only have been referring to Singleton, but he must also have had in mind the fact that when he made the statement, Robert Lincoln was Secretary of War and, had Thompson dared to emerge from the shadows, might have had some unflattering things to say about him.

On November 23, 1865, Clay wrote to President Johnson from his cell at Fortress Monroe that not only was he innocent, but he had at the time of the assassination been absent from Canada for over six months, and had never heard of or known of Booth. This was a lie; he had been in Canada until February 1, just two and a half months before the assassination, a fact readily proven by letters he had sent to Jacob Thompson signed "T. E. Lacy" on December 10, and in personal column messages in the NY *Daily News,* starting on December 15. There were other proofs, including an eyewitness account of a Canadian, Hiram Lewis Hall of Toronto, who met him at the New Year, and learned that he had unsuccessfully tried to run the blockade; he remained in jail.

A much vexed matter was this: did Jefferson Davis encourage Lincoln's murder?

On May 10, 1876, the Reverend J. William Jones, of the Southern Historical Society, which Davis had authorized to file, annotate and publish all proper records of the Civil War, wrote to him on the matter. Davis replied that he was well aware of the plans, and was "willing to entertain" the interesting idea of Presidential kidnap, because he believed there had been plots hatched against his life in the North.

On August 31, 1889, Davis corresponded on this issue with his former military aide, Colonel Walter H. Taylor; he reminded Taylor that he had rejected his plan to capture Lincoln in 1862 on the ground that such an attempt would involve killing instead of merely bringing the Northern President into captivity alive. On May 10, 1893, Virginia, Davis's wife, revealed to the reporter Henry T. Loutham that her husband had discussed the matter with her, saying that the kidnap plan was impracticable as it would result in Lincoln's death and that Taylor had agreed to abandon it.

AIDED BY HIS PRIESTLY FRIENDS AND WITH THE UNSTINTING SUPPORT OF the Archbishops of Montreal and Halifax, Surratt, on September 16, 1865, went to Quebec by boat up the St. Lawrence River, where he transferred to a tug to sail out to the Montreal Steamship Company vessel *Peruvian*. Aboard the tug were three good friends of the Confederacy: Beverley Tucker, Colorado Jewett, and Patterson McGee, the substitute White House coachman who had set fire to the barn as part of the February, 1864 attempt on Lincoln's life; Brigadier General Roswell S. Ripley was also aboard.

By prior arrangement, the *Peruvian*'s doctor, Lewis J. A. McMillan, kept Surratt under lock and key in his cabin until the ship sailed.

Once at sea, Surratt took a stroll with McMillan around the deck, often looking nervously over his shoulder. He picked out a passenger whom he thought was looking at him suspiciously and asked the doctor if he knew the man's name. McMillan replied that he did not. "Is he an American detective, do you think?" Surratt asked, nervously.

"I doubt it," McMillan replied, and, apparently oblivious of Surratt's true identity (he posed as a Mr. McCarty), said, "Why would you be afraid of such a person?" Surratt replied sharply, "I have done more things than you are aware of, and if you knew, you would stare." McMillan said that Surratt had nothing to fear, since he was on a British ship, and that if the man were really a detective, he would have arrested him before he went aboard.

As the trip progressed, Surratt admitted he was a Confederate trader and agent; that he had traveled with a woman spy who sounded like Sarah Slater; that when escaped Union prisoners asked them their business she told him to fire on the men and kill them; that Benjamin had given him $100,000 (equivalent to $1,090,000) to take to Montreal over a period of time; that when a Union gunboat on the Potomac intercepted him he had fired at and killed its occupants; that he and his companions had flushed a Union spy out of a Southern farmhouse when they heard tapping sounds from the attic.

The last day but one of the voyage, Surratt pointed to the Irish port of Londonderry, where the *Peruvian* was due to dock, and said, "A foreign land at last. I hope to return to my country in two years." Then he took out his revolver, saying, "I hope to God I shall live to see the time when I can serve Andrew Johnson as Abraham Lincoln had been served. If any man in England tries to arrest me I will shoot him. I would rather be hanged by an English hangman than by a Yankee, for if I go back [to America] I will swing."

Surratt broke the journey overnight in Londonderry, then went overland and took a ferry across the Irish Channel to Liverpool.

Instead of checking into a boarding house McMillan had recommended, he took sanctuary in the Oratory of the Holy Cross, where he remained until the end of September. McMillan, appalled by what Surratt had revealed to him on the trip, went to see Henry Wilding, the very able American consul who had replaced Beverley Tucker in March, 1861.

Wilding had him swear out a deposition and, with the words "such a wretch should not escape," and realizing that the most wanted man in America was in Liverpool, wrote to Seward in Washington with all the details. Seward went to see Stanton on the matter and the decision, shared by President Johnson, was that Surratt must be let go. In addition to the fact that a trial might reveal his involvement in trading with the enemy—and indeed that involvement came up when he was finally tried, though suppressed even by the prosecution—there was another matter to be considered: the unpopularity of the administration over the public execution of Mrs. Surratt.

Surratt left for Rome in October and enlistment as "John Watson" in the Zouave Papal guards, which he fondly expected would be a permanent cover. But an old Jesuitical schoolfriend, Henry de St. Marie, who had hoped to collect the $25,000 (equivalent to $274,000) reward on his head, and had been to Montreal to try to track him down, had also joined the Zouaves in an effort to entrap him.

A fellow pupil of Surratt's and Weichmann's at the Jesuit St. Charles College at Elliott's Mills, St. Marie, a florid, dark-haired Canadian who sang and played trumpet in Maryland concert halls, had left school for a woman he later made pregnant and abandoned in Montreal. He enlisted in a Delaware regiment, was caught thieving and spying and thrown into Castle Thunder and then became yet another trader with the enemy, mostly in cotton and tobacco.

In April 1863, Surratt arranged for him to go into Virginia for blockade running purposes; he worked like Weichmann in the Commissary of Prisons, and he shipped goods to England through the coastal blockade, earning enough money by October 1865 to undertake his long pursuit of Surratt through British North America to England and now to Rome.

St. Marie made sure he was in the same 9th Company of the Zouaves as Surratt, stationed at the small town of Valletri, playing the trumpet in the band but he soon learned the unhappy news that, as of November 25, President Johnson suspended all bounties on the surviving assassination conspirators. Determined to get some kind of reward, and perhaps the big one since he had initiated his search before the 25th, he introduced himself to Surratt, pretending surprise at so coincidental a meeting, reminded him of their schooldays together, their trading with the enemy, and joint service to the Confederacy, and, pretending continued support, wrung from Surratt an admission of his role in Lincoln's assassination.

Surratt told St. Marie that he had acted on orders from an immediate subordinate of Jefferson Davis, obviously Benjamin; that he wouldn't be drawn on whether Davis had been behind the plot, an obvious red herring; that he had acted under orders from men whose names he would not divulge, but who were in New York and London—the Woods, Belmont, Sanders, and Seymour of course—and that a "party in London" had offered him $10,000 if he would write an account of the assassination, but he had declined.

Then Surratt said, "Damn the Yankees, they killed my mother. We have killed Lincoln, the niggers' friend." He added, "Had it not been for that coward Weichmann, my mother would be living yet. It was fear made him speak. Had he kept his tongue there was no danger for him. If I ever return to America or meet him elsewhere, I shall kill him."

He said that he had been in the secret service of the South, and that Weichmann stole documents from the War Department and gave them to him and that he was in receipt of moneys from London; St. Marie saw letters evidencing this. Who else but Judah P. Benjamin and Sanders could have been the senders?

St. Marie took leave from Valletri to report the matter to U.S. Minister to Rome, Brigadier General Rufus King, the epileptic former trainer of the famous Iron Brigade. King successfully applied to the Vatican for an overruling of the non-extradition laws and had Surratt arrested on November 6 at the nearby town of Valeri, where he was on leave of absence.

Surratt was taken in irons to the Valeri fortress prison for questioning. After a night in solitary confinement he was awakened at 4 A.M. to start the journey to Rome. He asked if he could use the latrine, which he knew was situated at the back of the building. Given permission, he saw that the only way of escape was down a dangerously steep cliff and he had no rope to use. Once outside, he noticed that the privy's contents of years had been thrown down 28 feet to a ledge where they had solidified and could break his fall. He jumped and his pursuers, who as fellow Zouaves may well have wanted him to escape, told their German commander that they couldn't find him.

The jump injured his back and both of his arms. When the coast was clear, he clambered up the rocks and made his way to the Hospital of Sora Terra di Lavoro, run by nursing nuns. They took care of him but reported his presence to the police. Rufus King bungled by holding up his arrest until an identifying portrait photograph was obtained of him from the Zouave records files at Valletri, which gave him more than enough time to get to Naples.

With great boldness he went to the U.S. Consul in that city, stating that he had been expelled from the Zouaves for insubordination and wanted to return to the United States. Given the necessary papers, he proceeded to the British Consul with the same story, showing his Canadian passport issued in Montreal in January and asking for financial support and assistance in traveling to Alexandria, Egypt. This he was given and, on November 18, he boarded the Peninsular and Orient liner *Tripoli*, which was bound for Australia.

He had the devil's own luck: just out of Civita Vecchia, the port of Rome, a passenger came down with smallpox and the

Captain ordered a 15-day quarantine. This meant that William Winthrop, the United States Consul in Valletta, Malta, could not come aboard and look for him; only the local health officials were permitted. When Winthrop sent a note to the bridge to ask the skipper whether anybody was aboard in a Zouave uniform who answered that description, the Captain replied that there was only one such person, but his name was not Surratt, Watson, or Harrison; it was John Agostini. Incredibly, Winthrop took that response as sufficient and made no attempt to have Surratt arrested by the Captain and taken ashore under quarantine regulations; he realized his mistake too late. The British authorities in Valletta refused to take action—and the ship sailed.

By the time the *Tripoli* docked in Alexandria, Surratt had become "John Walters." Alerted by news from Malta, the local U.S. Consul Charles Hale defied the quarantine rule and boarded the ship. He took only seconds to discover Surratt in steerage with a number of bonded laborers and placed him in charge.

He held him under arrest in the quarantine station for the required number of days and then applied to the Pasha of Egypt for permission to ship him to America. The Pasha co-operated, and Rear Admiral Louis M. Goldsborough of the U.S. European Squadron, stationed at Villa Franca, Italy, telegraphed Commander William N. Jeffers to sail his corvette, the U.S.S. *Swatara*, from Marseilles to Alexandria to pick him up. Once aboard, Surratt was confined to the brig in irons. Jeffers refused to speak to him, even to ask him questions; a passionate admirer of Lincoln, Jeffers was disgusted by having him on board. He was still more disgusted when St. Marie, whom he had brought from Civita Vecchia, refused to meet Surratt face to face and charge him directly with his crime; when the *Swatara* docked at Villa Franca, St. Marie begged to be sent ashore. He undoubtedly feared Surratt might escape from the brig and kill him. Contemptuously, Jeffers let him go.

At a Johnson Cabinet meeting on October 16, 1866, Seward read out documents concerning the affair. In dealing with Surratt's statement that Booth had been in Richmond discussing the assassination with Benjamin, to whom Surratt and Booth had laid out their scheme, and that the matter had been discussed in the

Confederate Cabinet, Seward said that he believed Booth and Surratt had discussed the matter with Benjamin but he did not believe it had ever been discussed in Cabinet, or received the countenance of any other member save Benjamin.

When Surratt was jailed at the Old Capital Prison in Washington, he was approached by enemies of President Johnson to state that Johnson was behind the assassination. He refused to confirm the charge. His trial began on June 10, 1867; it ended on July 18th. The jury was conveniently accommodated at the weekends at the home of Francis Preston Blair, Sr., that leading peacemaker and trader with the enemy; any mention of trading was, as we have seen, quashed by prosecutor Edwards Pierrepont and Judge George Fisher, along with Surratt's connections to Judah Benjamin. Any mention of his crucial meeting of April 1, 1865 in Richmond was disallowed in its entirety, a severe and permanent blow to the cause of justice.

Late on the afternoon of July 2, something curious occurred. Henry de St. Marie, who had been well paid for his services but grumbled continuously that he had not, was without doubt the most important of witnesses against Surratt. Yet Edwards Pierrepont threw him away, and still more extraordinary, defense counsel Bradley did nothing to try to discredit his sworn statements in Rome relaying Surratt's confession of being directly responsible for Lincoln's death. Pierrepont wasted the court's time asking his key witness the name of the regiment he was in during his service with the Zouaves, what clothing he wore in that service, the dates on which he walked with Surratt and the names of the two men who walked with him; that Surratt said he was disguised as an Englishman in a scarf over the shoulders so that nobody could mistake him for an American; a nonsensical statement at best.

And there the matter ended, with no cross examination of the one man who could have settled the case, one way or another.

The only possible explanation, once again, is that St. Marie would have discussed his involvement in trading with the enemy with Surratt, and what Surratt would have said about it; and once again, that the information would cast a dark shadow over the present administration, of which both prosecutor and defending counsel were wholly in support.

The jury disagreed on the verdict; it announced that due to illness and concern over the conflicting evidence they could not reach a verdict and a mistrial was declared. Not content with that, Surratt demanded another hearing, even as defending counsel Bradley, who had turned much of the trial into a farce with his obnoxious and pointless interruptions, was disbarred on the spot, and when he challenged Judge Fisher to a duel, was sent to prison.

By now, Orville H. Browning was in the open as Surratt's attorney. When efforts were made by the government to try Surratt on new charges of conspiracy, that ever-helpful fellow trader with the enemy had him released on bail of $40,000. Such money can only have come from the wealthy Copperhead clique of New York and Washington, and then, in November, 1868, the case against John Harrison Surratt was finally dismissed.

In later life, he frequently gave a lecture, blending fact with fiction, entitled "A Plan Arranged to Kidnap not Kill President Lincoln," taught school, married, and maintained a considerable degree of popularity.

After the Surratt trial, Louis Weichmann joined the Philadelphia Customs House as a clerk, resigning on October 1, 1886. Following some criticism of his role in the Booth-Lincoln affair, he joined his brother, a Catholic priest, at Anderson, Indiana, married also, and set up the Anderson Business School in that town. He wrote (but it was not published until 1975) a well-written, if doctored, account of the events of 1864-1865.

BENNETT H. YOUNG, HEAD OF THE ST. ALBANS RAIDERS, AFTER RELEASE from prison in November 1865, flourished in Kentucky, first as President of the Louisville Public Library, then as commander in chief of the Kentucky United Confederate Veterans. At a ceremony at Louisville in 1905, on the anniversary of the October 19 raid, he and the surviving Retributors dressed in uniforms and rode in a parade through the streets, cheered by the citizens and flourishing the Confederate flag. On July 11, 1911, Kentucky Congressman Frank L. Greene gave a banquet for Young in the same city, at which the hero of St. Albans gave, somewhat exaggeratedly, an account of the attack; he ended with a lie that $208,000 of the stolen money was handed over to Richmond. None was.

In February 1867, on orders from President Johnson and Stanton, continuing as Secretary of War, the distinguished Brigadier General George H. Sharpe set off on an intelligence mission to London and Paris, of which he kept detailed records. His purpose was to trace Judah P. Benjamin's activities in England and to follow George Nicholas Sanders with a view to determining his contacts in London.

He discovered that Captain Thomas Courtney, inventor of a torpedo device used by the Confederacy, was maintaining the spendthrift Sanders in Paris; that despite the fact Sanders had written an introduction for Benjamin to at least one Earl (of Salisbury), he and Benjamin were in conflict; and that Sanders had so heavy a load of debt in London he could not return to that city.

Seeing the connection to the Lincoln assassination, Sharpe, with the aid of Sanders' old associate, the long term United States Vice Consul Benjamin Moran, unearthed the Napoleon III manifesto, reproduced in the London *Times* in 1858, naming Sanders as a fellow conspirator toward his death along with Hippolyte Magen. But Courtney was told only to collect such information; there was no way that Johnson or Stanton would dare bring Sanders in for arrest and trial, in view of all he knew.

Sharpe established from meetings with Courtney, who sought money and immunity from prosecution in return for his help to Washington, that the cash advanced for the Canadian operation was financed not directly from Richmond but from drafts drawn by Benjamin and Memminger on Fraser, Trenholm, thus proving outright cooperation in England for the entire murderous enterprise and that the payment was made in the form of cotton shipped north to Halifax for transfer to New York.

Sanders' situation worsened. He managed to get back to London, only to find that neither Benjamin nor Jefferson Davis, now out of prison, nor Clement C. Clay, nor any of his other associates, would lift a finger to help him. On March 10, 1866, he was, like Beverley Tucker, declared a bankrupt, with debts of over 10,000 pounds ($775,000 today).

Although his two surviving sons, Lewis and George, succeeded as lawyers, he suffered the loss of his daughter Virginia at
an early age and by the time he returned to New York, he was
completely broke. He died of congestive heart failure in Manhattan at age 62 on August 12, 1873; none of his former collaborators attended his funeral. He was interred in the cemetery of
St. Anne's Church, 18th Street, New York, in his wife Anna's family plot. *Requiescat In Pace*—but one doubts it.

POSTSCRIPT

Although I have supplied a selective bibliography, it is worth noting that scarcely a book on the list, or in the incomparable mass of Lincolniana which lies outside the scope of my study, mentions the vexed question of Lincoln, in direct contravention of the wartime laws, trading with the Confederacy while thousands of his troops died in what seemed to be an uncomplicated moral cause and while England and France were starved of cotton, tobacco and turpentine, throwing thousands out of work and bringing those countries' economies to the edge of ruin. Ironically, as I have pointed out in this chronicle, by allowing a blanket of opportunistic commerce to cover the movements of such figures as Booth, Surratt and their colleagues led by George N. Sanders, Robert E. Coxe and Beverley Tucker, Lincoln unwittingly wrote his own death warrant.

In order to trace this largely unknown story, I have relied in every instance not on published texts, except for the reports in Henry J. Raymond's peerless *New York Times,* but on original documents in English and French, including letters that supply primary evidence, internal police and governmental memoranda, trial transcripts with perjurers separated from tellers of the truth (the former unhappily outnumbering the latter), and diaries, most notably of such figures as Benjamin Moran, Edward Bates, Gideon Welles and, in particular, the unregenerate Orville H. Browning, conspirators' friend as well as Lincoln's, coolly detached recorder of treasonable trade and illegal political intercourse.

Many Civil War records, as any historian of the period can testify, contradict each other in the field; a disturbingly high percentage of the participants left accounts that oppose and deny each other. The hard-pressed chronicler of the most controversial of periods in American history has to make a choice, based upon the preponderance of evidence, as if he were reluctantly compelled to assume the mantle of a judge after some 139 years, in a trial that still continues and may always continue, as to which witness was telling the truth and whether defending or opposing counsel, namely the legion of previous authors, has, in the judge's opinion, reached the right conclusions.

The most consistent matter of controversy is the guilt or innocence of Mary Surratt and of her son. Because Mrs. Surratt was a woman, and in that age's peculiar mixture of anti-feminist condescension and gentlemanly "protectiveness" it was felt indecent to hang one of that "inferior" but in fact equal sex, she has had an army of supporters. Yet the evidence against her is, in my view, overwhelming.

Under the usual protections of trading with the enemy, her boarding house in Washington and her leased property at Surrattsville were entrepôts for enemy intelligence, where she entertained such Confederate trader-spies as Sarah Slater and Josephine Brown, and provided a haven for John Wilkes Booth, whom she called Pet, his childhood nickname. She had the guns hidden in the ceiling joists at the Surrattsville establishment along with the field glasses in the liquor storeroom, both needed for Booth and his associates' escape after the assassination, and she confirmed that the pickets would be removed on the road to and from Washington at 8 P.M. on the fatal night to allow the conspirators an uninterrupted journey of escape. And this is not to mention her incendiary remarks to Louis Weichmann, that classic example of a stool-pigeon, whom she was unwise enough to trust.

As for Surratt . . . there has been endless controversy as to whether he was or was not in Washington on the day of the murder. Witnesses in Elmira, New York, saw him in their town; more (and several knew him by sight) identified him as being in the nation's capital. On close analysis, it turns out that of the Elmira group, only one asserted without equivocation that he saw Surratt on the 14th, and he was quickly shaken on the witness stand. When documents were called for establishing Surratt's presence there, they could not be found. By a process of elimination, and re-examining the ignored or overlooked statements of a trusted

train superintendent and an Irish ferryman (whom the defending counsel at Surratt's trial, Joseph H. Bradley, didn't dare cross-
examine), it is possible today to find Surratt successively in both
places, and Appleton's Railroad Timetable does the rest.

Another, and related, matter of controversy for a century and
half has been who drilled the hole in the door of the Presidential
box that allowed Booth to peep through it to determine the chief
executive's exact position and who propped the Arsenal band
player's stand for his score against that hole to prevent immediate
exit of the victim's companions. For some inexplicable reason,
the evidence of the clockmaker, Theodore H. Rhodes, has been
ignored or dismissed by everyone, even though his witnessing of
Surratt's preparation of that helpful arrangement was carefully
recorded and remembered by him at the Surratt trial and the
defense was unable to shake him. Indeed, to have invented,
under bribes by the prosecution, so elaborate a story would have
taken the powers of a Victor Hugo, an Alexander Dumas, or a Sir
Walter Scott. Finally, then, I believe that the evidence of Surratt's
presence, to help coordinate Booth's final act and to make sure
that Booth himself did not run the risk of preparing the hole and
stick himself, is incontrovertible.

A similar weighing of evidence of the complicity of the New
York group of Copperheads, left out of the cotton deal (which
August Belmont at one stage actually proposed to Lincoln, only
to be ignominiously rebuffed) is in my view equally conclusive.
Ward Hill Lamon, himself a trader with the enemy, was, as Lincoln's intimate friend and Marshal of the District of Columbia, in
a position to determine, more than the not always reliable
Lafayette C. Baker, the plot against the President that was initiated by Belmont and the McClellan clique and when Manton
Marble, McClellan himself, Seymour and the Woods failed to
report the matter (or Booth's connection) to the authorities,
that across the board omission speaks for itself.

As for the evidence of Lincoln's sanctioning of trade with the
South, a direct contravention of the wartime Non-Intercourse
Act of 1861, the most surprising fact is that, with very rare excep-
tions, no historian has cited the eight-volume collection of Lincoln papers edited by Roy P. Basler and published at Rutgers in

1953, which so far from being discreetly weeded, contains a consistent record of smoking-gun evidence of his indulgencies of his inner circle. Indeed, the last meeting of his life, with his old friend George Ashmun, was on the cotton issue. It seems that he believed, or told himself he believed, that to supply the South with greenbacks and gold and to guarantee purchase of cotton, tobacco and rosin would somehow bring the Confederate citizens back into the fold in a show of gratitude; but in view of the fact that the cotton was bought at a premium and sold at considerable profit, and that it was of benefit only to a group of speculators in his intimate circle, he was proven entirely wrong. Some claim that he sought to undermine the South (as Ward Hill Lamon contended in his memoirs) by taking all of its cotton.

In sum, it seems that Lincoln's easy generosity and capacity to blind, as well as lend himself to the corruptions around him, led him into a situation which, far too late, he corrected by handing over control of the trade to Lieutenant General Grant.

WEARIED BY THE CONDUCT OF THE WAR AND A HORRIBLE MARRIAGE and haunted by premonitory dreams, Lincoln seemed by 1865 to be weighed down by an almost romantic degree of fatalism and, not believing in the survival of the human personality after death, he may even have longed, in some part of his being, for eternal sleep. And yet, at the very end of his life, so contradictory and unpredictable was his character, he sent a note to his wife that was filled with optimism and plans for the future—when at last his burdensome high office should have ended.

ACKNOWLEDGMENTS

The greatest of my debts is to James O. Hall, recognized by many scholars of the Civil War as a pre-eminent authority, who answered hundreds of questions with remarkable speed and generosity, and at the age of 90 is the liveliest of popular historians. His admirable colleague, Jane Singer, with whom I maintained an almost daily discourse, and David W. Gaddy, were indispensable mainstays in the considerable task of research. I owe a very great debt to a man whom I have not had the pleasure of meeting: Stewart Sifakis, whose magnificent *Who Was Who in the Civil War* (New York: Facts on File, 1988) has been my constant vade mecum, supplying correct designations for military leaders when the general soubriquet of "general" has been far too loosely used in histories of the time, and dates for each change of rank and assignment, even down to months of the year. Without Sifakis' diligent work, this book would not have been possible. Another indispensable work is Charles de Bussy's *Les Conspirateurs en Angleterre* (1858). Nobody in the field can give less than the highest praise to Joan Chaconas, of the Surratt Society at Clinton, Maryland, who, with unstinting good will, unearthed rare documents for me; or to Linda Crist, custodian and editor of the perennial project of publishing the papers of Jefferson Davis from her office headquarters at Rice University, Houston, Texas; or to those stalwarts of the Library of Congress, John Sellers, Bruce Kirby, and Clark Evans. All have helped me with countless difficult and abstruse matters despite their busy schedules.

At the National Archives, I have received unstinting aid from Yvonne Brooks, Michael Hussey, Mark Mollan, Michael Musick and Kate Snodgress. In London, Janice Robinson unearthed the Scotland Yard records on the Central Democratic Committee assassination bureau and the Victor Hugo records in the Channel Islands. Also in London, Melanie Aspey of the Rothschild

Archives was very helpful; and in Paris, Luc Nemeth did superb work trawling through the complex and forgotten records of the police, the Archives Nationale, and the domestic and foreign office records of the 1850s to uncover very rare materials.

In Ottawa, Douglas Campbell unearthed the previously undiscovered private hearings of the Police Commission on the St. Albans Raid, as well as accounts of the raid itself and the trials of George Sanders' fake kidnappers. Randall Haines in Cincinnati, despite illness in the family, was incomparably generous with both time and knowledge as the world authority on George Nicholas Sanders. Ned Comstock of the USC Doheny Library was unstinting in his help, as was Michael Sutherland, who gave me access to the vast and unexplored treasures of his collection of Lincolniana at Occidental College, Eagle Rock, California; his colleague Jean Paule assisted me in the task of filing thousands of documents. Professors William C. Cooper and David Donald and R.J.M. Blackett answered many questions patiently.

I am deeply grateful to Ron Davidson of the Sandusky Historical Society; to Fenton Bresler; to Matt Richardson and Christopher Thomas; to Deborah Stiff; to Arden Phair of the St. Catharines, Ontario Historical Society and museum; to Steven Smith, whose *Booth Day By Day* was often at my side; to Lois Gereghty, ace book finder; and to Jill Snyder, Hedy Sussman, Jeff Welles, Wayne Brent and to Udana Power under the supervision of Michael Clark Haney, who tackled the unenviable task of deciphering my typing and handwriting to produce readable results on their trusty word processors, Michael doubling as a superb director in the Los Angeles theatre. I am also deeply grateful to the staff of B.J.'s Printing Emporium, Glendale, California, and to Jessica Kaye for her impeccable editing and to Mary Aarons of New Millennium for her stewardship of the publication process.

NOTES ON SOURCES

Readers wishing to explore the subject of Lincolnian trading with the enemy and the names of those in governmental positions involved in it also, are referred to 38th Congress: Second Session; House of Representatives Report Number 24, *Trade with Rebellious States,* referred to below as the Washburne Report. Not previously used by scholars, it is available at the National Archive.

The published Lincoln papers also contain primary evidence. Titles of books are here given in abbreviated form; the reader is referred to the bibliography. *Diplomatic Correspondence* is the accepted title for the equally overlooked *Papers Relating to Foreign Affairs* published by the Government Printing Office in Washington D.C. and containing such previously unaccessed documents as letters from Clement C. Clay and Beverley Tucker to Judah P. Benjamin intercepted by Richard Montgomery, Union secret agent; the 1866 volume is the chief source, as these documents were apparently considered too sensitive to be published during the Civil War. The very large collection of George Sanders papers, all conveniently saved (though some were damaged by fire and water), in the Library of Congress and the National Archives are a conclusive source on his intrigues. Similarly, Clement C. Clay left much that was damaging in his papers, housed today at the University of North Carolina. Jacob Thompson, Judah P. Benjamin, James P. Holcombe and Beverley Tucker were smarter in their acts of self-protective incendiarism, but they unwisely left much that was damaging in other places. What follows is a kind of shorthand guide to scholars, and to the filed documents in my collection at Occidental College, Eagle Rock, California.

ONE: THE MISSION

RICHMOND CABINET: Over 50 sources including, most notably, the one printed, proper account in Burton J. Hendrick's shamefully neglected *Statesmen of the Lost Cause.*

TRENT INCIDENT: France: Archives Nationales; also see Case and Spencer: *The United States and France.* MISSION TO BRITISH NORTH AMERICA: Clay diaries, Chapel Hill; Cleary diary, same; WESTCOTT: Polk diaries, Pennsylvania Historical Society.

TWO: THE KILLER

SANDERS: Sanders papers; KOSSUTH: Spencer; *Kossuth;* U.S. AND DEMOCRATIC REVIEW: Files of the publication, Los Angeles Central Library; SOULE: Diplomatic Correspondence; BELMONT: D.C. also, BLACK: *The King of Fifth Avenue;* SANDERS IN LONDON: Scotland Yard files, Public Record Office; Foreign Office Records, Paris; Sanders papers; FROND: Foreign Office Records; Ledru-Rollin papers, Paris; Burhanan papers; files of *L'Homme,* Jersey; special reference: Charles de Bussy; *Conspirateurs;* TUCKER: Tucker, *The Life of Beverley Tucker;* NAPOLEON III ON SANDERS; The London Times, March 11, 1858; ATTEMPT ON LINCOLN IN CINCINNATI: Syracuse (NY) *Journal,* February 18, 1861; BELKNAP MUSKETS: Sanders papers, National Archives, Library of Congress; FRASER, TRENHOLM: Fraser, Trenholm archives, Merseyside, Lancashire; REID SANDERS MISSION: Sanders papers; TUCKER IN ENGLAND: Diplomatic Correspondence; ATTACKS ON LINCOLN: London *Times; Punch;* FLOUR: Diplomatic Correspondence; LONDON CONFEDERATE BANK: Diplomatic correspondence; RUFFIN CONTRACT: Official Records (O.R.) of the Union and Confederate Armies.

THREE: ALARMS AND EXCURSIONS

SANDERS IN B.N.A.: Clay papers; Sanders papers; VALLANDIGHAM: OR; KNIGHTS OF GOLDEN CIRCLE: OR; CARROLL: OR; ROBERT E. COXE: Coxe papers, collection of James O. Hall; BLACKBURN: New York *Times,* May-June, 1865; MOVEMENTS OF COMMISSIONERS: Reports by U.S. Consuls, Toronto, Montreal, Halifax, National

Archives, Washington; HINES: *Century Magazine,* January, 1891; DENI-
SON: D.C., MONTGOMERY: collection of James O. Hall; LEAKS OF
INTELLIGENCE IN PRESS: New York *Daily News;* JEWETT: Sanders
papers; GREELEY: *Lincoln and Greeley;* JAQUES/GILMORE: New York
Times July-August, 1864; BENNETT: New York *Herald* files, 1861-1865.

FOUR: THE NAME IS MURDER

SALA: New York *Times,* May 6, 1865; DIX/RICHMOND, ETC.: New
York *Times,* November 30, 1875; December 30, 1880; MARBLE: McClel-
lan papers, National Archives, August 22, 1864; PAYMENT TO BEN-
JAMIN WOOD: Clay papers; HOLCOMBE, CLAY: Clay papers; LEWIS
SANDERS: Sanders papers; OR; CHICAGO MISSION: OR; CAMP
DOUGLAS: Denney: Civil War Prisons; CONVENTION: New York
Times; all Chicago newspapers; COUP D'ETAT LETTER: Clay papers.

FIVE: RAIDS AND REBELS

PLANS FOR JOHNSON'S ISLAND: Official records of the Union and
Confederate Navy (ORN); FORT JOHNSON DETAILS: Sandusky
(Ohio) Historical Society files; ORN; BEALL, BURLEY: OR; ORN;
MICHIGAN INCIDENT: OR; ORN; HINE: Report to the War Depart-
ment, November 29, 1867; National Archives; BOOTH: *The Mad Booths
of Maryland,* Asia Booth Clarke: *The Unlocked Book;* De BAR: St. Louis
Provost Marshal report, April 24, 1864; KANE INCIDENT: John Joseph
Jennings; BAKER: *History of the Secret Service;* GIST/BLAIR/HELM/
WHITE: Baker, opt. cit; FLEMING: Provost Marshal Report, National
Archives, April 25; National Archives; ARNOLD/O'LAUGHLEN:
Arnold's signed confession, War Department related, National Archives;
ILES: *The Mad Booths of Maryland;* Hamilton, Ontario Times, May 4,
1865; SALA / BOOTH: Sala memoirs; Browning diaries; Washburne
Committee; HAMPTON ROADS CONFERENCE: *The Peacemakers of
1864;* the New York *Times;* Sandburg: Lincoln; CAMERON AT RICH-
MOND: Benjamin: *The St. Albans Raid;* KATE MCDONALD: Sanders
papers; reports from U.S. Consuls in Quebec and Montreal, National
Archives, CLAY TO SOUTH: Clay papers; also see memoirs of Virginia
Clay Clopton; CLEAVER: evidence at Surratt trial; SMOOT: Evidence at
Surratt trial; WEICHMANN: Evidence at Surratt trial; EDWIN G. LEE:
Lee papers, James O. Hall; DAVID PRESTON PARR: Parr interrogatories,

National Archives; Haines: *Life of George Sanders;* SURRATT Passport: Records of the State of Quebec; National Archives of Canada in Ottawa; SPANGLER: Spangler statements War Department file, National Archives; LINCOLN TO GRANT: Lincoln published papers, See Bibliography; RICHMOND EXAMINER COMMENT: March 9, 1865 issue; also see Pollard, Edward J. *Southern History of the War;* John Van Dien report: New York *Times* (and Cincinnati Commercial) June 24-25, 1865; INAUGURAL DAY INCIDENT: Weichmann: *A True History of the Assassination;* facts checked with James O. Hall; MORE TRADINGS: Washburne committee; STANTON/BROWNING: Browning Diaries; BOOTH TELEGRAMS/PAINE/SURRATT/WEICHMANN: Weichmann testimony, Surratt trial; TRIP TO THEATRE: Weichmann/Apollonia Dean/Honora Fitzpatrick testimonies; War Department file, National Archives; MATTHEWS: Matthews testimony, War Department records, files; National Archives; MEETING AT INN: Herold/Arnold/Atzerodt testimonies, War Department files; National Archives; MEETING AT INN: Herold/Arnold/Atzerodt testimonies, War Department, National Archives; HELM: John S. Goff: *Robert Todd Lincoln;* TELEGRAMS: Arnold/O'Laughlin testimonies, War Department files, National Archives DAVID BARRY: Barry testimony, Surratt trial; BROOKE STABLER: Stabler testimony, Surratt trial; SURRATT RICHMOND: Weichmann testimony, Surratt trial; FICKLIN: Roscoe: *The Web of Conspiracy.*

SIX: HOW TO BURN NEW YORK

Hinchen: *Confederate Activities;* trial of Bennett H. Young (National Archives) December, 1864; Headley memoirs; New York newspapers; TRAIN ATTEMPT: Headley; Buffalo newspapers; absence of generals from Johnson's Island established by Sifakis: *Who Was Who in the Civil War;* BRIBERY OF OFFICIALS/ST. ALBANS MATTERS: Montreal Police Commission hearings, December, 1864; Montreal police files; Lamothe files; all in National Archives of Canada, in Ottawa.

SEVEN: WINTER PLANS FOR DEATH

BOOTH/TRUNKS: William H. Ginley report, June 7, 1865; Tidwell, Hall, Gaddy: *Come Retribution;* US Consular reports from Quebec, Montreal, Halifax; Lloyds of London files, Guild Hall, London; National

Maritime Museum, Greenwich; COOKE: The Life of Jay Cooke; B AND O: Statement by William Prescott Smith, War Department files, National Archive; reports on Louis O'Donnell, War Department files, National Archive; EDWARD MARTIN: War Department files, National Archive; WILLARD SAULSBURY: War Department files, National Archive; PIERPONT: Washburne report; SURRATT: William Prescott Smith report; trial testimonies, Surratt trial; TIBBETT/LEE Testimonies at Surratt trial; GREENS: War Department files, National Archives; AFRICAN–AMERICAN AMNESTY: Washington newspapers; also see *Reveille in Washington;* JAMES HUGHES, SINGLETON: Orville H. Browning diaries; SWETT, ANDREW, ASHMUN, HELMICK: Washburne report; BOOTH: Simonds/Booth correspondence, National Archive; HEROLD: Herold confession, National Archive; CHESTER: Evidence at trial of the conspirators; COTTON/GRANT: Washburne committee; TUCKER LETTER: Sanders papers, National Archive; LINCOLN/COXE: Lincoln published papers; Browning diaries; CARTER, DEVENEY, WHEELER, FINEGAS: Statements at trial of the conspirators; authenticity confirmed by James O. Hall; BOURKE/McGEE: Wheeling, West Virginia *Record,* April 6, 1887; CAMPBELL: Testimony at trial of the conspirators; MONTGOMERY: Montgomery files, James O. Hall Collection; also see: Diplomatic Records; LETTERS FROM CLAY/TUCKER: Diplomatic Records; BAKER IN BRITISH NORTH AMERICA: Washburne reports; testimony by Lafayette C. Baker; also see his memoirs; CANBY/LINCOLN: Presidential directive, September 30, 1864; *Life of Canby* by Max L. Heman, Jr. St. ALBANS RAID: Diplomatic records; Benjamin: *The St. Albans Raid* (includes complete trial transcripts); eye witness accounts supplied by St. Albans Museum and Historical collection; Montreal and St. Albans newspapers, various; Clay papers; Sanders papers; Wright report/conspiracy/letter to George Ticknor Curtis is from Edward H. Wright, December 28, 1866; Also see HAMAND: *Ward Hill Lamon;* BELMONT AND BOOTH: Report in War Department files, May 15, 1865, national archives, reprinted and discussed in David Black's *King of Fifth Avenue;* BOOTH/THOMPSON MEDICAL LINK: War Department files, National Archive; HUDSPETH/SELBY: Her testimonies at Trial of the Conspirators and the Surratt Trial; BINGHAM REPORT: Diplomatic Records, June 27, 1878 letter from Tokyo, Japan to State Department; BATES/LETTERS: Bates: *Lincoln in the Telegraph Office;* HENRY HALL BROGDEN: Brogden testimony, Surratt trial: FIRE: Washington *Times,* April 3, 1865; SURRATT RETURN: Weichmann/Holahan testimonies, Surratt trial; LOU LETTER: Robert Purdy report, War Department files, National Archives; SURRATT IN MONTREAL: John J. Reeves testimony, Surratt trial; Weichmann to Surrattsville with Mrs. Surratt: Weichmann testimony, Surratt trial; BOOTH at Lincoln speech: Weichmann testimony, Surratt trial; also see Weichmann: *True History.*

EIGHT: BAD FRIDAY AND BEYOND

SURRATT'S JOURNEY SOUTH: testimonies at Surratt trial by Joseph Carroll, Frank H. Atkinson, Charles B. Stewart, New York *Times* November 1, 1867; Ezra B. Westfall; Morris Drohan; Charles H. M. Wood; Theodore H. Rhodes; James Lamb; David C. Reed; John Lee; STANTON/WEICHMANN/MRS. SURRATT/TRIP TO SURRATSVILLE: Weichmann testimony, Surratt trial; JOHN LLOYD: Lloyd testimony, Surratt trial; INCIDENT AT SUPPER: Weichmann/Olivia Jenkins; JOHN AND ELIZA HOLAHAN TESTIMONIES: Surratt trial; MRS. SURRATT IN PARLOR: Weichmann testimony, Surratt trial; police search: Clarvoe/McDevitt testimonies, Surratt trial; ANNA SURRATT RACISM: Weichmann testimony, Surratt trial; CASS: Cass testimony, Surratt trial; CANANDAIGUA: Frank O. Chamberlin testimony, Surratt trial; McDEVITT/CLARVOE/WEICHMANN: McDevitt, Clarvoe, Weichmann testimonies, Surratt trial; GREELEY: Harper: *Lincoln and the Press;* FERNANDO WOOD: London *Times,* April-May, 1865, JOSEPH SHAW: Harper: *Lincoln and the Press;* BROWNING: Browning diaries; JEFFERSON DAVIS: Cooper: *Jefferson Davis;* SLATER ARREST: War Department files, National Archives; also see: Chamlee: *Lincoln's Assassins;* AUGUSTUS HOWELL; RAYNOR: Raynor testimony, War Department files, National Archives; SURRATT IN MONTREAL: Diplomatic records; also see detailed records at Surratt Society, Clinton, Maryland; SANDERS/CLEARY/TUCKER/MANIFESTOES: New York *Times,* April-August 1865; HUNTER/CAMPBELL/TUCKER CONNECTION: Official Records of the Union and Confederate Armies; letters to and from Halleck and Stanton; KIDNAPPING: All Montreal newspapers; Canadian National Archives records, Quebec; JACOB/THOMPSON: *Life of Jacob Thompson* by Dorothy Oldham (unpublished); CLAY: Virginia Clay Clopton memoirs; WILLIAM JONES/DAVIS: Correspondence supplied by Linda Crist, Davis papers curator, Rice University; SURRATT TRIP TO ENGLAND, ITALY, ARREST, RETURN: Diplomatic Records; also see Surratt Society bound compile of letters, telegrams reports, Surratt Society, Clinton, Maryland; Blackburn, Headley, Sanders Future: Reports by Sharpe,

National Archives; Haines: *The Life of George Sanders;* information supplied by James O. Hall; Jane Singer; others.

NINE: AFTERMATH OF THE TRAGEDY

GREELEY: Various biographies; WOOD: London *Times;* BELMONT: Belmont papers: Rothschild Archives, London: SHAW: *Lincoln and the Press;* ST. LAWRENCE HALL: Haines: *Sanders;* HUGHES/HILL: Browning Diaries; also COXE, JOHNSON, EWING; TUCKER: OR.; THOMPSON: Oldham: Thompson; ASHMUN, HAWKES: Washburne Committee; PALLBEARERS: OR; ARRESTEES, COXE, PARR, SLATER: James O. Hall papers; RAYNOR: Weichmann evidence, Surratt trial; SURRATT adventures: Diplomatic Records; SANDERS/ TUCKER/LEE LETTERS: New York *Times;* SANDERS FAKE KIDNAP: Montreal papers/ Sanders papers/ New York *Times;* also Haines: Sanders; Benjamin in England: Public Record Office, Kew, England; THOMPSON memoirs: New York *Times;* DAVIS/JONES: Jefferson Davis archives, Rice University; SURRATT ABROAD: Diplomatic Records; Surratt Society archives; WEICHMANN: *History of the Assassination;* YOUNG: Louisville Public Library. History Collection; Louisville newspapers; SANDERS DECLINE: Haines: *Sanders.*

A warm acknowledgment and thanks to EH.Net, an invaluable resource for calculating the present value of 19th-century monies, which, for this book, was calculated by using the Consumer Price Index. Copyright © 2003 by EH.Net. All rights reserved. Used with permission of EH.Net administrator.

GOVERNMENT REPORTS

Trade with Rebellious States. Report by E. B. Washburne, Congressman, from the Committee on Commerce, 10,000 copies printed for private use only by members of the House. Followed by *Testimony on Trading With The Enemy.* Numerous witnesses, Statement of all contracts issued by H. A. Risley, Department of the Treasury, and index. March 1, 1865. (Referred to in notes on sources as the Washburne report).

Assassination of Lincoln. Report of the House Committee on the evidence, supplied by George S. Boutwell, Congressman, July, 1866. Contains details of the contents of the seized Confederate archives, threats against President Lincoln in intercepted documents, reports from witnesses, etc., etc.

GOVERNMENT ARCHIVES CONSULTED

Archives de la Marine, Paris.
Archives Nationales, Paris.
Archives de la Prefecture de Police, Paris
Archives du Ministere des Affaires Etrangeres, Paris.
Bibliotheque de la Prefecture de Police, Paris.
Bibliotheque de la Ville, Paris
Bibliotheque Thiers, Institut de France, Thiers.
Library of Congress, Washington D.C.
National Archives and Record Service, Washington, D.C.
Public Record Office, Kew, London

COLLECTIONS OF PAPERS

Adams, Charles Francis. Massachusetts Historical Society, Boston.
Belmont, August. Columbia University, NY.
Booth, John Wilkes. National Archive, Washington, D.C.
Buchanan, James. University of Pennsylvania, Philadelphia.
Clay, Clement C. University of N. Carolina, Durham, NC.
Davis, Jefferson. Rice University, Houston, TX.
DeBillet, Pacquet. Library of Congress.
Douglas, Stephen A. University of Chicago Library. Illinois State Historical Society Library.
Grant, Ulysses S. Illinois State Historical Society Library.
Greeley, Horace. Library of Congress, Washington D.C.
Lamon, Ward Hill. Huntington Library, California.
Lincoln, Abraham. Library of Congress.
Sanders, George Nicholas. Library of Congress; National Archive.
Trenholm, George. Merseyside Museum, Lancs, England.
Weed, Thurlow. University of Rochester, Rochester, N.Y.

(*Note:* Judah P. Benjamin, James P. Holcombe, Beverley Tucker and Jacob Thompson guiltily destroyed almost all documentary materials in their collections, and other documents were burned in the fire at the Provost Marshal's office in Washington, D.C. on April 2, 1865. But much has survived in other scattered collections and in libraries across the nation—materials that slipped through the conspirators' self-protective net.)

BOOKS

Abbott, John S. C. *The History of Napoleon III.* Boston: B.B. Russell, 1869.

Adams, James Truslow. *The March of Democracy.* Three Volumes. NY: Charles Scribner & Sons, 1932.

Allen, H.C. *Great Britain and the United States.* NY: St. Martins Press, 1955.

American Art Association. *The Political Correspondence of George N. Sanders.* NY: A.A.A., 1914.

Ancien Proscrit (Pseudonym). *La Verité sur Orsini à Paris.* Privately printed, 1858.

Anonymous. *The Diary of a Public Man.* New Brunswick, NJ: Rutgers University Press, 1946.

Baker, Lafayette C. *History of the U.S. Secret Service.* Published by the author. Philadelphia, 1867.

Baker, Lafayette C. *The United States Secret Service in the Late War.* Chicago: Thompson and Thomas. 1902.

Barton, William E. *The Life of Abraham Lincoln.* NY: Books Inc. 1943.

Basler (Roy P.) *The Collected Works of President Lincoln.* 8 volumes and index. New Brunswick, NJ: Rutgers University Press, 1953.

Bates, David H. *Lincoln in the Telegraph Office.* Lincoln, Na. And London: University of Nebraska Press, 1995.

Beale, Howard K. (Ed.) *Diary of Edward Bates, 1959-1866.* Washington DC: American Historical Society, 1933.

Benjamin, L. N. (Editor). *The St. Albans Raid. Or an Investigation into the charges against Lieutenant Bennett H. Young and Command for their Acts at St. Albans, Vermont.* Montreal: John Lovell, 1865.

Black, David. *The King of Fifth Avenue: The Fortunes of August Belmont.* NY: The Dial Press, 1981.

Blackett, R. J. M. *Divided Hearts: Britain and the American Civil War.* Baton Rouge, La.: University of Louisiana Press, 2001.

Blakey, Arch Fredric. *General John S. Winder, CSA.* Gainesville, Fla.: University of Florida Press, 1990.

Bowman, John S. (Ed.) *The Civil War Almanac.* NY: Gallery Books, 1983.

Brooks, Noah: *Washington in Lincoln's Time.* NY: Rinehart and Co., 1958.

Brown, Charles H. *Agents of Manifest Destiny: The Lives and Times of the Filibusters.* Chapel Hill, N.C.: The University of North Carolina Press, 1980.

Browning, Orville H. *Diaries*. Springfield, Ill.: Illinois State Historical Library, 1925.

Bryan, George S. *The Great American Myth*. NY: Carrick and Evans, 1940.

Calman, Alvin R. *Ledru-Rollin après 1848 et les Proscrits en Angleterre*. Paris: Presses Universaires de France, 1958.

Case, Lynn M. and Spencer, Warren F. *The United States and France: Civil War Diplomacy*. Philadelphia: University of Pennsylvania Press, 1970.

Chamlee, Roy Z. Jr. *Lincoln's Assassins*. Jefferson, N.C. and London: McFarland and Co., 1990.

Clarke, Asia Booth. *The Unlocked Book*. NY: G.P. Putnam's Sons, 1938.

Clay-Clopton, Virginia. *A Belle of the Fifties*. Tuscaloosa and London: University of Louisiana Press, 1999.

Cole, Arthur Charles. *The Era of the Civil War*. Springfield, Ill., Illinois Central Commission, 1919.

Cooper, William J. *Jefferson Davis, American*. NY: Vintage Books, 2001.

Crist, Linda Lasswell, and Dix, Mary Seaton (Eds.) *Jefferson Davis, the Papers*. Baton Rouge, La.: Louisiana State University Press, 1968-2004.

D'Ambès, Baron. *Intimate Memoirs of Napoleon III*. Tr. A. R. Allison. London: Duckworth, 1912.

Dana, Charles A. *Recollections of the Civil War*. NY: Collier Books, 1963.

Davis, William C. *Breckinridge: Statesman, Soldier, Symbol*. Baton Rouge, La.: Louisiana State University Press, 1974.

DeBussy, Charles. *Les Conspirateurs en Angleterre 1848-1858*. Paris: Legibre-Duquesne, 1858.

Denney, Robert E. *Civil War Prisons and Escapes*. NY: Sterling, 1993.

De Viel Castel, Comte Horace. *Memoirs*. London: Remington, 1888.

Dewitt, David Miller. *The Assassination of President Lincoln and its Expiation*. NY: Macmillan, 1909.

Donald, David, (Ed.) *Inside Lincoln's Cabinet. The Civil War Diaries of Salmon P. Chase*. NY: Longmans, Green, 1954

Donald, David H. *Lincoln*. NY: Touchstone, 1995.

Douglas, Henry K. *I Rode With Stonewall*. Chapel Hill, NC: the University of North Carolina Press, 1940.

Ettinger, Amos A. *The Mission to Spain of Pierre Soulé*. New Haven: Yale University Press, 1932.

Evans, Eli N. *Judah P. Benjamin, the Jewish Confederate*. NY: The Free Press, 1988.

Faust, Patricia L. (Ed.) *Historical Times Encyclopedia of the Civil War*. NY: Harper Perennial, 1986.

Fermer, Douglas. *James Gordon Bennett and the New York Herald*. NY: St. Martins Press, 1986.

Forrester, Izola Fox. *This One Mad Act.* Boston: Hale, Cushman and Flint, 1937.

Fürtwangler, Albert. *Assassin on Stage. Brutus, Hamlet and the Death of Lincoln.* Urbana and Chicago: University of Chicago Press, 1991.

Goff, John S. *Robert Todd Lincoln.* Norman, Oklahoma: University of Oklahoma Press, 1969.

Hancock, Harold Bell. *Delaware During the Civil War.* Historical Society of Delaware, 1961.

Hanna, A.J. *Flight Into Oblivion.* Bloomington: Indiana University Press, 1938.

Harper, Robert S. *Lincoln and the Press.* NY: McGraw Hill, 1951.

Headley, John W. *Confederate Operations in Canada and New York.* NY: Neale, 1906.

Hendrick, Burton J. *Statesmen of the Lost Cause: Jefferson Davis and His Cabinet.* NY: The Literary Guild, 1939.

Heyman, Max L. Jr. *Prudent Soldier: A Biography of Major General E. R. S. Canby.* Glendale, Calif.: Arthur H. Clark, 1959.

Horan, James D. *Confederate Agent.* Fairfax Press (not located): 1954.

Jennings, John J. *Theatrical and Circus Life.* St Louis: Sun Publishing, 1882

Jones, Howard. *Union in Peril.* Chapel Hill, N.C. University of North Carolina Press, 1992.

Jones, John B. *A Rebel War Clerk's Diary.* Two volumes. Philadelphia: J.P. Lippincott and Co., 1866.

Katz, Irving. *August Belmont: A Political Biography.* New York: Columbia University Press, 1968.

Kimmel, Stanley. *The Mad Booths of Maryland.* Indianapolis and New York: Bobbs, Merrill, 1940.

Kinchen, Oscar A. *Confederate Operations in Canada and the North.* North Quincy, Mass: Christopher Publishing House, 1970.

Kirkland, Edward Chase. *The Peacemakers of 1864.* NY: Macmillan, 1927.

Lamon, Ward Hill. *Recollections of Abraham Lincoln.* University of Nebraska Press, Lincoln, Nebraska, 1994.

Laughlin, Clara M. *The Death of Lincoln.* NY: Doubleday, Page and Co. 1909.

Leech, Margaret. *Reveille in Washington, 1860-1865.* NY: Harper and Brothers, 1941.

Levin, Alexandra Lee. *This Awful Drama.* NY: Vantage Press, 1987.

Lewis, Lloyd. *Myths after Lincoln.* NY: RC (The Readers' Club), 1929.

Logan, John A. *The Great Conspiracy.* N.Y: A.A.R. Hart, 1886.

Lowry, Don. *Towards an Indefinite Shore.* NY: Hippocrene Books, 1995.

McPherson, Edward. *The Great Rebellion* (Shortened title) Washington, D.C.: Philip and Solomons, 1865.

McPherson, James M. *Battle Cry of Freedom: The Civil War Era.* NY: Ballantine Books, 1988.

Meade, Robert D. *Judah P. Benjamin, Confederate Statesman.* NY: Oxford University Press, 1943.

Miller, Ernest C. *John Wilkes Booth—Oilman.* NY: Exposition Press, 1947.

Milton, George Fort. *The Eve of Conflict.* Boston: Houghton Mifflin, 1934.

Moran, Benjamin. *The Journal.* Two volumes. Chicago University Press, n.d.

Myers, Earl Schenck. (Ed.) *Lincoln Day by Day.* Dayton, Ohio: Morningside House, 1991.

Nevins, Allan. *The Emergence of Lincoln.* New York: Charles Scribner & Sons. 1950.

Niven, John. *Gideon Welles: Lincoln's Secretary of the Navy.* Baton Rouge, La: Louisiana State University Press, 1973.

Nuremberger, Ruth K. *The Clays of Alabama.* Lexington: University of Kentucky Press, 1958.

Oberholtzer, Ellie P. *Jay Cooke: Financier of the Civil War.* NY: Augustus M. Kelley, 1968.

Orsini, Felice. *Memoirs and Adventures of Felice Orsini.* Edinburgh: Thomas Constable and Co., 1857.

Ownsbey, Betty J. *Alias "Paine."* Jefferson, NC: McFarland and Company, n.d.

Owsley, Frank L. *King Cotton Diplomacy.* Chicago: University of Chicago Press, 1931.

Papers Relating to Foreign Affairs. Washington: Government Printing Office, 1864-1868.

Parker, Anna Virginia. *The Sanders Family of Grass Hills.* Madison, Ind.: Coleman Printing Co., 1966.

Patrick, Rembert W. *Jefferson Davis and His Cabinet.* Baton Rouge: University of Louisiana Press, 1944.

Payne, Howard C. *The Police State of Louis Napoleon Bonaparte.* Seattle: University of Washington Press, 1966.

Pleasants, Samuel A. *Fernando Wood of New York.* NY: AMS Press, 1966.

Pollard, Edward A. *Southern History of the War.* NY: Two Volumes. C. B. Robinson, 1866.

Ramage, James A. *Rebel Raider: The Life of General John Hunt Morgan.* Lexington, Ky: University Press of Kentucky, 1986.

Rhodehamel, (John) and Taper (Louise). *Right or Wrong, God Judge Me: The Writings of John Wilkes Booth.* Urbana and Chicago: University of Chicago Press, 1997.

Roscoe, Theodore. *The Web of Conspiracy.* Englewood Cliffs, NJ: Prentice Hall, Inc. 1959.

Ross, Ishbel. *Rose O'Neil Greenhow, Confederate Spy.* Marietta, Ga.: Mockingbird Books, 1992.

Saint-Ferreól, Amédéé. *Les Proscrits Français en Belgique.* Brussels: C. Murquardt, 1870.

Sala, George Augustus. *The Life and Adventures written by himself.* NY: Charles Scribner & Sons, 1895.

Samples, Gordon. *Lust for Fame: The Stage Career of John Wilkes Booth.* Jefferson, NC and London: McFarland, 1998.

Sandburg, Carl. *Abraham Lincoln.* NY. Harcourt, Brace and Co., 1926.

Sanders, George Nicholas. *George N. Sanders on the Sequences of Southern Secession.* NY: George Sanders, 1860.

Scharf, J. Thomas. *History of the Confederate Navy.* NY: Rogers and Sherwood, 1887.

Sheil, Richard. *The Apostate: A Tragedy in Five Acts.* London: John Murray, 1817.

Spence, Edward F. *Bar and Buskin.* London: Elkin Matthews and Marriott, 1930.

Spencer, Donald S. *Louis Kossuth and Young America.* Columbia, Miss.: University of Missouri Press, 1977.

Steers, Edward Jr. *Blood on the Moon: The Assassination of President Lincoln.* Lexington, Ky.: The University Press of Kentucky, 2001.

Tenot, Eugene and Dubost, Antonin. *Les Suspects en 1858.* Paris: Armand de Chavalier, 1868.

Tidwell, William A. *April, '65.* Kent, Ohio: Kent University Press, 1995.

Tidwell, William A. with James O. Hall and David Winfred Haddy. *Come Retribution.* NY: Barnes and Noble, 1998.

The Trial of the assassination and conspirators at Washington DC, May and June 1865, for the Murder of President Lincoln. Philadelphia: T.B. Peterson, 1865.

The Trial of John Surratt. Two volumes. Washington D.C.: Government Printing Office, 1867.

Trindal, Elizabeth S. *Mary Surratt: An American Tragedy.* Gretna, La.: Pelican Publishing Co. 1996.

Tucker, Jane Ellis. *Beverley Tucker, A Memoir by His Wife.* Richmond, Va.: Privately printed, 1893.

Turner, Thomas R. *Beware the People Weeping.* Baton Rouge, La.: Louisiana State University Press, 1982.

U.S. War Department. *The War of the Rebellion: A Compilation of the Official Records of the Union and Confederate Armies and Navy.* Washington D.C.: U.S. Government Printing Office, 1880-1906.

Walsh, William S. *Abraham Lincoln and the London Punch.* NY: Moffat, Yard, 1909.

Washburne, Mark. *A Biography of Elihu B. Washburne.* Published by the author, 2001.

Weichmann, Louis J. *A True History of the Assassination of Abraham Lincoln.* NY: Alfred A. Knopf, 1975.

Williams, Ben Ames. (Ed.) Chesnut, Mary Boykin. *A Diary from Dixie.* Boston: Houghton Mifflin, 1949.

Wilson, Dennis K. *Justice Under Pressure.* NY: Lanham, 1992.

Winks, Robin W. *The Civil War Years: Canada and the United States.* Montreal: McGill-Queens University Press, 1998.

UNPUBLISHED MANUSCRIPTS

Cleary, William C. Diary. University of North Carolina, Chapel Hill, N.C.

Oldham, Dorothy. *Jacob Thompson*. University of Mississippi, Oxford, Miss.

Haines, Randall. *George Nicholas Sanders*. Author's property, Cincinnati, Ohio.

Hamand, Lavern Marshall. *Ward Hill Lamon*. University of Illinois, Urbana and Champaign, Illinois.

INDEX